D1274645

Law and the Underprivileged

Law and the Underprivileged

Chris Smith
Lecturer in Law
University of Sheffield

and

David C. Hoath
Solicitor, Lecturer in Law
University of Sheffield

London and Boston
Routledge & Kegan Paul

First published in 1975
by Routledge & Kegan Paul Ltd
Broadway House, 68-74 Carter Lane,
London EC4V 5EL and
9 Park Street,
Boston, Mass. 02108, USA
Set in Journal by Autoset
and Printed in Great Britain by
Unwin Brothers Ltd
ISBN 0 7100 8259 2 (C)
ISBN 0 7100 8260 6 (P)

Contents

Tables

Preface

The ceaseless outpourings of legislation concerning the rights and liabilities of the poorer sections of the community can achieve little, unless there are enough trained advisers to bring home its meaning to those for whom it is primarily intended. The lawyer, social worker or other adviser who has to refer clients straight to the local DHSS office for advice on social security problems, or to the local housing department on council housing matters, may seek to justify his action by saying that his training has not equipped him with the necessary knowledge, and that he now has no time to acquire it; but there are refreshing signs that this attitude is changing, with a growing awareness on the part of advisers of the general importance of poverty law, and of its relevance even in the traditional lawyers' fields such as divorce and personal injury litigation.

The number of voluntary advice centres in deprived areas is steadily increasing, and lawyers have now been given the following solemn judicial warning: 'None of us can afford ... to make the always suspect separation between lawyer's law that we have to know, and the other law which we have to look up when necessary. The law of pensions and supplementary benefits requires as much expertise and demands as much study ... as any other branch of the family law, of which it is, essentially, a part' (Reiterbund v Reiterbund [1974] 2 A11 ER 455, 461). Trainee solicitors sitting the Law Society examination in Family Law are now required to know about supplementary benefit, and the Central Council for Education and Training in Social Work urged in August 1974 that all courses for social workers should include basic legal studies.

This book seeks to provide a not too forbidding account of some of the major areas of the law of England and Wales relating to the underprivileged. We hope it will prove useful to students and advisers concerned with law or social work, and to the general reader; also, we trust it will prove useful 'in the field': it is not meant to be an academic treatise.

Many will quarrel with our choice of topics: this was dictated by the need to limit the size of the book, and in deciding what to include or omit we have drawn on our experiences of solicitors' practice, voluntary legal advice centres, tribunal advocacy and the teaching of undergraduates and social workers.

The method of printing adopted has not permitted the traditional cross-referencing in the text by the use of page numbers: since a considerable amount of cross-referencing is nevertheless unavoidable in a work of this nature, we have adopted a system of referring to other parts of the book by what is hopefully a logical lettering and numbering system: at its most gruesome, a reference to another chapter could read: 'see ch 12(A)(4)(b)(iii)', but we have used wherever possible the shortest reference consistent with clarity: thus e.g. 'see (b)(iii) above' is a reference to the earliest preceding passage of the current chapter satisfying that description. We hope this system will not be found too confusing when used with the table of contents and index (which do use page numbers).

We have received help from individuals and bodies too numerous to list individually, but we must particularly express our debt to the Legal Action Group, whose monthly bulletin performs such an excellent service for advisers in this area; to the secretarial staff of Sheffield University Law Faculty for wrestling with a baffling manuscript which was subject in places to almost daily variations; to Peter Hopkins of Routledge for his enthusiasm and support; and to our long-suffering wives.

The law is stated as at 1 April 1975, but it would be a miracle if it remained static for long: changes of substance occurring since that date and before going to press are mentioned in outline below.

Lastly, we hope that the collaboration of a public lawyer and a property lawyer in a venture designed for a wider readership than their fellow lawyers has not resulted in too many infelicities and inconsistencies of style, or in an excess of 'legalese'.

Recent developments

p.7

The review of NI benefit and contribution rates is currently being undertaken more frequently than once a year, though it is intended to return to annual reviews when inflation allows.

pp.7-8

The rates of NI contributions given in the text are under review at the time of writing and may be increased in late 1975.

pp.10-11, 78

Clause 100 of the Employment Protection Bill 1975, when enacted, will abolish the 'grade or class' provision of the trade—dispute disqualification for NI unemployment benefit. The SB disqualification will also be amended accordingly.

p.17
NI non-contributory invalidity pension will come into force on 17 November 1975.

p.52
The aggregation of a dependent child's resources and requirements with those of a SB claimant relates only to the 'necessaries of life'; therefore substantial resources of a child to be used for other purposes will not prevent a parent receiving SB for his own requirements (K v JMP Co Ltd [1975] 1 All ER 1030, CA).

p.57
The share of rent attributed to a non-dependant in a SB claimant's household, when the non-dependant cannot afford the share calculated by the 'headcounting' method (p.56), is now such as to leave him £10 per week (£17 if married) plus £4 for each dependent child of his.

p.61
Resources generally must be calculated arithmetically; the SBC does not possess an 'arbitrary discretion' to treat resources in the way it thinks fair and reasonable.

Arrears of periodical payments must be treated as relating to the weeks when they should have been paid, and current SB is not affected. (R v West London SBAT, ex p Taylor, 'The Times', 12 May 1975).

p.64
By June 1975, the capital limit has not, as previously expected, been raised to £1,200, but remains at £300. The assumed tariff income is £0.05 per week for every £25 between £300 and £800, and £0.12½ per week for every £25 over £800 (for quick calculation see the tables in Handbook, para 29 and Lynes, 1974, p.70). References to '£1,200' on pp.62,63,67 should be read as '£300'. The change to £1,200 may be made later in 1975.

pp.69-73
The wage-stop will be abolished when clause 18 of the Child Benefit Bill 1975 is enacted. This also affects pp.56, 183, 187.

pp.92-6
Family Allowances will be abolished from April 1977 and replaced by child benefit of £1.50 for each child in a family including the first, when the Child Benefit Bill 1975 is enacted. One-parent families will receive FA in respect of the first child from April 1976 to April 1977.

p.100

The maximum FIS payment has been increased to £7 for a one-child family plus £0.50 for each additional child.

pp.178-81

The Court of Appeal held in Bristol CC v Clark ('The Times', 3 July 1975) that a local authority seeking possession of a council house in the county court does not have to show that it requires the house for housing purposes, but it must have regard to Circulars as to what matters are relevant in deciding whether to evict, even though the Circulars have no statutory force.

pp.196-200, 206

In R v Kerrier DC, ex p Guppys (Bridport) Ltd ('The Times', 2 July 1975) it was held by the Divisional Court that where a local authority is requested to make an order for the repair or reconstruction of an unfit house under HA 1957, s9 or s16, then it must take positive action: it cannot do nothing, nor does it have the option of merely using the provisions of the public health legislation; the importance of this case lies in the fact that there is a duty to rehouse where the authority operates the housing provisions on the house proving beyond reasonable repair (pp.199-200), but there is no duty to rehouse where the building is closed under the public health provisions (pp.208-9).

pp.205-8

The decision in Salford CC v McNally, mentioned briefly in the text, has been confirmed by the House of Lords ('The Times', 25 June 1975), which made some important observations on the difference between the housing legislation and the public health legislation: it was emphasized that a house might well be 'unfit for human habitation' under the housing legislation without being either 'prejudicial to health' or a 'nuisance' under the public health legislation: the public health question should thus not be decided by the test of fitness for habitation.

(N.B. there have also been changes since 1 April 1975 in the rates of, and financial conditions for, various benefits: we have managed to incorporate these changes in the text.)

C.S.
D.C.H.

Cases

NI Commissioners' Decisions

Since 1950 Commissioners' Decisions have been prefixed by the letter 'R' and the appropriate symbol in brackets indicating one of the following series:

(A) attendance allowance series

(F) family allowance series

(G) the general series—maternity benefit, widow's benefit, guardian's allowance, child's special allowance and death grant

(I) industrial injury series

(P) retirement pension series

(S) sickness benefit series

(U) unemployment benefit series

The cases are numbered by series and year, e.g. R(P)1/70 is the first reported retirement pension decision of 1970.

Prior to 1951, most cases were prefixed by 'C' and a series symbol and numbered in order of case within a year, e.g. CP 21/49 is the twenty-first retirement pension decision of 1949. In this period Welsh and Scots decisions carried an additional prefix 'W' or 'S' and were separately numbered, e.g. CWS 3/48, CSG 9/49.

Series A

R(A) 1/72 19

CA 5/72

(unreported) 18

R(A) 1/73 18

Series F

R(F)3/61 96

R(F)8/61 94,96

R(F)9/61 94

R(F)10/61 94

R(F)11/61 94

R(F)12/61 93

R(F)2/62 94

R(F) 3/62 94

R(F) 3/63 94

R(F) 5/63 95

R(F) 1/64 96

R(F) 1/71 94

R(F) 1/73 94

Series G

CG 3/48 28

CG 4/48 28

CG 5/48 28

CG 15/48 30

CG 3/49 19

Statutes

Abbreviations

AC	Appeal Cases
All ER	All England Law Reports
App	Appendix
BWCC	Butterworth's Workmen's Compensation Cases
CA	Court of Appeal
CABx	Citizens' Advice Bureaux
Ch	Chancery Reports
CHAC	Central Housing Advisory Committee
CLY	Current Law Year Book
Cmd,Cmnd	Command Papers
CPAG	Child Poverty Action Group
Crim LR	Criminal Law Review
CYPA	Children and Young Persons Act
D of Em	Department of Employment
D of En	Department of Environment
DHSS	Department of Health and Social Security
EA	Education Act
E(MP)A	Education (Miscellaneous Provisions) Act
ECA	Exceptional Circumstances Addition
ENP	Exceptional Needs Payment
ER	English Reports
ERS	Earnings-Related Supplement
FA	Family Allowances
FAA	Family Allowances Act
FIS	Family Income Supplement
FISA	Family Income Supplements Act
HA	Housing Act
HFA	Housing Finance Act
HL	House of Lords
HO	Home Office
HRSA	Housing Rents and Subsidies Act
II	Industrial Injuries
JPL	Journal of Planning Law

KB	King's Bench Reports
LAA	Legal Aid Act
LAG BUL.	Legal Action Group Bulletin
LCA	Land Compensation Act
LEA	Local Education Authority
LGA	Local Government Act
LGR	Local Government Reports
LHA	Local Health Authority
LJ Ch	Law Journal Chancery Reports
LSG	Law Society's Gazette
LT	Law Times
L&TA	Landlord and Tenant Act
MHLG	Ministry of Housing and Local Government
MOH	Ministry of Health
MPNI	Ministry of Pensions and National Insurance
NAA	National Assistance Act
NAB	National Assistance Board
NHS	National Health Service
NHSA	National Health Service Act
NI	National Insurance
NLJ	New Law Journal
P&CR	Property and Compensation Reports
para	paragraph
PC	Privy Council
PHA	Public Health Act
Pt	Part
QB	Queen's Bench Reports
RA	Rent Act
reg	regulation
s	section
SB	Supplementary Benefit
SBA	Supplementary Benefit Act
SBAT	Supplementary Benefit Appeal Tribunal
SBC	Supplementary Benefits Commission
Sch	Schedule
SI	Statutory Instrument
SJ	Solicitors Journal
SR&O	Statutory Rules and Orders
SSA	Social Security Act
WLR	Weekly Law Reports

Whether he welcomes the development or not, no lawyer can deny that recent years have seen an unprecedented interest in the legal status of the underprivileged, interest which embraces both access to the law and those areas of law (collectively termed poverty law) of immediate concern to the underprivileged. This book describes the most important of these areas of law. In doing so the relevant law has been grouped under two principal headings, income and accommodation; though this does not reflect any coherent legislative division—on the contrary the law is often diverse in subject-matter and contradictory in principle.

(A) Income

Public maintenance of the poor in this country dates from before the Act of 1601 which is commonly viewed as the precursor of much subsequent poor relief legislation (Act for the Relief of the Poor 1601). From that date to the present day the law has distinguished sharply between the 'deserving' poor—the sick, injured, orphaned and aged whom the law assists with relative generosity—and the 'undeserving' poor—the idle, unemployed or workshy whom the law assists and coerces at the same time.

  The present form of income maintenance legislation dates from the Beveridge Report of 1942 (Cmd 6404) which proposed a 'universal' scheme of social insurance—subsistence level benefits paid in return for contributions—and a 'safety-net' of means-tested non-contributory National Assistance. Pre-conditions of this scheme included universal Family Allowances to avoid family poverty and a free health service. Contrary to the Beveridge proposal, social insurance (National Insurance) benefits have always remained below the level of National Assistance (now Supplementary Benefit) to which many NI claimants must therefore turn. The triumph of public assistance has been accompanied by an extension of 'selective' (as opposed to universal) benefits in cash, kind and services which are thus free only to those who prove their poverty via the means-test. Whether as a result or in spite of these trends, poverty studies have demonstrated that our income maintenance legislation has not reduced the numbers in poverty, particularly children and pensioners (Abel-Smith and Townsend, 1965; Atkinson, 1969).

By and large, it can be stated that the universal schemes of social security—National Insurance, Industrial Injuries and Family Allowances—accord greater rights to claimants and more satisfactory means of challenging administrative decisions; while entitlement to selective benefits either turns exclusively on size of income or turns on that question plus the exercise of administrative discretions subject to less satisfactory appeal mechanisms (in some cases even subject to no independent appeal).

(B)   Accommodation

There has been a complete shift in home ownership patterns over the last sixty years: in 1914, of the eight million dwellings in England and Wales, about 90 per cent were let to tenants of private landlords, and the number of local authority dwellings was trivial; but by 1971, of seventeen million dwellings, over half were owner-occupied, more than a quarter were rented from local authorities, and a fifth were rented from private landlords ('Fair Deal For Housing', Cmnd 4728, para 1). Thus there are now more council tenants than tenants of private landlords, and the government admitted in 1973 that the decline in the numbers of privately rented dwellings 'is unlikely to be reversed' ('Widening The Choice: The Next Steps in Housing', Cmnd 5280, para 37).

The second part of the book deals with the law relating to homelessness, private and public sector landlord and tenant, housing related benefits, and defective housing (in 1973 almost one household in six lived in a property which was unfit or lacked one or more of the basic amenities: 'Better Homes—The Next Priorities', Cmnd 5339, para 3).

Most of the law surveyed consists of legislative responses to the sorry fact that demand for housing far exceeds supply: as the Francis Report recognized in 1971, 'the only solution in the long term is the provision of more and better homes' (Cmnd 4609, p.212). Further, the policy behind this legislation has varied with changes of government, producing a statutory morass often unintelligible to lawyers let alone to the victims of the housing problem.

(C)   Procedures

For the most part no attempt is made to describe standard court procedures familiar to most lawyers and common to fields of law outside the scope of this work. On the other hand, there are in poverty law a number of statutory jurisdictions, often vested in tribunals, and the powers and procedures of these bodies are detailed at the appropriate points in the text. Additionally, the final chapter includes consideration of the statutory legal services which at present concern courts more than tribunals, for no survey of poverty law can exclude these services which are classic examples of selective benefits.

Reference is made at several points to the three prerogative orders as means of challenging decisions of statutory agencies or tribunals, and a brief explanation of these remedies may be helpful, especially for the non-lawyer.

(1) Certiorari
This is an order quashing a decision, available if the decision-making authority has exceeded its jurisdiction (e.g. made a decision it has no competence to make); acted contrary to the rules of natural justice (which require that the decision-maker must not be biased and must afford a party the right to put his case); or if the record of the proceedings reveals an error of law. It was formerly the case that certiorari would only issue to quash decisions of bodies acting judicially; although this position has been liberalized by recent decisions, the scope of the order in this respect remains unclear.

(2) Prohibition
Prohibition is an order issued to prevent a course of action in excess of jurisdiction or contrary to the rules of natural justice. The confusion over the 'acting judicially' requirement also applies to this order.

(3) Mandamus
This order compels the performance of a duty. In this book, the duties to which it may apply are statutory and are generally indicated by the word 'must', though mandamus may lie to compel the proper exercise of a discretionary power. Unlike certiorari and prohibition, the question of 'acting judically' has not arisen.

All three orders are issued at the court's discretion and are bedevilled by procedural difficulties; also, there are differences in time-limits and other matters between them. Although in urgent need of reform (Law Commission Working Paper No. 40, 'Remedies in Administrative Law', 1971), they remain major remedies for challenging decisions in poverty law and carry the advantage of the availability of civil legal aid (see ch 13 (A) (2)). In some situations, however, an action for a declaration may be a more convenient remedy. Both the prerogative orders and declarations are fully covered in the leading work on administrative law remedies (de Smith, 1973).

(D)   Maladministration

Poverty law is a field where the administrator often reigns supreme. Viewed in the context of the problems aimed at by the legislation, it is unsurprising that frustrations arise, mistakes are made and delays occur. While negotiation or adjudication may resolve many cases of friction, instances of maladministration can be referred to the appropriate 'ombudsmen'—the Parliamentary Commissioner for Administration, the Commissions for Local Administration and the Health Service Commissioners (Parliamentary Commissioner Act 1967; Local Government Act 1974, Pt III; National Health Service Reorganisation Act 1973, Pt III). While reference to the ombudsmen does not usually lead to the alteration of an unfavourable decision, it can produce more satisfactory procedures for the general public.

The Council on Tribunals, which has a statutory brief to supervise the constitution and working of tribunals (Tribunals and Inquiries Act 1971, s1(1)(a)), also receives complaints and comments about tribunals from the public and, while not able to alter decisions, is sometimes able to secure improvements in procedures as a result.

References

'Social Insurance and Allied Services', Report by Sir W. Beveridge, Cmd 6404 (1942).

Abel-Smith, B. and Townsend, P. (1965), 'The Poor and the Poorest', Bell, London.

Atkinson, A. B. (1969), 'Poverty in Britain and the Reform of Social Security', Cambridge University Press.

'Fair Deal for Housing', Cmnd 4728 (1971).

'Widening The Choice: The Next Steps in Housing', Cmnd 5280 (1973).

'Better Homes—The Next Priorities', Cmnd 5339 (1973).

'Report of the Committee on the Rent Acts', Chairman: H. E. Francis QC, Cmnd 4609 (1971).

de Smith, S. A. (1973), 'Judicial Review of Administrative Action', 3rd ed., Stevens, London.

Part1 **Income**

In principle the National Insurance scheme provides benefits in return for contributions on the private insurance model; in practice the NI fund, from which benefits are paid, is also financed by general taxation (Social Security Act 1975, s1 (5)). When a particular 'risk' materializes, benefit is not automatically forthcoming: claimants must satisfy specified conditions of entitlement including, for most benefits, payment of the appropriate number of contributions.

After several major amendments and consolidations, the NI scheme is still largely based on the Beveridge Report proposals (Cmd 6404). Since April 1975 the principal statute is the Social Security Act 1975 which consolidated earlier legislation. Transitional provisions allow for continuity of contributions and benefits paid under the two acts (Social Security (Consequential Provisions) Act 1975, s2 and Sch3). The amounts of contributions and benefits must be reviewed annually in the light of changes in the general level of earnings; contributions may also be varied to take account of the state of the NI fund (SSA 1975, ss120-6).

(A) Contributions

(1) Liability to Pay Contributions
There are four classes of contributions (SSA 1975, s1(2)).

(a) Class 1   These are paid by employed earners—those 'gainfully employed in Great Britain under a contract of service'—if over sixteen and earning between the upper and lower earnings limits (currently £69 and £11 per week); those earning above the upper limit must pay contributions related to earnings up to that limit (SSA 1975, ss2(1), 4(1)–(3)). Earners' contributions (called 'primary contributions') are currently 5.5 per cent of weekly earnings, or 2 per cent in the case of married women and widows electing to pay at the lower rate (SSA 1975, ss4(6), 5, 130; SI 1973/1376). No contribution is required from those who have retired or those over pensionable age (sixty for women, sixty-five for men) but not retired and not entitled to a category A retirement pension on reaching pensionable age (SSA 1975, s6(1); see (10) (b) below).

The employer of any employed earner must pay a further 'secondary contribution' of 8.5 per cent of earnings not exceeding the upper earnings limit (SSA 1975, s4(3)–(6)).

(b) Class 2   These contributions (£2.41 per week) must be paid by self-employed earners—those 'gainfully employed in Great Britain' except as employed earners—if over sixteen unless were they in Class 1, they would be exempt or only liable at the lower rate (SSA 1975, ss2(1), 7 (1)(2)). There is no liability to contribute if annual earnings are less than £675 provided an exception certificate is obtained (SSA 1975, s7(5); SI 1973/1264, regs 21-3). There is automatic exemption from liability for any week in which a self-employed earner receives sickness or invalidity benefit (see (B)(2) (3) below), injury benefit or unemployability supplement (see ch 3 (2) (3) (a) below), maternity allowance (see (10) (b) below) or is incapable of work or in prison or legal custody (SI 1973/1264, reg 20(1)).

Both Class 1 and 2 contributions must only be paid by the 'gainfully employed'. The corresponding phrase under the National Insurance Act 1965, 'gainfully occupied in employment', was interpreted to cover cases where an employee's remuneration did not exceed his expenses (Vandyk v MPNI [1954] 2 All ER 723), or was a small gratuitous payment (Benjamin v MPNI [1960] 2 All ER 851). What distinguishes employed (Class 1) from self-employed (Class 2) earners? The former must be a party to a contract of service, but doubtful cases can arise which are decided by the Secretary of State for Social Services, who may order an inquiry before deciding (SSA 1975, s93(1) (a), (3)). Some of his decisions (known as 'M Decisions') are published which, together with reported appeals to the High Court, offer examples of cases falling either side of the line (e.g. M40, M34; Gould v MPNI [1951] 1 All ER 368; Whittaker v MPNI [1966] 3 All ER 531). The commonest test, sometimes used alone but often in conjunction with others, is whether the contract of employment gives the alleged employer that degree of control over the work normally associated with a contract of service. Certain categories of earners may be deemed employed for contribution purposes by regulations (SSA 1975, s2 (2) (b)).

(c) Class 3   These contributions (£1.90 per week) may be paid voluntarily by Class 1 or 2 contributors solely to acquire the necessary 'earnings factor' (see (3) below) for entitlement to benefits for which their Class 1 or 2 contribution record would be insufficient (SSA 1975, s8). A Class 3 contribution may be credited to a Class 1, 2 or 3 contributor if his earnings factor for a year is fractionally insufficient (SI 1973/1264, reg 31).

(d) Class 4   These contributions (8 per cent of profits or gains in the range £1,600-£3,600 a year) must be paid by the self-employed in addition to Class 2 contributions (SSA 1975, s9).

(2)   Payment of Contributions

All Class 1 contributions must be paid by employers who may recover primary contributions by deduction from pay; to deduct a secondary contribution is an offence (SSA 1975, Sch 1, para 3). If an employer fails to pay primary contributions these may still be treated as paid so his employees are entitled to benefit (SI 1973/1264, regs 18, 19). Failure by anyone to pay a contribution for which he is liable is an offence (SSA 1975, s146 (1)). Ensuring compliance with contribution liabilities is the principal task of NI inspectors (SSA 1975, ss144-5).

Contributions are collected through the Inland Revenue, by the sale of stamps to be fixed to contribution cards, or by other methods authorized by the Secretary of State (SSA 1975, ss9, 10 and Sch 1, 2)

(3)   Contribution Conditions

Entitlement to most NI benefits depends, among other conditions, on satisfying contribution conditions: payment of sufficient contributions in a year to produce an 'earnings factor' (calculated from tables produced by the DHSS) which must be at least as large as the multiples of the current lower earnings limit specified for each benefit.

Some benefits are restricted to Class 1 or 2 contributors and unemployment benefit to Class 1 only.

Table 1 shows for each benefit the classes of contributors eligible to claim, the contribution conditions and the multiple of the lower earnings limit to which the earnings factor must equate. Where two contribution conditions are listed, both must be satisfied. Certain benefits (marked * in table 1) may be paid at a reduced rate if a claimant has not paid sufficient contributions to be fully entitled, though increases of benefit for dependent children (see (13) (a) below) are paid in full (SSA 1975, s33).

Class 1 contributors at the reduced rate cannot claim any benefits; their contributions only provide entitlement to benefits under the Industrial Injuries scheme (see ch 3).

(B)   Benefits

(1)   Unemployment Benefit

(a) Entitlement   A claimant is entitled to unemployment benefit for 'any day of unemployment which forms part of a period of interruption of employment' (SSA 1975, s14(1) (a)). Any two days of unemployment in one week, consecutive or not, and any two periods separated by thirteen weeks or less constitute one period of interruption (SSA 1975, s17(1) (d)).

Additionally on each day of a period of interruption the claimant must be 'capable of work' and 'available to be employed in employed earner's employment' (SSA 1975, s17(1) (a) (i)). 'Capable of work' is not statutorily defined but, being juxtaposed with the contrary requirement of incapability of work for sickness benefit, must have the contrary meaning to that phrase (see (2) (a) below).

Availability for employment must be proved by the claimant (R(U)12/52, R(U)3/65). He must

> show that he is able and willing to work in an employment on conditions and for hours similar to those on and for which persons are employed in the area within which the claimant was prepared to work . . . ability to work must not be hedged about with restrictions which will render his chance of obtaining employment negligible (R(U) 12/52).

The claimant must be ready to accept 'any offer of suitable employment, and not only offers in his particular vocation' (R(U) 1/53). Refusal of a suitable offer is 'strong evidence' of unavailability (R(U)44/53), but is not necessary for a claimant to be judged unavailable.

A claimant must also either

(i) be under pensionable age and satisfy the contribution conditions (see table 1); or

(ii) be over pensionable age and entitled to a category A retirement pension had he retired on reaching pensionable age (see (10)(b) below);

(iii) be a woman over pensionable age and entitled to a category B retirement pension, whose husband is dead and who has elected to resume work after retirement (see (10)(c) (d) (ii) below) (SSA 1975, s14(2)).

(b) Disqualifications   Although otherwise entitled a claimant may be disqualified for unemployment benefit in several circumstances. While disqualified he must resort to SB but the disqualification is reflected there also (see ch 4(F)(3), (G)(1)).

(i) Trade-disputes   A claimant is disqualified for unemployment benefit if he participates in or finances or has a direct interest in a trade-dispute which caused the stoppage of work making him unemployed (SSA 1975, s19(1)(a)). This disqualification is defended as affording the D of Em neutrality in industrial disputes though it must be some deterrent to strikes and an incentive to lock-outs. But there is a further provision which disqualifies a far larger group: those who belong to a 'grade or class of workers of which, immediately before the stoppage, there were members employed at (the) place of employment any of whom are participating in or financing or are directly interested in the dispute' (SSA 1975, s19(1)(b)). This embraces the non-trade unionist laid off when his colleagues strike and those on the 'passive' side of a demarcation dispute if thrown out of work. The interest of a grade or class may be the possibility of higher or lower wages or variations in the volume of work available as a result of the dispute (R(U)14/64; Punton v MPNI (No. 2) [1964] 1 All ER 448, CA). A Royal Commission proposal in 1969 to abolish the 'grade or class' provision has not been enacted (Cmnd 3623, paras 953-92).

The disqualification is not easily avoided, but possible 'defences' include identifying the claimant's department or section of an enterprise as a separate 'place of employment' as the statute allows (SSA 1975, s19(2)(a)); questioning the meaning of 'grade or class' in a particular context, referring to different types of work, degrees of skill and rates of pay; and questioning the nature of the interest of a grade or class if no likely outcome of the dispute will affect its conditions of work.

The disqualification lasts for the duration of the trade-dispute, unlike the remaining disqualifications which last for a maximum of six weeks.

(ii) Misconduct   A claimant is disqualified if 'he has lost his employment through his misconduct' (SSA 1975, s20(1)(a)). The purpose of this disqualification is avowedly 'not to punish the insured person but to protect the insurance fund from claims in respect of unemployment which the insured person has brought upon himself' (CU190/50). This should mean that decisions are made without reference to criminal charges or convictions, but while 'it is not necessary that a claimant be prosecuted to conviction in a court of law . . . the fact that a person had been convicted would be extremely cogent evidence of his misconduct' (R(U)10/54).

What constitutes misconduct? Dishonesty, both at work and elsewhere, is sufficient and even an acquittal in court may not help (CU190/50, R(U)20/59, R(U)8/57); offensive behaviour such as drunkenness or insulting workmates may also be misconduct (R(U)14/57, R(U)12/56), as may breach of workplace rules (R(U)24/56) and negligence, mistakes or inefficiency in performing work, although low output by a naturally slow worker is not in itself sufficient (R(U)34/52). Driving incidents may fall either side of the line: an isolated accident in an otherwise clean record has been called 'an isolated error of judgement and not misconduct' (R(U)10/52), whereas a similar accident caused by the claimant's negligence was misconduct but, with mitigating circumstances, penalized by only three weeks' disqualification (R(U)13/53). The period of disqualification is discretionary and an appeal may be made solely with a view to reducing this.

(iii) Voluntary unemployment   Disqualification results if a claimant has left his last employment 'voluntarily without just cause' (SSA 1975, s20(1)(a)). It must first be proved against him that he lost his job voluntarily and then, to avoid disqualification, proved by him that he had just cause (R(U)20/64). It has been held that provoking one's dismissal (e.g. by refusing to carry out a reasonable request) is leaving voluntarily (R(U)16/52), but to anticipate an inevitable dismissal for other reasons may not be (R(U)1/58).

'Just cause' is a question of fact in each case; possible just causes may be personal such as the need to tend a family or invalid relative (R(U)6/59, R(U)32/59), or related to the employment, such as distance from the claimant's home or a substantial cut in wages (R(U)14/52, R(U)15/53). As with misconduct there may be mitigating circumstances which should reduce the disqualification period, and factors unsuccessfully pleaded as just cause may suffice to achieve this.

(iv) Neglecting a reasonable employment opportunity   If a claimant 'has neglected to avail himself of a reasonable opportunity of suitable employment', he is disqualified (SSA 1975, s20(1)(c)). There is no 'defence' of 'just cause'. Apart from proving that an offered employment is unsuitable, this is a difficult disqualification to challenge. Mere refusal to attend an interview is sufficient to attract disqualification, as is attending in a state which leads to refusal of employment (R(U)28/55) or placing unreasonable restrictions on an acceptance of offered employment (R(U)23/51). Since the question is usually clear-cut there is little scope for mitigation of the six weeks' disqualification except personal hardship.

(v) Refusal or failure to follow certain courses of action   Refusal or failure to apply for or accept suitable employment, to carry out official recommendations aimed at finding suitable employment, or to take advantage of D of Em approved training all lead to disqualification; in all three cases the refusal or failure must be 'without good cause' (SSA 1975, s20(1)(b)(d)(e)).

Employment is not 'suitable' in this context if it consists of a vacancy created by a trade dispute; employment in the locality similar to the claimant's normal occupation but at a lower rate of pay or on less favourable conditions than might reasonably be expected; or employment in another locality at a lower rate of pay or on poorer conditions than those generally observed by employers and trade unions in the district; but after a reasonable lapse of time, employment is not considered unsuitable merely by not being in keeping with a claimant's occupation provided pay and conditions are compatibile with local norms (SSA 1975, s20(4)). These are, however, only qualifications of 'suitability'—if none of them apply in a particular case, all other relevant matters must be considered (R(U)5/68).

The D of Em must initially prove an employment prima facie suitable; the claimant must then prove it unsuitable (R(U)26/52). Convincing the D of Em that it knows less of the local labour market than the claimant is naturally difficult and avoiding disqualification by proving 'good cause' where possible is a sounder line of defence. Unlike 'just cause' (see (iii) above), 'good cause' is related to the terms of employment (or, presumably, the training) offered (R(U)20/55). Therefore a refusal may with good cause be based on the nature of the work (e.g. its suitability with regard to the claimant's qualifications, experience, age or health), the place of work (e.g. distance from home, the effect of outdoor work on health), or the hours of work (R(U)20/60). The length of time a claimant has been unemployed may affect the decision; in particular it may defeat the objection that offered employment is not within his usual occupation. To refuse an offer solely to avoid an income below unemployment benefit level is not 'good cause' (R(U)10/61). Circumstances insufficient to establish good cause may suffice to reduce the disqualification period.

(c) Rates and duration of unemployment benefit   There are two rates of unemployment benefit (SSA 1975, s14(4)-(6)).

(i) A higher rate is paid to claimants under pensionable age who satisfy the contribution conditions: a married woman, however, can only receive the higher rate while she receives an increase for a husband incapable of self-support (see (13)(a) below); or is living with her husband who receives invalidity pension (see (3) below), category A, C or D retirement pension (see (10)(b)(e) below), or who does not contribute to her maintenance at a weekly rate more than the difference between the higher and lower rates.

(ii) A lower rate is paid to all married women under pensionable age. Those over pensionable age are paid at the rate of retirement pension they would have received had they retired, disregarding the earnings rule and possible increases of pension (see (10)(b)(c)(d)(i) below). The current rates are shown in table 2.

Unemployment benefit is not paid for the first three days of a period of interruption, known as waiting days, but is paid thereafter for up to 312 days of an interruption (SSA 1975, ss14(3), 18(1)). Thereafter a claimant cannot be entitled to unemployment benefit again, in either the same or a subsequent period of interruption, until he has been employed for a further thirteen weeks and worked twenty-one hours or more in each week (SSA 1975, s18(2)).

(d) Earnings-related supplement   A claimant under pensionable age entitled to unemployment benefit is also entitled to a weekly ERS for up to 156 days after the thirteenth day of a period of interruption of employment (SSA 1975, s14(7)). In the case of a claimant suspended but not dismissed by his employer, days of unemployment are for ERS purposes only taken into account from the seventh day in a continuous period of suspension (SSA 1975, s17(3)(a)).

ERS is computed by first calculating a claimant's 'reckonable weekly earnings' by dividing by fifty the earnings factor of Class 1 contributions paid in the last year before that including the first day of the period of interruption of employment. He then receives as ERS the lesser of two sums:

(i) one-third of the aggregate of the amount by which his reckonable weekly earnings exceed the current lower earnings limit but do not exceed £30, and 15 per cent of the excess of reckonable weekly earnings over £30 but below the upper earnings limit: or

(ii) the amount by which his unemployment benefit, including increases for dependants (see (13) below), falls short of 85 per cent of his reckonable weekly earnings (SSA 1975, Sch 6, paras 1-3).

(2) Sickness Benefit

(a) Entitlement   A claimant is entitled to sickness benefit for any day of 'incapacity for work' which forms part of a period of interruption of employment (SSA 1975, s14(1)(b); see (1)(a) above).

A day of incapacity for work means a day on which the claimant is 'incapable of work by reason of some specific disease or bodily or mental disablement' (SSA 1975, s17(1)(a)(ii)). A claimant must prove he is incapable of work (R(S)13/52) by producing evidence establishing incapacity (R(S)1/53). In the absence of conflicting evidence the prescribed medical certificate (Form Med 3) from the claimant's doctor is sufficient; an employer's certificate that a claimant is absent through illness is not enough (R(S)13/51). A doctor's certificate is not conclusive if other evidence contradicts it; Insurance Officers are particularly suspicious of doctor's certificates obtained at traditional holiday periods (R(S)13/55, R(S)4/60, R(S)5/60); and a medical certificate influenced by non-medical factors may be refused (R(S)13/54).

The test of incapacity has been summarized thus:

A person is incapable of work if, having regard to his age, education, experience, state of health and other personal factors, there is no work or type of work which he can reasonably be expected to do. By 'work' we mean remunerative work whether part-time or whole-time (R(S)11/51).

Availability of work in a locality is immaterial, since the incapacity must result from a specific disease or disablement (R(S)11/51). Although confined to personal factors, the test is rigorously applied. A claimant who remains at work even on crutches or in a wheel-chair is not entitled (R(S)13/52, R(S)5/51). One permitted exception is work under medical supervision designed as therapy for a claimant who is otherwise accepted as incapacitated.

'Specific disease or bodily or mental disablement' includes an unspecified psychological condition (R(S)4/56), hospitalization, even if only for observation (R(S)1/58), and regular out-patient treatment which prevents work between visits (R(S)24/51). Pregnancy is not a specific disease or disablement, but a medical certificate citing 'sickness of pregnancy' has been allowed (CS 221/49).

After a period in receipt of sickness benefit a claimant is visited by a DHSS officer or required to be examined by a DHSS-appointed doctor, and subsequently the award of benefit is reviewed (see (C)(4) below). The majority of awards are not terminated on review, but where benefit is discontinued an appeal should be considered especially if the claimant's doctor and the DHSS investigations produce conflicting opinions.

(b) Disqualifications   There are three disqualifications for sickness benefit; in all cases the period of disqualification is up to six weeks, during which penalized claimants must rely on SB (SSA 1975, s20(2)).

(i) Misconduct   This disqualification penalizes a claimant who is incapable of work as a result of his own misconduct. Venereal disease and pregnancy are specifically excluded from the operation of this provision. The only reported example of misconduct is self-induced alcoholism (R(S)2/53). Short of self-inflicted injury there seems to be little other conduct (except misuse of drugs) which could lead to this disqualification.

(ii) Medical treatment   Failure to attend for or submit to a medical or other examination or treatment (apart from vaccination, inoculation and all but minor surgery) if required under regulations leads to disqualification. Medical examinations are usually required only when cases are reviewed; three days' notice must be given.

The failure must be 'without good cause', which covers reasons such as religious objections but not refusal to attend except on the claimant's own conditions (R(S)9/51, R(S)1/64). Refusal to undergo non-medical treatment is not penalized if it does not relate to recovery from the disease or disablement (R(S)3/57–blind claimant refused vocational training which would not cure her blindness).

(iii) Rules of behaviour   A claimant in breach of any of the rules of behaviour, prescribed by regulations, without 'good cause' is disqualified. There are three rules.

First, the claimant must refrain from behaviour calculated to retard his recovery, and answer reasonable inquiries as to whether he is doing so. 'Calculated' is interpreted subjectively, so a claimant's reasonable belief that his behaviour would not retard recovery is good cause (R(I)26/51).

Second, a claimant must not be absent from his residence without leaving word where he may be found. This is contravened if he is out when a DHSS officer calls, even if he is ignorant of the rule (R(S)21/52). But 'good cause' will assist the claimant out for a few hours at a time, particularly if his doctor has instructed him to go out or if there is no one with whom to leave a message (R(S)6/55).

Third, a claimant must not do remunerative work, except as part of medical treatment or as a non-employed person. To work on medical advice for very little remuneration is either no breach of this rule, or is a breach with good cause (CWS2/48, R(S)10/60). But to do regular work for which others might be paid is a breach (CWS5/50), as is doing remunerative work because no one else could (R(S)5/33).

Since the length of the disqualification period is discretionary, a trivial breach of the rules or a 'first offence' may be visited with only a token penalty such as one day (R(S)4/61).

(c) Rate and duration of sickness benefit   The rates of sickness benefit are as for unemployment benefit (see (1)(c) above). No payment is made for the first three days, and is limited to 168 days in a period of interruption of employment; thereafter claimants still incapable of work qualify for invalidity benefit (SSA 1975, ss14(3), 15(1)).

(d) Earnings-related supplement   Sickness benefit payable to Class 1 contributors is augmented by ERS in the same way as unemployment benefit (see (1)(d) above). A claimant receiving injury benefit (see ch3(A)(2)) who would otherwise receive sickness benefit, is paid ERS with injury benefit (SSA 1975, Sch 6, paras 5, 6).

(3)   Invalidity Benefit

Invalidity benefit consists of invalidity pension and an additional invalidity allowance. It is only conditional on contributions in as much as it replaces sickness benefit for which claimants under pensionable age must satisfy contribution conditions. Unlike sickness benefit it has no specified duration. Despite its name, it is not confined to invalids.

(a) Entitlement and disqualifications   A claimant is entitled to an invalidity pension for days of incapacity for work after the 168th day of a period of interruption of employment; he must be under pensionable age or, if over that age, not retired and able to satisfy the same conditions required of his age group for unemployment benefit (see (1)(a) above) (SSA 1975, s15 (1)(2)).

If a claimant is more than five years below pensionable age on the first day of incapacity for work he is also entitled to invalidity allowance while in receipt of invalidity pension (SSA 1975, s16 (1)).

The sickness benefit disqualifications all apply to invalidity benefit (see (2)(b) above).

(b) Rate of invalidity benefit   There is a standard rate of invalidity pension for those below pensionable age (see table 2). For those over pensionable age, the rate is that of the retirement pension they would receive if retired, disregarding increases for dependants and working after pensionable age (SSA 1975, s15 (3)(4)).

Invalidity allowance is paid at higher, middle and lower rates to those who on the first day of incapacity for work were under thirty-five, forty-five and sixty (fifty-five for women) respectively (SSA 1975 s16 (2); see table 2).

No ERS is payable with invalidity benefit, so despite invalidity allowance the change from sickness to invalidity benefit often causes a noticeable reduction in benefit.

(4)   Non-contributory Invalidity Pension

Like invalid care allowance (see (5) below), this benefit was introduced by the Social Security Benefits Act 1975, though immediately consolidated in the SSA 1975. It will come into force on a day appointed by regulations.

(a) Entitlement and disqualifications   A claimant is entitled to the pension for any day on which he is incapable of work if he has been so incapable for at least the preceding 196 consecutive days (SSA 1975, s36(1)). 'Incapable of work' is to be defined by regulations, which will also prescribe residence qualifications (SSA 1975, s36(3)(7)). Regulations will also provide that a person who has previously been entitled to the pension may be entitled afresh by reference to a period ending before the first day of fresh entitlement and not consisting of consecutive days (SSA 1975, s36(6)).

The following persons are disqualified from receiving the pension:

(i) a person under sixteen or receiving full-time education;

(ii) a married woman either living with her husband or receiving maintenance from him at a rate not less than the weekly rate of the pension, and a woman 'cohabiting with a man as his wife' (see (8)(d) below); unless in either case she is 'incapable of performing normal household duties' (also to be defined by regulations);

(iii) a person who has reached pensionable age, unless he was entitled to the pension immediately before reaching that age;

(iv) a person disqualified by one of the disqualifications for sickness benefit, which all apply to this pension (see (2)(b) above) (SSA 1975, s36(2)(4)(7)(9)).

As the name implies, there are no contribution conditions. In effect, it is a parallel benefit to invalidity benefit for those not qualifying for that benefit (see (3) above).

(b) Rate   The pension is paid at a standard weekly rate (see table 2).

(5)   Invalid Care Allowance

Like the non-contributory invalidity pension, this is a non-contributory benefit due to come into force on a day to be appointed.

(a) Entitlement and disqualifications   A claimant must establish that he is 'regularly and substantially engaged' in caring for a severely disabled person and that he himself is 'not gainfully employed'; both expressions in quotes are to be defined by regulations (SSA 1975, s37(1)(8)). A 'severely disabled person' means a relative of the claimant or other person in respect of whom an attendance allowance (see (6) below) or 'other payment out of public funds on account of his need for attendance' is being paid (the categories of relatives, other persons and payments will be specified by regulations; the payments will presumably include II constant attendance allowance: see ch 3(A)(3)(c)) (SSA 1975, s37(1)(2)).

Residential qualifications will also be prescribed by regulations (SSA 1975, s37(4)). A claimant will only be entitled to one allowance at a time so, for example, a daughter caring for two invalid parents will only receive one invalid care allowance. Where two or more persons qualify for an allowance in respect of one severely disabled person, they may elect who shall be the recipient; in default of such agreement, the Secretary of State will decide who will receive the allowance (SSA 1975, s37(7)).

The first three categories of person disqualified for non-contributory invalidity pension are also disqualified for invalid care allowance (see (4)(a) (i)-(iii) above) (SSA 1975, s37(3)(5)).

(b) Rate   The allowance is paid at a standard weekly rate (see table 2).

(6)   Attendance Allowance

(a) Entitlement   An attendance allowance is payable to a person who is 'so severely disabled physically or mentally' that he requires from another person either 'frequent attention throughout the day' or 'prolonged or repeated attention during the night' in connection with his bodily functions or 'continual supervision' throughout the day or night 'to avoid substantial danger to himself or others' (SSA 1975, s35(1)). This is the only condition of entitlement, there being no contribution conditions.

With only a few reported decisions to date there is little available guidance to the meaning of this condition, except that 'continual supervision' includes 'regularly receiving supervision' (CA5/72 unreported); that if supervision or attention is being provided that is 'strong evidence that it was required'; and that whether supervision to avoid danger is required is to be decided in the circumstances of each case (R(A)1/73). The term 'night' has been held to mean 'that period of inactivity through which a household went in the dark hours' beginning 'from the time at which the household, as it were, closed down for the night'; thus undressing a paraplegic claimant prior to going to bed was not a service required at night (R v NI Commissioner, ex parte Secretary of State for Social Services, [1974] 1 WLR 1290).

(b) Rate and duration of attendance allowance   There are two rates of the allowance; a higher rate if attention or supervision is required day and night and a lower rate if either is required only by day or night (SSA 1975, s35(2)(3)).

Attendance allowance is payable for the period certified by the Attendance Allowance Board as one in which the claimant fulfils the condition of entitlement and which is preceded by six months during which it was also satisfied (SSA 1975, s35(2)). An allowance cannot be backdated but may be claimed and an award made during the preliminary six months subject to a review if it is discovered that subsequently the condition has not at some time been fulfilled (SSA 1975, s35(4)). An allowance is not paid while a claimant is in Part III accommodation (see ch 8 (A)(2)) or other accommodation provided out of public funds (SSA 1975, s35(6)).

(c) Procedure   The Attendance Allowance Board is entrusted with all decisions relating to attendance allowances (SSA 1975, ss105-6 and Sch 11). In practice it delegates its functions to doctors and initially the claimant's own doctor completes a form about his patient and a doctor delegated by the Board decides from this form whether the statutory condition is fulfilled. If an award is made the Board certifies the period of the award and if attention or supervision is required day or night or both.

Either on a claimant's request or of its own volition the Board may review a decision and consequently issue, revoke or alter a certificate. The review procedure takes the form of a visit by a delegated doctor who completes a form similar to the original, on the basis of which another delegated doctor makes a written decision (Carson (1972) NLJ 973). On any question of law arising from a review or refusal to review, an appeal lies to a NI Commissioner with his leave. One commissioner has appeared to confine 'questions of law' to 'errors of law' but included within that term decisions exposing a false legal proposition or unsupported by evidence or absurd, breaches of natural justice and failure to give adequate written reasons for a decision (R(A)1/72).

(7)   Maternity Benefit

There are two forms of maternity benefit: a lump sum payment (maternity grant) and a short-term weekly allowance (maternity allowance).

(a) Maternity grant   A woman is entitled to the grant if she has been confined in Great Britain or her pregnancy has advanced to within nine weeks of expected confinement (SSA 1975, s21(1)(3)(5)). Confinement includes, as well as labour after the normal term of pregnancy resulting in a normal birth, labour after twenty-eight weeks resulting in a live or still birth (SSA 1975, s23(1)(a)).

In addition either the claimant or her husband must satisfy the contribution conditions; this follows automatically if she satisfies the contribution conditions for maternity allowance (see table 1).

A claim can be made on a husband's contribution record regardless of the child's paternity (Scott v Northumberland and Durham Miners Permanent Relief Fund [1920] 1 KB 174), or on a late husband's record in the case of a posthumous child (SSA 1975, s 21(2)); but not on that of the child's father if he is not married to the claimant (CG 3/49) or that of a husband she marries after the confinement (R(G)1/52). In the event of twins or a multiple birth a grant is paid for each child (SSA 1975, s21(4)).

(b) Maternity allowance   Maternity allowance can only be claimed by women who have paid full-rate Class 1 or Class 2 contributions. A claimant, whose pregnancy must have reached the fourteenth week before the expected week of confinement, must satisfy the contribution conditions (see table 1) (SSA 1975, s22(1)). The allowance is payable for eighteen weeks from the eleventh week before the anticipated confinement (the 'maternity allowance period'), though this may be extended in cases of late confinement (SSA 1975, s22(2)(7)). As with maternity grant, stillbirths are not excepted, but an allowance ceases if the claimant dies or her pregnancy ends otherwise than by confinement (SSA 1975, s22(5)(6)).

There are three disqualifications for maternity allowance: working during the maternity allowance period, failing to observe rules of behaviour, and failing to attend or submit to a required medical examination—all correspond to sickness benefit disqualifications (see (2)(b) above) (SSA 1975, s22(9)). The second and third disqualifications can be avoided by showing 'good cause'. The first is less flexible; thus a woman confined much earlier than expected who thus only stops work a few days before may only receive allowance from the day after she stops work (CG 266/49).

A Class 1 contributor in receipt of maternity allowance is also entitled to ERS from the thirteenth day without work for a maximum of 156 days in a period out of work, including days for which she has received an ERS of unemployment or sickness benefit (SSA 1975, s22(4)). The ERS is calculated as for those benefits (see (1)(d) above).

(8)   Widow's Benefit

There are three forms of widow's benefit: widow's allowance paid for the period following a husband's death; widowed mother's allowance paid to a widow with children; and widow's pension paid to widows who qualify until they reach sixty. A claimant can only receive one form of widow's benefit at once (SSA 1975, ss25(3), 26(3)). All three forms of benefit are related to husbands' contributions, so a widow whose husband's contribution record is deficient must rely on SB (see ch 4), as must the 'widow' of a common law marriage and a woman whose former husband dies after a decree absolute of divorce or nullity.

(a) Widow's allowance   A woman may claim widow's allowance if on her husband's death she was under pensionable age or if her husband was not at his death entitled to a category A retirement pension (see (10)(b) below). In addition her late husband must have satisfied the contribution condition (see table 1)(SSA 1975, s 24(1)).

The allowance is payable for twenty-six weeks from and including the date of a husband's death (SSA 1975, s24(2); R(G)3/52). An earnings-related addition is also payable for each week that a Class 1 contributor's widow is entitled to widow's allowance (SSA 1975, s 24(3)). This is calculated like ERS of unemployment benefit but on the basis of a late husband's reckonable weekly earnings in the year before that in which he died; and the addition paid is the first of the two amounts used in relation to unemployment benefit, whereas ERS is the lesser of the two (see (1)(d) above)(SSA 1975, Sch6, paras1-3).

(b) Widowed mother's allowance   A widow is entitled to this allowance if either:

(i) she has a family including a child living with her or in respect of whom she is making contributions to maintenance at the specified weekly rate, and this child was either a child of her late husband's family under the Family Allowances Act (FAA 1965, Sch, para 3) or a child of the claimant and her husband or of the claimant and a previous husband who also died; or

(ii) she has residing with her a person under nineteen who is or has been a child as defined in (i), or would have been were he under sixteen or in Great Britain when her husband died; or

(iii) she is pregnant by her late husband (SSA 1975, s25(1)(2)).

In addition her late husband must have fulfilled the contribution conditions (see table 1).

Widowed mother's allowance is payable for as long as the claimant satisfies one of these conditions, but not while she receives a widow's allowance (SSA 1975, s25(3)). A widow with children, therefore, normally receives widow's allowance for six months after her husband's death, then a widowed mother's allowance until her children reach nineteen.

(c) Widow's pension   Widow's pension is paid to a widow whose late husband satisfied the contribution conditions (see table 1) either if on her husband's death she was over forty and under sixty-five or if she has ceased to be entitled to a widowed mother's allowance between those ages (SSA 1975, s26(1)).

The rate of the pension is reduced, in the case of a woman under fifty, by 7 per cent of the normal rate times the number of years or part of a year by which her age was less than fifty at her husband's death or when her entitlement to widowed mother's allowance ceased (SSA 1975, s26(2)).

Widow's pension is paid until a claimant reaches sixty-five (when she qualifies for a category B retirement pension: see (10)(c) below), but not while she receives other forms of widow's benefit (SSA 1975, s26(3)).

(d) Cohabitation   A claimant is disqualified for any form of widow's benefit after she remarries or 'for any period during which she is cohabiting with a man as his wife' (SSA 1975, ss24(2), 25(3), 26(3)). The same disqualification applies to non-contributory invalidity pension, invalid care allowance and child's special allowance (see (4)(5) above, (11) below) and, though differently phrased, to II death benefit (see ch 3 (A)(5) and SB (see ch 4(A)(2)).

Unlike cohabitation in SB cases, there is a volume of NI case-law which offers some guidance. It is for the DHSS to prove cohabitation (R(G)1/53). How must it be proved? In 1971, a Commissioner held that the question 'requires an examination of three main matters: (1) their relationship in relation to sex: (2) their relationship in relation to money: (3) their general relationship. Although all three are as a rule relevant, no single one of them is conclusive' (R(G)3/71). However, it is clear that sex once admitted nearly always leads to disqualification; a later decision holding it necessary 'to look at the whole picture' stated that 'important elements include living together, habitually sharing a bed, being the parents of a child, having sexual intercourse, and the pooling of financial resources'—three sex-related criteria out of five (R(G)2/72). Earlier cases show that, against confessed sexual relationships, financial arrangements and the use of different names by a man and woman carry little weight (R(G)2/64, CP 97/49, R(G)5/68), but sharing accommodation and the same name, for whatever reason, are also 'cogent evidence of cohabitation' (R(G)5/68).

Proving that cohabitation has ended is yet more difficult. The burden of proof is now apparently on the claimant (R(P)6/52). Where cohabitation has in the past been clearly established by admitted sex and the birth of a child, it is necessary to consider other circumstances (CG 214/50, R(G)2/64). Separation for business or holiday reasons does not end cohabitation since it would not mean that a married couple had ceased to live together, but separation after a quarrel does end cohabitation (R(G)11/59). If a man returns to a woman he formerly lived with there must be clear evidence of a change in their relationship to avoid a presumption of resumed cohabitation (R(G)11/59, R(G)14/59, R(G)6/52). A widow who purportedly remarries but later obtains a decree of nullity is cohabiting as long as she lives with her 'husband' as his wife (R(G)1/53).

As a survey of cohabitation cases showed, many common situations such as landlady and lodger or employer and housekeeper may attract allegations of cohabitation (Lister, 1973, pp.9-12). In such cases an appeal should be made. A common complication is the simultaneous disqualification for widow's benefit and SB and it is not unknown for tribunals to reach different decisions on the two benefits (Lister, 1973, pp.30-1).

(9)   Guardian's Allowance
A claimant is entitled to guardian's allowance in respect of a child of his family (within the meaning of the Family Allowances Act (see ch5(A)(1)) if either:
    (a) both the child's parents are dead (in the case of adopted children, the adoptive parent or parents; in the case of illegitimate children, the

mother and, if paternity has been established, the father); or

(b) one parent is dead and the claimant proves he was at the date of death unaware of, and has failed after all reasonable efforts to discover, the whereabouts of the other parent (some attempt to trace the missing parent must be made (R(G)4/59), and there is no entitlement if that parent is discovered other than by the claimant (R(G)3/68)); or

(c) one parent is dead and the other is in prison (SSA 1975, s38(1)(2)).

The child must either be living with the claimant or the claimant must contribute weekly to the child's maintenance at the prescribed rate (SSA 1975, s43(1)(2)). There are no contribution conditions.

A parent cannot claim the allowance in respect of his own child (SSA 1975, s38(6)). Where a child is a member of a family of a man and his wife, only the wife is entitled to the allowance but either may receive it (SSA 1975, s38(5); FAA 1965, s4(2)-(6)). The allowance is paid as long as the conditions of entitlement are satisfied.

(10)   Retirement Pensions and Age Addition

The last Conservative government's legislation envisaged widespread changes in the provision of pensions: from 1975 all insured persons would contribute towards both NI pensions and either approved occupational pensions or a second state pension (SAA 1973, Pts II, III). The Labour government of 1974 did not bring the latter provisions into operation and proposed in their place a different scheme to be operational by 1978 at the latest (Cmnd 5713). This scheme, incorporated in the Social Security Pensions Bill 1975, seeks to relate not only retirement but also widow's and invalidity pensions to claimants' earnings, and also to maintain the value of pensions in the face of inflation. Partial contracting out of this scheme will be permissible if an occupational pension scheme meets certain statutory requirements. When operational, the new scheme will make considerable changes to NI contributions and benefits. In the meantime only the NI basic scheme pensions are in operation. There are four such pensions (one for contributors, one for their wives and two for the very old) and an age addition.

(a) General provisions   It is a condition of entitlement to any retirement pension that the claimant has reached pensionable age (sixty-five for a man, sixty for a woman) and retired from regular employment. A person may be treated as retired on reaching pensionable age whether or not he was previously earning or is or intends to continue earning, provided he does so 'only occasionally or to an inconsiderable extent or in circumstances not inconsistent with retirement' or his earnings cannot be expected to exceed or will only occasionally exceed the amount which would reduce his pension (SSA 1975, s27(3)). Regular excess of earnings over this amount invokes the earnings rule (see (d)(i) below). It is important to note that these tests are alternatives: only one needs to be satisfied for a person to be classed 'retired'.

To continue to earn requires the receipt of 'remuneration or profit' (SSA 1975, s3(1)), which is more liberally treated than in the context of classification of contributors (see (A)(1) above) (R(P)5/55). 'Occasionally' earning on the other hand is interpreted literally; work for several months at a time is not occasional nor is intermittent work for a substantial proportion of the year (R(P)8/52, R(P)10/53).

Whether work is only 'to an inconsiderable extent' is often judged by the time spent at work—less than twelve hours a week or less than a quarter of the normal working week, whichever is more favourable to the claimant, has been used as a guideline (CP 33/49). But a small amount of actual working time while employed for a larger period is not 'inconsiderable' (CP 126/49, R(P) 12/53); though claimants working long hours may still be treated as retired by the 'not inconsistent' test (R(P)9/54). A Commissioner has held that the self-employed should be judged by that test and not the 'inconsiderable extent' test (R(P)2/53).

Whether an occupation is 'not inconsistent with retirement' requires consideration of all the circumstances; although the hours worked are relevant, so is the type of work: if it is an occupation which a retired person might reasonably engage in the test may be satisfied (R(P)8/54). The claimant must prove consistency with retirement (R(P)11/55). Most of the reported examples indicate the need for a change on retirement. Thus to continue in the same job for no payment but in return for board and lodging is inconsistent with retirement (R(P)3/53), but to do the same work as before but only occasionally or for purely personal reasons is not (R(P)5/51, R(P)3/52). On the other hand a change of occupation to one merely more suited to an older person is not necessarily sufficient to satisfy the test (CP 21/49).

Whether he works after pensionable age or not, a claimant can only be treated as retired after giving notice in writing of the date of his retirement (SSA 1975, s27(4)). Notice after the date of retirement may only be back-dated one month with a possible extension of up to one year with good cause for delay. Notice should be given in advance so that the pension can be paid from the date of retirement. The date of retirement is the day work ceases, even if the claimant is paid thereafter (e.g. holiday pay: R(P)17/52). Anyone is deemed retired five years after pensionable age (SSA 1975, s27(5)).

A claimant may only receive one category of pension; if otherwise entitled to more than one, he receives that most favourable to him (SSA 1975, s27(6)).

(b) Category A retirement pension   This is payable from the date of retirement for life to a claimant satisfying the contribution conditions; a married woman is only entitled if she married at fifty-five or later, or if she can satisfy a further contribution condition (see table 1) (SSA 1975, s28(1)(2)). In the case of a woman widowed before pensionable age, her husband's contributions may be treated as her own to make good any deficiency in her record (SSA 1975, s28(3) and Sch 7).

Category A pensions may be increased in two ways (other than in respect of dependants).

(i) Increments for deferred retirement   The weekly rate of pension is increased by $\frac{1}{8}$ per cent for every six days (except Sundays) between pensionable age and a deferred date of retirement, subject to a minimum of forty-eight such days of increment. A widow is entitled to a $\frac{1}{16}$ per cent increase for every six days which provided her husband with an increment, or would have so provided him had he retired on the date he died. Percentage increments for deferred retirement are based on the basic weekly rates disregarding increases for dependants but including invalidity increases (SSA 1975, s28(4)-(6),(8)).

(ii) Invalidity increase   If a claimant was entitled to an invalidity allowance (see (3) above) at any time in the thirteen weeks and a day before reaching pensionable age, the rate of category A pension is increased by the rate of that allowance, as uprated periodically (SSA 1975, s28(7)(8)).

(c) Category B retirement pension   This pension is solely for wives and based on their husband's contributions. A woman is entitled if she is or has been married, has reached pensionable age and can satisfy one of four sets of conditions:

(i) she is married when she reaches pensionable age to a husband who is also of pensionable age, and satisfies the contribution conditions (see table 1), and both are retired; or

(ii) as (i) but she marries after pensionable age; or

(iii) her husband has died after she reached pensionable age, she was married to him at his death and he satisfied the contribution conditions; or

(iv) her husband died before she reached pensionable age, she has retired, was a widow immediately before reaching pensionable age and is entitled to a widow's pension (see (8)(c) above) as a result of her husband's death (SSA 1975, s29(1)-(5)).

Once entitled a claimant receives the pension for life (SSA 1975, s29(9)). There are two rates of payment. The lower is paid to women qualifying under (i) or (ii) while their husbands are alive. The higher rate is paid to those claimants after their husband's death and to women qualifying under (iii). The rate for those qualifying under (iv) is that of their widow's pension (SSA 1975, s29(7)). The appropriate rate may be increased in two ways (apart from increases for dependants).

(i) Increments for husband's deferred retirement   This is paid, while a claimant's husband is alive and married to her, at the rate of $\frac{1}{16}$ per cent for every six days of increment after she married him or reached pensionable age; to this is added, after a husband's death, a further $\frac{1}{16}$ per cent for every six days of increment for which he himself qualified for an increase of category A pension (SSA 1975, s29(10)).

(ii) Invalidity increase   If, but for the bar on the receipt of two pensions, a married woman would also be entitled to a category A pension with an invalidity increase (see (b)(ii) above), she is entitled to receive that increase with her category B pension (SSA 1975, s29(8)).

(d)Working after retirement   Category A and B pensions may be affected in the five years after pensionable age by two provisions relating to work after retirement: the earnings rule and election to return to work.

(i) The earnings rule   Claimants entitled to category A or B pensions while working after pensionable age (see (a) above) have their pensions reduced, if earnings exceed £20 per week, by half the excess under £4 and all the excess over £4 (SSA 1975, s30(1)). From April 1976, the earnings limit will be raised from £20 to £35 and, from April 1977, to £50 (SSA 1975, s30(2)).

(ii) Election to return to work   A category A or B pensioner can elect to return to work and forego his pension; instead he will accrue increments of his ultimate pension for deferred retirement (see (b)-(c) above). If a husband and wife are entitled to category A and B pensions respectively, the wife must consent to her husband's election unless she unreasonably withholds consent (SSA 1975, s30(3)(4)). This provision only applies to the five years after pensionable age; thereafter all persons are treated as retired (SSA 1975, s27(5)).

(e) Category C and D retirement pensions   These pensions are for the very old. Category C pensions are payable to:

(i) those over pensionable age on 5 July 1948 (paid at the higher of two rates);

(ii) wives of those in (i), if over pensionable age and retired (paid at a lower rate, but increased to the higher rate if marriage ends);

(iii) widows or former wives of husbands over pensionable age on 5 July 1948 (at the rate prescribed by regulations) (SSA 1975, s39(1)(2)(4)).

Category D pensions are paid, at the same rates as category C, to claimants over eighty and unentitled to category A, B or C pensions or only entitled to one of those pensions at a rate less than the appropriate rate of category D pension (SSA 1975, s39(1)).

There are no contribution conditions for either pension and both are paid for life (SSA 1975, s39(3)).

(f) Age addition   Any claimant receiving a retirement pension of any category who is over eighty is entitled to an age addition, payable for life (SSA 1975, s40(1)(3)). There are no contribution conditions.

(11)   Child's Special Allowance
This benefit can be claimed by a divorced mother if:

(a) her former husband, who is dead, satisfied the contribution conditions (see table 1); and

(b) her family includes a child who at her husband's death was either a child of her family or her husband's under the Family Allowance Act 1965 (see ch5(A)(1)) or would have been if in Great Britain; and

(c) she was receiving from her husband before his death payments for the child of at least the prescribed weekly amount (SSA 1975, s31)). An annulled marriage may be treated as a divorce (SSA 1975, s162(a)).

As with guardian's allowance, the child in question must live with the claimant or she must contribute to the cost of providing for the child at the prescribed weekly rate; only one child may be the subject of an allowance (SSA 1975, s43(1)-)3)).

The purpose of the allowance is to compensate for the end of maintenance payments for children; thus no entitlement exists if a husband made no payments for a lengthy period before his death, though temporary and involuntary lapses may be ignored (R(G)5/59, R(G)6/59, R(G)15/59, R(G)3/60). A claimant whose husband's undertaking to make payments could not materialize because of his death is entitled (R(G)17/59).

Like widow's benefit, child's special allowance is not paid while a claimant cohabits with a man as his wife (see (8)(d) above).

(12)   Death Grant
A death grant is paid in respect of the death of a person in one of four categories:

(a) a contributor who satisfied the contribution condition (see table 1);

(b) the wife, husband, widow, widower or child of a person in (a);

(c) a child of the family of a person in (a) who predeceased him or a posthumous child of such a person;

(d) a person over nineteen who at his death either has been incapacitated for regular employment since reaching nineteen, or was living (or would be were he not in an institution for disabled persons) with a near relative who satisfies the contribution condition or is the wife or widow of a man who satisfies that condition (SSA 1975, s32 (1)-(3)).

The grant is not payable in respect of a person who reached pensionable age before 5 July 1948 or died outside Great Britain (SSA 1975, s32(5)) or in respect of a stillborn child (R(G)3/51). The amount of the grant depends on the age of the deceased on death (see table 2).

(13)   Increases of Benefits for Dependants
The rate of most weekly NI benefits is increased if a claimant has dependants to support. There are separate provisions for children and

adult dependants.

(a) Children   Unemployment or sickness benefit, invalidity pension, widow's or widowed mother's allowance and category A, B or C retirement pensions are increased for each child in a claimant's family, including the child of a woman living with him if the child is their illegitimate child or is at least six months old and has been maintained by the claimant for six months prior to the claim for an increase or the date of the claimant's retirement (SSA 1975, ss41(1)(2)(4), 42(1)-(3)). An increase may also be paid with a maternity allowance and relate to the child in respect of whose birth the allowance is paid, and with a child's special allowance in relation to any child except the older or eldest. No increase is payable for a child who is the subject of a guardian's or child's special allowance (SSA 1975, s41(1)(3)(5)). Increases for children may also be paid with a non-contributory invalidity pension or invalid care allowance in circumstances to be prescribed by regulations (SSA 1975, s49).

A further condition of entitlement is that the child must live with the claimant or he must be contributing at a prescribed weekly rate to the cost of providing for the child (SSA 1975, s43(1)(2)).

A married woman claimant can only receive an increase if her husband is 'incapable of self-support', defined as 'incapable by reason of physical or mental infirmity and likely to remain so for a prolonged period' (SSA 1975, s41(6) and Sch 20). This does not mean incapable of work; the question is whether a husband could secure 'a reasonable standard of living' (CG4/48, CG5/48), which is not to be judged by SB standards (CG3/48, R(G)2/57, R(G)3/57).

If a husband and wife are both entitled to category A, B or C pensions and to an increase for the same child, only one may receive the increase; and if they are separately entitled in respect of different children, the rate of increases paid is as for one family (SSA 1975, s42(4)). Increases are included for the purpose of the earnings rule (see (10)(d)(i) above)(SSA 1975, s41(1)).

Unlike SB, where the amount of requirements for a child depends on the child's age, increases of NI benefits are at a flat rate for first and subsequent children (see table 2).

(b) Adult dependants   Certain benefits may be increased in respect of adult dependants but only one increase may be paid at any time (SSA 1975, ss44(4), 48(1)).

(i) Unemployment or sickness benefit, category A or C retirement pension or invalidity pension is increased if a claimant's wife lives with him or if he contributes not less than the weekly amount of the increase to her maintenance (SSA 1975, ss44(1), 45(2)). Neither a woman cohabiting with a claimant nor a divorced wife may be treated as a wife (CS11/48, R(S)9/61).

(ii) Unemployment or sickness benefit, maternity allowance, category A or C retirement pension (with some exceptions) or (if the claimant is under pensionable age) invalidity pension is increased if either

the husband of a woman claimant is incapable of self-support (see (a) above), and either lives with her or receives from her maintenance of at least the amount of the increase; or

the claimant maintains a relative living with him; or

a woman has the care of the claimant's child or children: she need not have sole care of a child or even more care than the claimant provided she performs to a substantial extent duties necessary for a child's care (CS 726/49); an increase may be paid in respect of a child-minder if a wife goes out to work but not in respect of a woman living with the claimant as his wife (R(S)20/54,CS55/49) (SSA 1975, ss44(2)(3), 46, 47(1)).

(iii) A non-contributory invalidity pension or invalid care allowance may be increased in respect of an adult dependant in circumstances to be prescribed by regulations (SSA 1975, s49).

Increases of category A or C retirement pensions or invalidity pension in respect of a wife living with the claimant or a woman looking after his child or children are subject to an earnings rule: the wife's or woman's earnings in excess of £20 per week and under £4 lead to a reduction of the increase by half the excess; and any excess of £4 or more is deducted from the increase in full (SSA 1975, s45(3)). (From April 1976, the earnings limit will be raised from £20 to £35 and, from April 1977, to £50 (SSA 1975, s45(4).) Moreover, any increase of a category A or B pension in respect of an adult dependant is subject to the earnings rule for those pensions (see (10)(d)(i) above) (SSA 1975, s48(2)).

(14)   General Disqualifications
As already noted, several NI benefits may not be paid despite fulfilment of the conditions of entitlement because of disqualifications particular to those benefits. In addition there are three general disqualifications for all NI benefits: absence from Great Britain; imprisonment or detention in legal custody; and claiming after expiry of the time limit (subject to a 'defence' of 'good cause': see (C)(1) below) (SSA 1975, s82(1)(5)). Benefits may be suspended if a claimant receives hospital treatment as an in-patient (SSA 1975, s82(6)(b)).

(C)   Procedure, Payment and Appeals

In relation to all NI benefits except Attendance Allowance (see (6)(c) above), the manner of claiming, payment and the appeal structure is standard.

(1) Claims

A separate claim form is provided for each benefit and for increases of benefits for dependants. Forms are supplied by local DHSS offices, employment exchanges and often by other services. In respect of some benefits a claim form need not be sought. Unemployment benefit is usually claimed as part of the normal procedure on first registering at an employment exchange and is administered by the D of Em. Sickness benefit is claimed by completing the reverse of a doctor's medical certificate. Registrars supply special death certificates for NI purposes containing a request for the supply of widow's benefit and death grant claim forms. Retirement pension claim forms are sent to claimants a few months before they reach pensionable age. Evidence in support of a claim, such as birth certificates in relation to child-related benefits, may be required (SI 1971/707, reg 5). Claims may be treated as if made for another NI or II benefit (SI 1971/707, regs 7, 8 and Sch 1).

Claims must be made within specified time-limits to avoid disqualification, unless a claimant shows 'good cause' for delay (SSA 1975, s82(1); SI 1971/707, reg 11 and Sch 3). Good cause is not a 'good excuse' but 'means some fact (or combination of facts) which having regard to all the circumstances would probably have caused a reasonable person of his age or experience to act (or fail to act) as the claimant did' (CS 371/49, R(S)2/63). Ignorance of one's rights is not good cause; in such cases inquiries should be made (R(S)2/63, CWS 3/48, CWS 2/49), unless a claimant bona fide believes he is unlikely to be entitled (R(S)2/63). Misinformation or insufficient information from a competent source, such as a solicitor or DHSS local office, but not a neighbour or doctor, is good cause (CS 50/50, R(U)3/60, CSG 9/49, R(S)5/56), as is misunderstanding of DHSS leaflets or advice or a change in the law since refusal of an earlier claim (R(G)4/68 and (1973) LAG BUL. 20, R(S)14/54, R(U)6/52). Personal reasons such as severe illness or 'educational limitations', but not mere negligence, have also been permitted as good cause (CS 51/49, R(P)10/59, CG 15/48), as has the failure of a solicitor, parent, interpreter or other person entrusted with claiming (CG1/50, R(S) 4/52, CS 100/49).

A claim is considered first by an Insurance Officer who is nominally independent of the Departments and who is in practice bound by the Commissioners' Decisions as well as the legislation (SSA 1975, s99(1)-(2)). The Insurance Officer decides whether the conditions of entitlement exist. Certain questions (known as 'Minister's questions') must be referred to the Secretary of State for Social Services (in practice a Departmental official) for decision:

(a) whether a claimant is an earner and if so his contribution class (see (A)(1) above);

(b) satisfaction of contribution conditions (see table 2);

(c) which of two or more persons should receive an invalid care allowance (see (5)(a) above);

(d) increases of benefit where two or more claimants satisfy the conditions of entitlement (see (13)(a) above);

(e) whether a claimant is maintaining a child or which family a child is to be treated as in under the Family Allowances Act 1965 (see ch 5(A)(1));

(f) the treatment of a claim for a particular benefit as a claim for another benefit (SSA 1975, ss 93(1), 95(1)).

Questions arising under (a), (b) or (d) may be referred to the High Court or taken there on appeal from the Secretary of State's decision; an appellant's costs may be awarded against the DHSS regardless of the outcome (SSA 1975, s94). If a Minister's question arises on appeal to a NI local tribunal or Commissioner, it may be referred through an Insurance Officer to the Secretary of State (SSA 1975, s103). The Secretary of State may review and alter decisions in categories (a)–(e) (SSA 1975, ss95(2), 96).

(2) Payment

Payment of NI benefits is now either by girocheque for unemployment and sickness benefit, maternity benefit and death grant or, for other benefits, by books of orders encashable at a post office for up to twelve months from the date on the face of an order (SI 1971/707, regs 9-10A, 12). At the claimant's request, or to protect his interests, payment may be made to a third party (SI 1971/707, reg 15A). On the death of a claimant, the Secretary of State may appoint a person to make or pursue a claim to benefit to which the deceased may have been entitled and payment may be made to his personal representatives, legatees, next of kin or creditors (SI 1971/707, reg 15).

(3) Appeals

An Insurance Officer may refer a case to a NI local tribunal for decision (SSA 1975, s99(2)(3)). This rarely happens but may arise if an undecided point of law is involved. Otherwise cases come before the tribunals on appeal by claimants. An appeal may be made whenever there is a decision adverse to a claimant which includes refusal of benefit, payment of less than full benefit, disqualification or the length of a disqualification period but not Minister's questions (SSA 1975, s100(1). Appeals must be made in twenty-one days of an Insurance Officer's decision by written notice to a local office which should specify the grounds of appeal though this is not normally insisted on (SSA 1975, s100(4) (5); R(I)15/53). An appeal may be heard if made after the time-limit if the tribunal chairman allows 'for good cause' (SSA 1975, s100(4)). A refusal to hear a late appeal cannot be appealed against (R(U)21/64, R(U)44/59). The meaning of good cause in this context is not defined but the late claim decisions are arguably analogous (see (1) above).

A NI local tribunal consists of a lawyer chairman and one member from each of two panels representing employers and employees. Hearings are informal and in public though chairmen have the power to order, and appellants may request, in camera hearings. The Insurance Officer changes from decision-maker to advocate but often adds little to a written submission which, with the claimant's notice of appeal, is sent to all present a few days in advance. The appellant and Insurance Officer may be asked to withdraw while the tribunal deliberates and a written decision must be sent to both parties giving reasons and any dissenting opinion.

From a tribunal decision a further appeal may be made to a NI Commissioner by an Insurance Officer, claimant or an association 'which exists to promote the interests and welfare of its members' if the appeal concerns a member: this includes trade unions and claimants' unions and perhaps law centres (see ch13(B)(2)) and similar bodies (SSA 1975, s101(1)-(4)). Appeals must be made in writing to a local office within three months of a tribunal decision but a Commissioner may allow a late appeal 'for special reasons' (SSA 1975, s101(5)). In practice, many months may elapse before a Commissioner's hearing.

The Commissioners' hearings are in London, Cardiff and Edinburgh. They usually sit individually but occasionally as a tribunal of three in important cases. An oral hearing must be requested and may be dispensed with at a Commissioner's discretion. The Insurance Officer is usually represented by a DHSS solicitor. An Insurance Officer's written submission is sent to the appellant some weeks in advance of a hearing. Proceedings are more formal than before the local tribunals; hearsay evidence is admissible but treated more guardedly than in local tribunals. A Commissioner's decision can only be questioned by use of the prerogative orders (see ch 1(C)).

Before both tribunals and Commissioners skilled representation is desirable; though legal aid is not available, some assistance can be sought from solicitors and other sources (see ch 13).

(4) Review
The decision of an Insurance Officer, tribunal or Commissioner can be reviewed by an Insurance Officer, or by a tribunal on an Insurance Officer's reference, if:

(a) the decision was made in ignorance of or based on a mistake as to a material fact (a Commissioner's decision can only be reviewed in this way if fresh evidence is produced); or

(b) there has been a relevant change of circumstances since the decision; or

(c) a decision of the Secretary of State or Attendance Allowance Board has been reviewed (see (1) and (B)(6)(c) above) (SSA 1975, s104(1)).

A review can be requested by writing to an Insurance Officer stating the grounds (SSA 1975, s104(2)). Reviews are dealt with in exactly the same way as claims and are subject to the same rights of appeal (SSA 1975, s104(3)(4)). Payment of a benefit may be suspended until the resolution of doubts as to entitlement during a review (SSA 1975, s82(3)).

References
'Social Insurance and Allied Services', Report by Sir W. Beveridge, Cmd 6404 (1942).
'Report of the Royal Commission on Trade Unions and Employers' Associations', Chairman: Lord Donovan, Cmnd 3623 (1969).
Lister, R. (1973), 'As Man and Wife? A study of the Cohabitation Rule', CPAG, London.
'Better Pensions', Cmnd 5713 (1974).

Chapter 3

Industrial Injury Benefits

Statutory provisions for compensation for injury at work date from the Workmen's Compensation Acts 1897-1906, which were replaced in 1948 by the NI Industrial Injuries scheme which paralleled that of NI benefits; the Beveridge proposal for complete integration was not implemented (Cmd 6404, paras 77-105), but by 1975 the contribution, administration and appeals provisions had been merged with the main NI scheme. The II scheme however only extends to Class 1 NI Contributors (see ch 2(A)(1)(a)) and there are some procedural differences. The distinctive characteristics of the II scheme are the absence of contribution conditions (insurance begins on the first day of employment), conditions of entitlement common to all benefits, and higher rates of benefit than under the NI scheme. The II scheme has also inherited some of the wording of the Workmen's Compensation Acts with the effect that much pre-1948 case-law, as developed by the Commissioners, remains authoritative today. As with NI benefits, the principal legislation is the Social Security Act 1975, though separate provisions deal with pre-1948 injuries (see (C) below).

(A)   Benefits

(1)   General Provisions

The II scheme provides three forms of benefit—injury benefit, disablement benefit, and death benefit. As with NI benefits, increases may be made in respect of dependants (see (4) below). Disablement benefit only may also be increased by virtue of additional allowances paid in certain circumstances (see (3) below).

A claimant of any of these benefits must have suffered either 'personal injury caused after 4 July 1948 by accident arising out of and in the course of employment' (SSA 1975, s50(1)), or 'any prescribed disease (or) any prescribed personal injury not so caused, being a disease or injury due to the nature of that employment and developed after 4 July 1948' (SSA 1975, s76(1)).

(a) Personal injury by accident arising out of and in the course of employment   Few provisions of social security law have been more disputed than this. Under the Workmen's Compensation Acts the courts expounded at length on this phrase and the Commissioners have added to the case-law.

An accident in respect of which benefit is claimed must have happened while the insured person is in Great Britain (SSA 1975, s50(5)).

What is 'injury' for this purpose? Basically, the term has its normal meaning of physical injury or 'hurt' (Woodcock v L & NWR [1913] 3 KB 139,148). The injury must be 'to the living body of a human being. Damage to some artificial appendage, such as spectacles, false teeth or a wig or an artificial limb, may well cause incapacity for work, but such damage cannot constitute "personal injury", (R(I) 7/56). Any physiological change for the worse may constitute injury, and there is no need for a violent act or exceptional exertion to have caused the change (CI 5/49). There is still an injury within the 1975 Act even if 'the injury or change be occasioned partly or even mainly by the progress or development of an existing disease, if the work which (the claimant) is doing at or about the moment of the occurrence of the physiological injury or change contributes in any material degree to its occurrence' (Oates v Earl Fitzwilliam's Collieries Co [1939] 2 All ER 498,502,CA). This principle extends to previous injuries which are reactivated by or cause a proneness to the injury prompting a claim (CI 5/49, CI 27/49, CI 39/49).

How is the condition that an injury is caused 'by accident' satisfied? As with 'injury' the term 'accident' is accorded its normal meaning. 'It signifies an event which, although it may be one of several similar events, is capable of being reasonably clearly identified as the cause of the trouble' (R(I) 52/51). 'Accident' also embraces two situations: '(1) Personal injury sustained under circumstances which can be referred to as an "accident", and (2) cases in which there are no such circumstances capable of being so described but in which the results of the occurrences are so unexpected that they may be fairly considered as accidental' (CI 123/49). The occurrences must be 'unexpected' from the point of view of the person injured (Trim Joint District School Board of Management v Kelly [1914] AC 667,HL); this includes unforeseen occurrences caused by others (CI 63/49). The case-law abounds with examples of accidents held to be within the Act, and offers illustrations of similar cases falling either side of the line (e.g. Maskrey v Lancashire Shipping Co Ltd (1914)7 BWCC 428; Pyper v Manchester Lines Ltd [1916] 2 KB 691,CA).

While it is possible, in certain circumstances, to base a claim on a 'prescribed disease' (see (b) below), it is also permissible to claim on the grounds of 'injury by accident' if a disease is caused by an accident or accidental circumstances. 'It does not appear that by calling the consequences of an accidental injury a disease one alters the nature of the consequential results of the injury that has been inflicted' (Brintons Ltd v Turvey [1905] AC 230,233,HL). But it is important to distinguish between diseases resulting from an accident and those resulting from a continuous process.

> Two types of case have not always been sufficiently differentiated. In the one type there is found a single accident followed by a resultant injury, or a series of specific and ascertainable accidents followed by an injury which may be the consequence of any or all of them. In either case it is immaterial that the time at which the accident occurred cannot be located. In the other type, there is a continuous process going on substantially from day to day, though not necessarily from minute to minute, or even from hour to hour, which gradually over a period of years produces incapacity. In the first of these types, the resulting incapacity is held to be injury by accident. In the second it is not. There must come a time when the indefinite number of so-called accidents and the length of time over which they occur take away the element of accident and substitute that of process (Roberts v Dorothea Slate Quarries Co Ltd [1948] 2 All ER 201, 205-6,HL).

To bring a disease within the 'accident' head of claim, therefore, the evidence must point to an event or events which can be said to have caused the disease. Otherwise the claim is caught by this 'process' doctrine and the only possible claim is under the prescribed disease provisions.

The borderline between accident and process is very fine. Twenty years' inhalation of silica dust in a slate quarry leading to silicosis was held to be a process: but each of many inhalations of tuberculosis bacilli in a hospital was treated as an accident (Roberts v Dorothea (above); Pyrah v Doncaster Corp [1949] All ER 883, CA).

While the Commissioners have explicitly adopted the formulation of the process doctrine expressed in Roberts's case (CI 257/49), they have placed some qualifications on its operation. A tribunal of Commissioners stressed that the question whether a series of incidents amounts to accident or process depends on their continuity rather than their duration (CI 83/50). And a Commissioner has criticized 'a tendency unduly to extend the conception of injury by process in opposing claims for injury benefit', and while suggesting that the doctrine contemplates 'a length of time very much longer than two or three days', stated 'Each case has to be decided on its own facts' (R(I) 43/61). In another case, the Commissioner suggested that the doctrine frustrated the primary purpose of the legislation, 'to provide benefit when insured persons are injured or killed by their work' (R(I) 7/66). His invitation to Parliament to reform the law has not been heeded.

Having established both personal injury and accident as the cause of such injury, a claimant must finally show that the accident arose 'out of and in the course of his employment'. There are three general limits placed on the 'scope of employment' (as this requirement is often termed).

First there is the limit of time. Thus an accident outside normal working hours will usually not arise 'out of and in the course of employment'. But some fine distinctions arise. A worker injured in the works canteen while taking his meal break is within the scope of his employment (CSI 6/49), but not if the canteen is across a public road from the place of work and the claimant is injured on the road (R(I) 74/52). While the question of time, meal and other breaks apart, may raise few problems where working hours are clearly determined, difficulties may arise if working hours are not specified. Thus work necessarily done after normal working hours may qualify (R(I) 64/51).

Second, there is the limit of place. If the place of employment is clearly delineated, there are few problems. But this is not true, for example, of those whose work takes them onto the public highway. In R(I) 11/51, the Commissioner upheld the claim of a lorry driver injured while helping another motorist to remove a partial obstruction of the highway; this was reasonably incidental to his employment 'having regard to the recognised behaviour of give and take between all persons using the highway'. In a later case, the principle inherent in that decision—that an injury qualifies if sustained while lending assistance on the highway—was confined to cases 'where there was some similarity of function between the helper and the person helped, as in the case of fellow motorists'. So a claimant visiting a private house in the course of his work, and injured when stopping a runaway child's tricycle, failed in his claim (RI) 52/54). In certain circumstances, the 1975 Act brings accidents while travelling to or from work within the scope of employment (see (iii) below).

Third, there is the limit of the claimant's contract of employment. What if a claimant is required to perform certain duties, but is injured while performing others? Is it relevant to such a decision whether he performed these tasks out of curiosity, excess zeal or in disobedience to orders? Several claims have been allowed by workers injured as a result of smoking at work where this has been permitted by employers (R(I) 2/63, R(I)21/60, R(I)4/64); but the worker who was injured while waiting after the end of his permitted tea-break to use a 'smoking-booth', smoking being forbidden elsewhere, failed (R(I) 4/66, R v II Commissioner, ex p AEU [1966] 1 All ER 97, CA). In certain circumstances, unauthorized or forbidden acts are brought within the 1975 Act (see (ii) below).

Against these limits placed by the case-law on the requirement that an accident must arise 'out of and in the course of employment' must be placed five statutory provisions which tend to widen the 'scope of employment'.

(i) General presumption   'An accident arising in the course of an employed earner's employment shall be deemed, in the absence of evidence to the contrary, also to have arisen out of that employment' (SSA 1975, s50(3)). The effect of this presumption is to distribute the burden of proof between the claimant and the Insurance Officer. The claimant must prove that his accident arose in the course of his employment; the Insurance Officer may then question whether it arose 'out of' the same employment. It need not be proved that the accident did not arise out of the employment—merely adducing evidence to that effect is sufficient to remove the statutory presumption (R v NI (II) Commissioner, ex p Richardson [1958] 2 All ER 689), though such evidence must be 'something more than speculative inference' (R(I) 1/64). Similar cases have fallen either side of the line (CI 195/49, CSI 23/50).

(ii) Disobedience   An accident is deemed to arise out of and in the course of employment if it occurs while the claimant is 'acting in contravention of any statutory or other regulations applicable to his employment, or of any orders given by or on behalf of his employers, or (if) he is acting without instruction from his employer, if—

(a) the accident would be deemed so to have arisen had the act not been done in contravention of any such regulations or orders or without such instructions, as the case may be; and

(b) the act is done for the purpose of and in connection with the employer's trade or business' (SSA 1975, s52).

The Commissioners have emphasized the need to satisfy both provisos in order to bring an unauthorized act within this provision (R(I) 7/57, CI 11/49).

(iii) Travelling to or from work   An accident while travelling to or from work is deemed to arise out of and in the course of employment if the injured claimant travels with his employer's express or implied permission in any vehicle, even if not obliged to travel by that vehicle, subject to the following provisos:

'(a) the accident would have been deemed so to have arisen had he been under such an obligation: and

(b) at the time of the accident the vehicle—

(i) is being operated by or on behalf of his employer or some other person by whom it is provided in pursuance of arrangements made with his employer; and

(ii) it is not being operated in the ordinary course of a public transport service' (SSA 1975, s53(1)).

These conditions are strictly observed. Thus the necessary permission of an employer must relate to the part of a journey where the accident takes place—an accident while taking an unauthorized detour is outside the section (R(I) 40/55). 'Travelling' includes boarding and alighting from a vehicle (R(I) 48/54, CI 182/48) but not walking from the place of work to the vehicle, or from one vehicle to another (R(I) 79/51, R(I) 67/52, R(I) 48/54). 'Vehicle' includes 'a ship, vessel or aircraft' (SSA 1975, s53(2)), buses, a motor-cycle (R(I) 8/51), a railway carriage (R(I) 67/51) and a farm tractor (R(I) 42/56).

Cases of accidents while travelling to or from work which do not fall within the conditions of s53(1) may still be within the II scheme provided they occur within the scope of employment. Thus accidents while travelling within the grounds or premises of the workplace are normally within the scope of employment (R(I) 41/57, R(I) 20/58), unless a claimant is not there for the purposes of his employment, as for example if he arrives early in order to have some refreshment before work (R(I) 1/59). Similar considerations attach to travel in the course of a working day. An accident must arise while travelling as part of the job the claimant is employed to do: if a claimant is permitted to travel direct from home to make a visit in connection with his work, an accident en route may ground a claim (R(I) 18/55): but in some cases, the Commissioners have held that such a claimant does not enter the sphere of his employment until he reaches the place of his first visit (R(I) 19/57, R(I) 2/67).

(iv) Emergencies   An accident in or about the employer's premises is deemed to arise out of and in the course of employment if the claimant, while employed there for the purpose of the employer's trade or business, is injured 'while he is taking steps, on an actual or supposed emergency at those premises, to rescue, succour or protect persons who are, or are thought to be or possibly to be, injured or imperilled, or to avert or minimise serious damage to property' (SSA 1975, s54). The effect of this section is to bring cases which satisfy its conditions within the scope of employment; but other cases of emergencies are not excluded simply because they do not satisfy those conditions (CI 280/49). The Commissioners have identified a more general class of emergency cases, in which claimants have, for example, helped fellow workmen in difficulty with their work or taken steps to remove obstructions, and their claims have succeeded wherever their actions have been incidental to their employment (R(I) 11/56, R(I) 62/51, R(I) 46/60). A claimant need not be working on the premises in question, provided he is present there on his employer's trade or business (R(I) 6/63). Once the conditions of s54 are fulfilled, it cannot be argued that the accident does not arise out of and in the course of employment, on the grounds that but for this section it would not so arise (R(I) 6/63).

(v) Misconduct, skylarking and negligence   An accident is within the scope of employment if caused by the 'misconduct or skylarking or negligence' of a person other than the claimant, or by steps taken in consequence of any such behaviour, 'or by the behaviour or presence of an animal (including a bird, fish or insect), or is caused by or consists in the injured person being struck by any object or by lightning' (SSA 1975, s55(1)(b)). Such accidents must also satisfy three conditions. First, the claimant must not have directly or indirectly induced or contributed to the accident by conduct outside his employment or by acts not incidental to his employment (SSA 1975, s55(1)(c)). Second, the accident must arise after 19 December 1961 (when this provision first came into force). And lastly, the accident must have been in the course of employment (SSA 1975, s55(1)(a)). If the section as a whole is satisfied, the effect of this last condition is to allow a claim to succeed in respect of an accident of the type covered by the section which, although in the course of employment, did not arise out of the employment (R(I) 3/67).

(b) Prescribed diseases and injuries   Part II, ch V of the 1975 Act extends the II scheme to certain prescribed diseases and injuries. The contracting of such a disease or sustaining of such an injury may therefore ground a claim for benefit (SSA 1975, ss76(1), 77(1)). The detailed provisions of this part of the II scheme are contained in regulations made under Part IV of the Act (SI 1959/467). The diseases and injuries are prescribed by the Secretary of State, who can add to the list (SSA 1975, s76(2)). A claim may be made in respect of a disease developed before it is prescribed, as long as it did not develop before 5 July 1948. The prescribed diseases provisions do not prevent the making of claims on the grounds of 'personal injury by accident' if a non-prescribed disease results from an accident (SSA 1975, s76(5)). Since diseases are prescribed in relation to occupations, this allows a person in a certain occupation who develops a disease prescribed only for other occupations to claim, provided it results from an 'accident arising out of and in the course of employment'.

The prescribed diseases and injuries are listed in regulations (SI 1959/467, reg 2(a) and Sch 1, Pt I; the list is reproduced in DHSS leaflet NI 2). A prescribed disease includes a condition resulting from a disease, although the condition is not itself prescribed (SI 1959/467, reg 3). With three exceptions (SI 1969/467, Sch 1, Pt I, diseases Nos 38, 41, 42) a claimant suffering from a disease prescribed for his occupation is presumed to be so suffering due to the nature of his employment, unless the contrary is proved, if he was working in that occupation on the date the disease developed or during the preceding month (SI 1959/467, reg 4(1)). The date of development is taken as the first day of incapability of work, loss of faculty or the date of death, depending on whether the claim is for injury benefit, disablement benefit or death benefit respectively (SI 1959/467, reg 6(2)).

Disputes over claims based on prescribed diseases almost invariably turn on medical evidence. There is a considerable volume of case-law relating to both certain types of injuries and certain diseases and the appropriate title in the 'Digest of Commissioners' Decisions' should be consulted (Jenkins (ed), 1964). The procedure for claims based on prescribed diseases and injuries is discussed below (see (B) below).

(2) Injury Benefit

Injury benefit is paid to a claimant for any day after the first three days in the 'injury benefit period' which forms part of a period of interruption of employment and on which he is incapable of work as a result of his injury or disease (SSA 1975, s56(1)(5)). 'Period of interruption' and 'incapable of work' have the same meanings as for unemployment and sickness benefit (see ch 2(B)(1) (a), (2)(a)), though 'work' means only work which the claimant 'can reasonably be expected to do' (SSA 1975, s56(2)). Injury benefit is limited to 156 days from and including the day of the accident and is not available if disablement benefit (see (3) below) is available (SSA 1975, s56(4)). As with sickness benefit, a medical certificate from the claimant's doctor will usually suffice as evidence of incapability and also serves as a claim form. A claimant who can prove incapability but not an injury or disease as its cause may be entitled to sickness benefit.

(3) Disablement Benefit

Disablement benefit is payable if a claimant 'suffers as the result of the relevant accident (or disease) from loss of physical or mental faculty' or disfigurement amounting to not less than 1 per cent disablement under the statutory formula for the assessment of disability (SSA 1975, s57(1)(2)). This benefit is only payable from after the third day following an accident or development of a disease and is not payable if the claimant receives injury benefit (SSA 1975, s57(4)). Unlike injury benefit, disablement benefit does not require incapacity for work and is not limited to a fixed period of time (though it may be granted for a provisional period: see below).

The following principles of assessment of disability are laid down (SSA 1975, Sch 8, para 1; SI 1964/504, reg 2 and Sch 2):

(a) account is taken of all disabilities, whether or not involving loss of earning power or additional expense, to which the claimant may be subject, having regard to his physical and mental condition, as compared with a person of the same age and sex whose condition is normal;

(b) account is taken of disabilities resulting from congenital defects and prior injuries or diseases except to the extent which claimants would be subject thereto during the assessment period;

(c) account is taken of disabilities resulting from injuries or diseases caused after and otherwise than by the accidents in question to the extent to which claimants are subject thereto during the assessment period;

(d) in the case of two accidents within the II scheme, assessment is confined to the later;

(e) the particular circumstances of the claimant are ignored except for age, sex and physical or mental condition.

The assessment of disablement is on a percentage basis. The prescribed degrees of disablement range from 1 per cent for loss of a toe to 100 per cent for loss of two limbs. Some latitude is allowed for a different assessment than that prescribed for a particular loss of faculty if reasonable in the circumstances. Disablement assessed at less than 1 per cent does not lead to any entitlement to benefit (SSA 1975, s57(1)).

Assessment is made for the period during which the claimant 'has suffered and may be expected to continue to suffer from the relevant loss of faculty'. This is known as a final assessment, and leads to uninterrupted payment of benefit. If a final assessment is not possible a provisional assessment is made for a limited period at the expiry of which a further assessment is made (SSA 1975, Sch 8, para 4). Assessments of disability between 20 and 100 per cent are rounded to the nearest multiple of ten, multiples of five being rounded up (SSA 1975, Sch 8, para 5). If disablement is assessed at less than 20 per cent, the benefit takes the form of a lump sum gratuity, determined according to the degree of disablement and length of the period for which the assessment is made (SSA 1975, s57(5)). The amount of gratuity is fixed subject to a maximum by reference to a prescribed table (SI 1964/504, reg 3 and Sch 3). In cases of 20 per cent disablement or above, the benefit is known as disablement pension and paid weekly, like injury benefit, at the specified rate (SSA 1975, s57(6) and Sch 3, para 3). If a claimant receives increases of disablement gratuity on the grounds of special hardship (see (b) below), he may receive the increased sum as a disablement pension.

Apart from increases in respect of dependants (which also apply to injury benefit: see (4) below), disablement pension or gratuity may be increased by one or more of five provisions.

(a) Unemployability supplement   A claimant may receive an increase of disablement pension (but not of a gratuity) 'if as a result of the relevant loss of faculty (he) is incapable of work and likely to remain so permanently' (SSA 1975, s58(1)). 'Incapable of work' has already been discussed (see ch 2(B)(2)(a)). But for the purposes of unemployability supplement, a claimant may still be treated as incapable of work if able to work, provided his loss of faculty is likely to prevent his earnings exceeding £104 per annum (SSA 1975, s58(3)). The Commissioners have held that incapability of work for unemployability supplement purposes is not entirely a medical question (R(I) 58/52). Receipt of unemployment benefit, a condition of which is being 'capable of work' (see ch 2 (B)(1)(a)), is not evidence of capability of work if the employment exchange has been unable to place the claimant in employment (CI 4/48).

A supplement is paid for a period determined at the time it is granted, but may be renewed at the expiry of that period (SSA 1975, s58(4)). Increases are made to unemployability supplement for those in certain age-groups at initial entitlement (SSA 1975, s59; see table 3). The supplement may not be paid for any period during which special hardship allowance is also paid (SSA 1975, s60(5); see below). The supplement is also reduced if the claimant spends more than eight weeks in hospital, but then entitlement to hospital treatment allowance may apply (see (e) below).

(b) Special hardship allowance   An increase of disablement pension or gratuity may be made if 'as the result of the relevant loss of faculty (the claimant)

(a) is incapable of, and likely to remain permanently incapable, of following his regular occupation; and

(b) is incapable of following employment of an equivalent standard which is suitable in his case, or if as the result of the relevant loss of faculty (he) is, and has at all times since (receiving injury benefit) been, incapable of following (such) occupation or employment' (SSA 1975, s60(1)(7)).

The claimant's 'regular occupation' does not include any subsidiary occupation—it must be his usual work; and an 'employment of an equivalent standard' must be one covered by the II scheme (SSA 1975, s60(2)). If a claimant's disability has deprived him wholly or partly of prospects of advancement he must be treated as incapable of following his occupation (SSA 1975, s60(2)(3)). 'Regular occupation' must be determined without regard to particular circumstances, such as place of work or employer, but prospects of advancement should be assessed in the light of such circumstances (R v II Commissioner, ex p Humphreys [1953] 3 All ER 885, 891-2). Work in the claimant's normal occupation following his disablement is disregarded if undertaken for the purpose of rehabilitation, training, ascertaining recovery or done prior to surgery (SSA 1975, s60(4) and SI 1964/504, reg 5). Provided the conditions are satisfied, no special hardship need be proved in addition (CI441/50, R(I) 14/62).

In calculating the allowance, the amount of disablement benefit in payment must be disregarded, even though that benefit and the allowance together provide a higher income than the claimant would have enjoyed but for his disablement (CI 330/50). An allowance, paid for a fixed period but renewable, is determined by reference to the claimant's probable income in a suitable employment which he is capable of undertaking as compared with his regular occupation (SSA 1975, s60(6)). It cannot be paid in conjunction with unemployability supplement (SSA 1975, s60(5); see (a) above).

(c) Constant attendance allowance   A disablement pension (but not a gratuity) paid to a claimant whose disablement is assessed at 100 per cent is increased if as a result of the relevant loss of faculty he requires constant attendance (SSA 1975, s61(1)). 'Constant attendance' is not statutorily defined but a DHSS leaflet instances 'those who are bedridden, blind or paralysed. It is not paid for help with ordinary housework or for similar domestic purposes, nor is it paid simply for help with dressing and undressing. Anybody who applies has to prove that daily attendance is needed and is likely to be needed for a long period' (DHSS leaflet NI 6, p.17). There are two maximum rates of payment depending on the severity of the disablement (SI 1964/504, reg 7). The allowance is paid for a determined period but may be renewed, or increased if the need for attendance has grown (SSA 1975, s61(2); see (d) below). It is not payable to recipients of NI attendance allowance (see ch 2(B)(6)), unless the claimant qualifies for a rate higher than the NI allowance, in which case the balance of constant attendance allowance over the NI allowance is paid.

Unlike other II benefits, entitlement to constant attendance allowance is decided entirely by the Secretary of State (see (B) below). Therefore there can be no appeal (CI 2/48).

(d) Exceptionally severe disablement allowance   If a disablement pensioner receives a constant attendance allowance (or would receive the allowance were he not in hospital) at a rate higher than the lower maximum and his need for constant attendance is likely to be permanent, his disablement pension is further increased (currently by £7.60) for a specified period and the increase can subsequently be renewed (SSA 1975, s63).

(e) Hospital treatment allowance   An award of disablement benefit (pension or gratuity) following an assessment of disablement at less than 100 per cent may be paid as if the assessment were 100 per cent for any period which the claimant spends as an in-patient in a hospital or similar institution receiving medical treatment for his injury or loss of faculty (SSA 1975, s62(1)). So during such a period the claimant receives the maximum rate of benefit (see table 3). In cases of disablement gratuity the effect of the hospital treatment allowance is to convert the gratuity into a pension, reduced by that portion of the gratuity attributable to the period of hospitalization (SSA 1975, s62(2)). The claimant must be an in-patient; so if the institution at which he is receiving treatment closes temporarily, he is not entitled to the allowance while discharged (R(I) 14/56). Similarly, a claimant for whom there is insufficient hospital accommodation is not entitled, even if he attends all day every day and not as a normal out-patient (R(I) 27/59). The allowance is payable for the day of discharge but not the day of admission (CSI 131/49).

(4)   Increases of Injury Benefit and Disablement Pension for Dependants
A claimant receiving injury benefit is entitled to an increase of benefit for

children in his family, as is a disablement pensioner receiving unemployability supplement (SSA 1975, s 64(1)). Children must be living with or maintained by the claimant (SSA 1975, ss 64(4),65(1)(2)). A married woman claimant is not entitled to an increase in respect of her children if living with her husband unless he is incapable of self-support (see ch 2(B)(13)(a)) (SSA 1975, s 65 (4)).

The same categories of claimants may receive increased benefit in respect of a wife, husband, certain other prescribed relatives (as for death benefit: see (5)(e) below) or a woman who has the care of the claimant's child or children (SSA 1975, s 66(1) and SI 1964/504, reg 10 and Sch 5). The increase may only be made in respect of a husband or other male relative if he is residing with or maintained by the claimant and 'incapable of self-support' (see ch 2(B)(13)(a)) (SSA 1975, s 66(1)(b) and SI 1964/504, reg 10 (2)); and is reduced or not granted in respect of a dependant's earnings (SSA 1975, s 66(3)—(5) and SI 1964/504, reg 9—11).

(5)   Death Benefit

If an insured person dies as the result of an industrial injury or disease death benefit is payable to one or more persons (SSA 1975, ss 50(2)(c), 67-75). It may often be the case that if a claimant of injury or disablement benefit dies, death benefit is payable; and if a claimant dies while he is entitled to constant attendance allowance (or would be so entitled were he not in hospital) he is regarded as having died as a result of the injury for which disablement pension was paid (SSA 1975, s 75(1)). But this does not follow automatically. A claim for death benefit requires investigation to determine whether the death itself, as opposed to the injury or disease giving rise to payment of other benefits, has resulted from an 'injury by accident arising out of and in the course of employment' or from a prescribed disease (R(I) 4/57). Where a previous claim for injury benefit (or presumably, disablement benefit) has been disallowed, a claim for death benefit in respect of the same accident should be treated as a review of the earlier decision (R(I) 19/61).

There are six forms of death benefit.

(a) Widows   The widow of an insured person is entitled to death benefit if at his death she was either residing with him or would but for his accident or disease have received from him periodical maintenance of not less than the prescribed amount (currently £0.25 per week) (SSA 1975, s 67(1) and SI 1964/504, reg 18(a)), not including maintenance payments in respect of children (Stevens v Tirard [1939] 4 All ER 186, CA) but only payments provided or procured by her husband which she receives or is entitled to receive under a court order, trust or agreement which she has taken reasonable steps to enforce (SSA 1975, s 67(3)). The benefit comprises a pension from the deceased's death for life or until remarriage;

and a gratuity equal to fifty-two times her current pension if she remarries (SSA 1975, s 67 (2)). The pension is not payable during any period of cohabitation with 'a man not her husband' (SSA 1975, s 67(2); see ch 2(B)(8)(d)) but the right to the remarriage gratuity remains (SI 1964/504, reg 19). For the first six months following her husband's death, the pension is paid at a higher rate and thereafter at one of two rates (SSA 1975, s 68 and SI 1964/504, reg 18(b); see table 3).

(b) Widowers   The widower of a deceased insured woman is entitled to death benefit in the form of a pension from the date of death for life, if at his wife's death he was or would but for her accident have been maintained by her and if he is permanently incapable of self-support (see ch 2 (B)(13)(a))(SSA 1975, s 69).

(c) Children   Death benefit in the form of a weekly allowance is payable to any person (widow, widower or other) who has living with him or is maintaining a child or children who were in the deceased's family at the time of his death (SSA 1975, s 70(1)(3)). In the case of a widow who receives a widow's pension (see (a) above), this allowance is paid at a higher rate (SSA 1975, s 70(2); see table 3).

(d) Parents   The parent of a deceased insured person is entitled to death benefit if at his or her child's death the parent was or would but for the accident have been maintained by that child (SSA 1975, s 71(1)). Depending on the degree of maintenance by the deceased, the benefit takes the form of a small pension or gratuity (SSA 1975, s 71(2)(4)). 'Parent' for this purpose includes a step-parent, parent by adoption and the mother but not the father of an illegitimate child (SSA 1975, s 71(6)). A pension is not payable to a mother if she marries or remarries or cohabits 'with a man not her husband' (see ch 2 (B)(8)(d)), unless she marries or is cohabiting with a man with whom she was cohabiting immediately before her child's death (SSA 1975, s 71(3)).

(e) Relatives   Certain prescribed relatives of a deceased insured person are entitled to death benefit in the form of a pension or gratuity subject to the usual conditions concerning maintenance, and, in the case of a man, incapability of self-support, and, in the case of a woman, marriage or cohabitation. The pension is paid for a period fixed when first granted but can be renewed from time to time (SSA 1975, s 72). The list of prescribed relatives includes lineal ascendants and descendants in direct line of the deceased; step-parents and children; sisters, brothers, and half-sisters and brothers; and parents of the spouses of deceased insured persons or deceased recipients of death benefit (SI 1964/504, reg 20 and Sch 5).

(f) Woman looking after children   Subject to the same familiar conditions, a woman residing with the deceased at his death who had the care of one or more of his children is entitled to death benefit by way of a weekly allowance (SSA 1975, s 73).

The 1975 Act and regulations prohibits the payment of the same form of death benefit to more than one claimant and payment to the same person of both a relative's pension and child-minder's allowance (see (e) and (f) above). Persons otherwise entitled to a relative's pension are accorded a gratuity. Priority among claimants 'competing' for an allowance in respect of a child is also determined by regulations (SSA 1975, Sch 9; SI 1964/504, reg 25 and Sch 8).

(6) Disqualifications

There are several general disqualifications for II benefits. With some exceptions (SI 1964/504, reg 28-32), absence from Great Britain and imprisonment or other legal detention are absolute disqualifications, lasting for the period of absence or detention (SSA 1975, s 82(5)). Disqualification for up to six weeks may be imposed if the claimant has:

(a) if a claimant of injury benefit (see (2) above), behaved in a manner calculated to retard his recovery; or

(b) failed to attend or submit himself to medical examination; or

(c) failed to furnish information required to determine his claim; or

(d) failed to give notice of a change of circumstances affecting his right to benefit; or

(e) wilfully obstructed or otherwise been guilty of misconduct in connection with any medical examination he has been required to undergo (SSA 1975, s90 and SI 1964/73, reg 19).

Disqualifications (a) and (b) correspond to similar disqualifications for NI sickness benefit (see ch 2(B)(2)(b)). Disqualification under (c) or (d) will be a question of degree in each case. While there is no exemption for unintentional failures to furnish information or notify changes of circumstances, the degree of malice or thoughtlessness, if any, could be advanced on appeal as the reason for not imposing a disqualification, or at least for reducing the length of a disqualification. Benefit may be suspended while the claimant is a hospital in-patient (SSA 1975, s 82(6)(b) and SI 1971/1440). While disqualified a claimant must rely solely on SB.

(B) Procedure

The procedure relating to II claims and appeals is broadly that of the NI scheme (see ch 2(C)). As with NI benefits however, certain questions are determined exclusively by the Secretary of State for Social Services. In the case of II benefits, these 'Minister's questions' are:

(a) whether a person is or was employed in insurable employment;

(b) whether constant attendance allowance or exceptionally severe disablement allowance (see (A)(3) above) should be granted or renewed;

(c) how the limitations preventing the concurrent payment of certain forms of death benefit (see (A)(5) above) are applied to particular cases;

(d) questions relating to the maintenance of children, or the family in which children are treated as included for II benefit purposes (SSA 1975, ss 93(1),95(1)).

As under the NI scheme, decisions on Minister's questions may be reviewed by the Secretary of State and questions of law under (a) may go to the High Court (see ch 2(C)(1)).

Certain medical questions are not decided by Insurance Officers but referred to Medical Boards:

(a) whether an accident has resulted in a loss of faculty;

(b) the degree of disablement to be assessed and the period of the assessment (see (A)(3) above);

(c) whether a claimant is suffering from a prescribed disease (see (A)(1)(b) above) (SSA 1975, ss 108(1)(2), 113(1)(2) and SI 1959/467, reg 27).

In the case of prescribed diseases, the Insurance Officer first obtains a report from one or more doctors, and may either then refer the case to a Medical Board or decide it himself. In the latter eventuality, the claimant may appeal to a Medical Board.

From decisions of Medical Boards, an appeal lies within three months to a Medical Appeal Tribunal but, in the case of 'provisional' decisions (see (A)(3) above), only after two years' provisional assessment. The Insurance Officer must also refer a Medical Board decision to a Medical Appeal Tribunal if the Secretary of State is of the opinion that this should be done (SSA 1975, s 109). From a Medical Appeal Tribunal, a further appeal lies to a NI Commissioner, but only on the ground that the tribunal decision is wrong in law and only with leave of either the tribunal or a Commissioner. Leave must first be sought from the tribunal within three months of its decision; if this application is refused, leave must be sought from a Commissioner within twenty-one days of the refusal. The appeal itself must be made within three months of leave being granted (SI 1967/1571, reg 15). A Medical Appeal Tribunal may also refer a question of law for decision by a Commissioner (SSA 1975, s 112).

Medical Boards are composed of two doctors, Medical Appeal Tribunals of two doctors and a lawyer chairman. At the Boards' hearings, which are private, claimants are medically examined and questioned and a decision posted to them. The tribunal hearings are in public and more formal. Papers are circulated beforehand as for NI Local Tribunals (see ch 2(C)(3)), the claimant and Insurance Officer present their cases and the claimant is examined afterwards by the tribunal doctors. Decisions are sometimes announced and always sent later by post. Representation is permitted before both bodies and desirable at tribunal hearings. Medical Boards and Appeal Tribunals are bound by a decision of an Insurance Officer, NI Local Tribunal or Commissioner that an accident arose out of and in the course of employment but are free, within that limit, to decide whether the accident caused a loss of faculty and the degree of disablement, if any, resulting from the loss of faculty (Minister of Social Security v AEU [1967] 1 All ER 210,HL; Jones v Secretary of State for Social Services [1972] 1 All ER 145,HL; R(I) 3/68; R(I) 5/68).

It is important to note that a claimant whose claim for any II benefit is refused may none the less be entitled to a declaration that his accident was an industrial accident; and such a declaration can be obtained even if no claim has been made. A declaration is conclusive for the purposes of any claim for benefit relating to the accident in question and can thus be relied on at a later date in a subsequent claim, even if an initial claim has failed. A declaration may only be refused if it is unlikely that the question will require determination in any future proceedings. A claimant's accident must be deemed an industrial accident if it arose out of and in the course of employment within the II scheme and if payment of benefit is not precluded because the accident happened outside Great Britain (SSA 1975, s 107).

(C) Old Cases

We have already seen that the II scheme only provides benefit in relation to accidents and diseases arising after 4 July 1948, the day on which the II scheme came into operation. In respect of cases, known as 'old cases', which would, before that date, have given rise to compensation under the Workmen's Compensation Acts those Acts continue to apply although repealed for all other purposes (Industrial Injuries and Diseases (Old Cases) Act 1975). The SSA 1975 enables unemployability supplement, constant attendance allowance and increases for dependants to be paid to recipients of workmen's compensation (SSA 1975, s 159); and schemes made under the Old Cases Act provide for further allowances and payment of benefits in respect of industrial diseases, including the 'prescribed diseases' (see (A)(1)(b) above), in old cases.

References

'Social Insurance and Allied Services', Report by Sir W. Beveridge, Cmd 6404 (1942).
Jenkins, E. (ed) (1964), 'Digest of Commissioners' Decisions', HMSO, London.

SB is the name given in 1966 to the scheme then known as National Assistance: a means-tested benefit unrelated to contributions and designed as a 'safety-net' in the Beveridge scheme of social security, to be of dwindling significance as NI increased to cover most of the population (Cmd 6404, paras 370-1). But the contrary has proved true: referring to the 'success' of the SB scheme, the chairman of the SBC wrote that in 1971 there were 6.4 million claims and 2.9 million persons in receipt of SB (introduction to 'SB Handbook', 3rd ed.). Another estimate suggests that in 1970 4.1 million persons relied directly or indirectly on SB (F. Field, 'Poverty', no. 20-1, p.3.)

While National Assistance was intended to mark a departure from all previous forms of poor relief, the survival of the means-test and the term 'assistance' were sufficiently reminiscent of pre-war policies to inhibit many claims and raise doubts about its effectiveness. The Supplementary Benefit Act 1966 thus introduced the new name, replaced the National Assistance Board with the SBC and stated plainly the right of an eligible claimant to SB and the duty of the SBC 'to exercise the functions conferred on them in such manner as shall best promote the welfare of persons affected by the exercise thereof' (SBA 1966, ss3(1), 4(1)). These changes can be viewed as a well-intentioned publicity exercise; not an entirely unsuccessful one, though the subsequent increase in applications can be ascribed partly to other reasons (Atkinson, 1969, pp. 61-77).

SB paid to a person under pensionable age (sixty for a woman, sixty-five for a man) is termed a supplementary allowance, that paid to a pensioner a supplementary pension.

The SBC operates in practice through local offices of the DHSS which determine claims; in doing so account is taken not only of the 1966 Act and regulations made under it, but also of SBC policy and administrative directions contained in the 'A' and 'AX' Codes, which are not made public at any stage—claim, decision or appeal. The SBC publishes the 'SB Handbook' giving some general indications of its policy (supplemented by a news-sheet 'SBC Notes and News'), and a few reports which explain the way it administers certain provisions of the Act. None of these publications, however, parallels the detailed and changing nature of the Codes. This poses a major problem for claimants and their advisers, who must learn the SBC's policies by experience; for while it is true that the Codes have no legal force, such an argument cuts no ice over the local office counter and SBATs are often unwilling to upset decisions based largely or even solely on SBC policy.

(A)   Entitlement

(1)   General Provisions

If a claimant's 'requirements' exceed his 'resources'—as defined by the Act and assessed by the SBC—he is prima facie entitled to SB if over sixteen, in Great Britain and neither in full-time employment nor still at school (SBA 1966, ss4(1), 8(1), 9(1)). The employment exclusion does not apply to the first fifteen days following a period of unemployment or a trade dispute (see (F)(8), (G)(4) below); nor does it apply to a self-employed disabled person whose earning power is 'substantially reduced in comparison with that of other (non-disabled) persons similarly occupied' (SBA 1966, s8(3)). The exclusion of secondary schoolchildren may be waived by the SBC in 'exceptional circumstances', a phrase liberally used in the 1966 Act but nowhere defined.

The amount of weekly SB payable to a claimant depends on the calculation of his requirements and resources under schedule 2 of the Act. While there is a clearly stated legal right to the benefit so calculated, we shall see that there are several ways in which the SBC by the exercise of discretions vested in it by schedule 2 may increase, reduce or even withhold the sum finally arrived at, except that a supplementary pension may not be reduced or withheld (SBA 1966, Sch 2, para 4(1)).

(2)   Cohabitation

A husband and wife, if they are living together, are treated as one unit for SB purposes—their 'requirements and resources shall be aggregated and treated as the husband's' (SBA 1966, Sch 2, para 3(1)). This has the effect of excluding claims to benefit by married women unless separated from their husbands (see (H) below).

The same rule applies 'as regards two person cohabiting as man and wife', unless there are 'exceptional circumstances' (SBA 1966, Sch 2, para 3(1)). Not only does cohabitation serve to exclude some claims by unmarried women, it also leads to withdrawal of benefit from, and sometimes prosecution of women who are suspected, rightly or wrongly, of undisclosed cohabitation. The SBC claims to use five main criteria in deciding whether cohabitation exists or not—public acknowledgment; stability of a relationship; sharing of accommodation; children of a relationship and financial support of a woman by a man—but concedes that other unspecified factors may be taken into account (Handbook, para 18). A survey of cohabitation cases suggested inconsistencies in the SBC's operation of its own criteria (Lister, 1973): whereas the SBC claims (in its report 'Cohabitation', 1971, para 28) public acknowledgment is the principal criterion, in the cases Lister studied it was alleged sexual relations which usually formed the basis for a withdrawal of benefit (Lister, 1973, p.8). This compares with the NI cohabitation rule (see ch 2(B)(8)(d)). Some claimants may fall foul of both the SB and the NI rules.

The 'exceptional circumstances' qualification permits the SBC to ignore cohabitation where to withdraw or refuse benefit to a woman might cause severe hardship. In fact, this discretion is used only as the basis for the provision in a few cases ('in the last resort': Cohabitation Report, para 32) of SB to a woman in respect of her children by a previous relationship only, not in respect of herself or her children by the relationship which causes the disqualification. Even where this is done, the benefit paid ceases after four weeks though this, like the whole practice, is an offspring of mere policy and can be appealed against. Both the Fisher and Finer Committees felt this power should be more generously exercised (Cmnd 5228, para 345; Cmnd 5629, para 5.276).

In challenging a cohabitation allegation, the SBC's evidence—which often only amounts to a report of a man seen leaving the house—must be carefully compared with its own criteria of cohabitation. While often impossible, admissions of casual sexual relationships should be avoided if possible since many SBAT members find this difficult to distinguish from cohabitation.

(3) Children

If there are children in a claimant's household their requirements and resources may also be aggregated with his and must be in the case of children under sixteen (SBA 1966, Sch 2, para 3(2)).

(B) Requirements

(1) The Scale Rates

With the exception of certain categories (see (4) below), the requirements of all claimants are those appropriate to their age, marital and household status and size of family as contained in the 'scale rates' (SBA 1966, Sch 2, paras 9, 10: see table 4). There are slightly higher rates for some blind persons.

The A, B and C rates shown in table 4 apply to different categories of claimants. Rate A applies to all claimants for supplementary allowances, except those who have been in receipt of an allowance for two years without being required to register for employment (see (F)(1) below). Rate B applies to this latter category (the two year qualifying period may be an aggregate of two or more periods interrupted by breaks of thirteen weeks or less or by hospitalization), to all supplementary pensioners under eighty years of age, and to those so severely disabled that, after two years, they can be regarded as unemployable (Handbook, paras 37-8, 41). A widow under sixty and not required to register for work is allowed to count her husband's period in receipt of SB towards her two year qualification, provided he was not required to register for work (Handbook, para 41). Rate C applies to pensioners aged eighty or over. A married pensioner claimant qualifies for rate C if his wife is over eighty.

Rates B and C do not apply to claimants in hospital, Part III accommodation or lodgings (see (4)(a)-(c) below). Assessment of requirements at Rates B and C can affect entitlement to ECAs (see (5) below).

There is no statutory indication of the needs of claimants which these scale rates are designed to meet. They do not cover housing costs for which separate provision is made (see (3) below). The SBC views the scale rates as sufficient for 'all normal needs which can be foreseen, including food, fuel and light, the normal repair and replacement of clothing, household sundries (but not major items of bedding and furnishing) and provision for amenities such as newspapers, entertainments and radio and television licences' (Handbook, para 44).

The requirements of claimants who are unemployed in certain circumstances or affected by trade-disputes are subject to special rules (see (F)(3), (G)(1) below). In all other cases, the scale rate requirements are assessed automatically by the SBC according to the rates in table 4, and to these are added attendance requirements (if any) and rent requirements.

(2)   Attendance Requirements
Attendance requirements—the amount of a NI attendance allowance—are added if a claimant or dependant is entitled to the NI allowance (see ch 2(B) (6)) (SBA 1966, Sch 2, para 12). Advisers of claimants who are or may be entitled to attendance requirements should examine whether there are related grounds for claiming ECAs or ENPs (see (5), (D) below).

(3)   Rent
Rent requirements are added to scale rate requirements if a claimant or claimant's dependant is a householder; a non-householder receives a flat-rate addition of £1.00 (SBA 1966, Sch 2, para 13(1)), though this can be increased at the SBC's discretion (SBA 1966, Sch 2, para 4 (1)(a)).

'Householder' is only defined incidentally by the 1966 Act, in relation to the scale rate requirements for single persons, as someone 'who is directly responsible for household necessities and rent (if any)' (SBA 1966, Sch 2, para 9(b)). Classification as a householder is crucial, since it attracts not only the addition of housing costs to the requirements calculation but also higher scale rate requirements for single persons (see table 4). The statutory definition seems to contemplate according household status to persons living rent-free as long as they are responsible for 'household necessities', but in practice the SBC restricts the status to 'normally the person responsible for rent (or who owns the house in case of an owner-occupier) and other household expenses . . . irrespective of his age' (Handbook, para 43). In practice, therefore, householders include home-owners, tenants and sub-tenants, but not persons living with relatives or persons not paying a share of the rent to a landlord (or boarders, lodgers or persons in certain other types of accommodation, for whom separate provision is made: see (4) below).

Problems have arisen where, for example, two or more persons share rented accommodation, all in fact contributing equal shares of the outgoings but only one of them being nominally responsible for the rent (or even for just the gas or electricity accounts). In some such cases, the SBC has treated this one person as the householder and the others, when claiming SB, have been accorded neither the householder level of scale rate requirements nor their actual rent shares. Such decisions can be challenged by production of a rent book (if there is one and if it names the rent-sharers as joint tenants), by evidence of separate payment of rent shares to the landlord; and a landlord, if obliging, can be asked to acknowledge that those sharing premises are joint tenants—this last tactic has been known to work a change of heart by the SBC, even after an adverse tribunal decision ('Poverty', no. 27, p. 22; for further examples see S. Weir (1974) LAG BUL. 81). The Court of Appeal has held that, in the case of joint tenants, none should be regarded as a householder, but 'each should get an allowance in respect of his contribution to rent and each may be granted a special addition to take account of the exceptional circumstances' (R v Sheffield SBAT, ex p Shine, 'The Times', 5 March 1975, CA); thus a joint tenant should receive the £1.00 non-householder rent allowance plus an ECA (see (5) below) to bring the rent element of his SB up to his share of the total rent. This formula, however, denies such a claimant the benefit of the householder scale rates which he needs to meet his share of other household expenses.

The amount of a householder's rent requirement is his 'net rent', which is defined as the rent payable for one week in the case of a tenant, or the weekly amount of mortgage interest (but not capital) repayment in the case of an owner-occupier; and the weekly cost of rates in both cases (unless a landlord is responsible for rates). In all cases, the annual cost of rent or mortgage interest and rates is calculated as a weekly sum, even if paid on a monthly or other basis. A home-owner is also permitted the amount of any ground rent and 'a reasonable allowance towards any necessary expenditure on repairs or insurance' (SBA 1966, Sch 2, para 13(3)); the SBC relates this allowance to rateable values: Handbook, para 48). As a result of this formula, many tenants receive the equivalent of their actual rent and rates expenditure in their SB, and many home-owners all their housing costs except mortgage capital repayments (though the SBC sometimes prefers to meet repairs as they arise by use of exceptional needs payments (see (D) below) rather than by a weekly allowance as directed by statute. The problem of mortgage capital repayments may be solved by persuading a mortgagee to accept only interest repayments while the mortgagor is receiving SB. A claimant who is prepared to sub-let part of his house (if the mortgagee permits this) can apply the proceeds of sub-letting towards capital repayments, in which case the SBC does not deduct the proceeds in calculating 'net rent' (Lynes, 1974, p.52; see (b) below). The SBC also ignores any charitable payments to claimants for the specific purpose of repaying mortgage capital (Handbook, para 49).

'Net rent' may be less than actual outgoings related to accommodation for one of six reasons. In some of these cases, the difference may be supplied from another source; in others it is not and the claimant is out of pocket.

(a) Services provided by landlords   If a claimant's full rent includes payment, for example, in respect of heating and lighting, the 'net rent' does not take account of this since the scale-rates are supposed to cover it (see (1) above). Where the sum for services is known, this is deducted; otherwise the SBC deducts a standard estimated sum—£1.20 per week for heating and hot water, £1.35 if lighting is also included (Handbook, para 50; Lynes, 1974, p.41). Where these estimates are clearly too large their use should be questioned. Where a known charge is more than the estimates, an ECA should be claimed (see (5) below).

(b) Sub-letting   If the claimant receives any proceeds from sub-letting any part of his accommodation, the amount of those proceeds is set against his assessed rent requirements (SBA 1966, Sch 2, para 13(3)). Since it is only 'proceeds' which are set off, a tenant who derives no profit from sub-letting should not be affected by this provision. In practice the SBC has drawn up a scale of allowances for sub-letting expenses, and sets these off against actual receipts. These allowances range from £1.80 per week for furnished accommodation with heat and light provided down to £0.30 per week for unfurnished accommodation without the provision of any services (Handbook, para 51; for details, see 'Poverty', no. 30, p.29). This scale, like all SBC policy, has no legal force, so a claimant who is not allowed his actual expenses incurred by sub-letting should always appeal, and provided he produces evidence of his actual costs (such as insurance, repairs and other overheads) should succeed. It must be noted, however, that while a claimant can cover his outgoings the law does not allow him to make a profit from sub-letting.

(c) Rent rebates and allowances   If a tenant in receipt of SB becomes eligible for a rent rebate or allowance, this does not reduce his SB (see ch 11(A)(1)(b)(i)). In the converse situation in which a tenant in receipt of a rent rebate or allowance applies for SB he continues to receive the rebate or allowance from the local authority for eight weeks and his SB rent requirements are reduced accordingly (SBA 1966, Sch 2, para 13(4)). If still receiving SB after eight weeks, he ceases to receive the rebate or allowance and the SB rent requirements increase to take its place.

These arrangements do not apply to a SB claimant subject to the 'wage-stop' (see (F)(2) below), who continues to recceive or can claim a rent rebate or allowance as long as he receives SB.

(d) Rate rebates   Since full rates are included in the calculation of SB rent requirements, a claimant already receiving SB cannot apply for a rate rebate (with one exception: see ch 11 (B)(1)(b)(i)). A claimant in receipt of a rate rebate when he applies for SB continues to receive the rebate for eight weeks if he is a council tenant also in receipt of a rent rebate or, in other cases, until the end of the rebate period (see ch 11(B)(5)). During this time, the SBC reduces the rent requirements by the amount of the rebate (SBA 1966, Sch 2, para 13(4)).

A SB claimant subject to the 'wage-stop' is also entitled to claim and receive a rate rebate; the DHSS should inform the local authority of the amount of rebate which can be paid without reducing his SB (D of Em Circular 41/74, para 20).

(e) Other residents   A claimant may find his 'net rent' to be less than his actual rent if there is another person resident in the premises to whom a share of the rent may be attributed (SBA 1966, Sch 2, para 13(2)). It is important to note that this provision only applies to residents whose requirements are not aggregated with the claimant's for SB purposes (e.g. lodgers or adult children) and not to wives or children. Nor does it apply if the claimant or his wife is blind or, a concession of SBC policy, if the non-dependant is under sixteen. Again, the SBC has designed a rule of thumb formula for calculating such contributions by other residents. Under this formula, the number of persons living in the premises is totalled, children under sixteen counting as half. The rent is then divided by the total number of persons so calculated and the result is the share attributed to the non-dependant resident (Handbook, para 52). SBC policy only allows for a smaller 'contribution' where the non-dependant is unable to pay the sum so calculated, in which case the non-dependant's 'share' of the rent is calculated so as to leave his weekly income at least £1 over the scale rates; if he is under twenty-one he is allowed to keep £7 of his weekly income and half the excess over £7, the rest being regarded as available for rent if this is more favourable to him (Lynes, 1974, pp.42-3). This manner of calculating rent contributions, however, is based entirely on the 'A' Code and should always be challenged on appeal if hardship results to the claimant.

(f) The rent-stop   A claimant will fall foul of the 'rent-stop' if the SBC decides his 'net rent' should be less than his actual rent because the latter is not 'reasonable in the circumstances' (SBA 1966, Sch 2, para 13(1)). In deciding whether a rent is reasonable, the SBC's general policy is to consider both the type of accommodation and any information from local authority housing departments and rent officers (Handbook, para 53). Adverse decisions based solely on such information should always be challenged, since the information will usually be of a general nature and it is ultra vires for the SBC effectively to surrender its discretion to another body (Ellis v Dubowski [1921] All ER 272).

SBC policy differs in detail according to type of accommodation.

(i) Local authority rents   Rents for local authority accommodation (see ch 10(C)) 'will almost invariably be met in full' (Handbook, para 54).

(ii) Private sector rents (Handbook, para 55)   The rent of unfurnished accommodation rented from a private landlord is regarded as reasonable for the accommodation if it is a registered fair rent (see ch 9(B)(1)) or not in excess of registered rents for comparable local accommodation, or if a local authority has based a rent allowance (see ch 11(A)) on the full rent. A fair rent or 'comparable' is not taken as necessarily reasonable for the claimant, but local authority use of the actual rent for rent allowance purposes is (see below).

The rent for privately rented furnished accommodation is treated as reasonable for the accommodation if registered but again the SBC may feel the accommodation, and thus the rent, is not reasonable for the claimant.

Rents registered after rent tribunal hearings (see ch 9(B)(2)) are presumably treated in the same way as fair rents determined by rent officers.

In relation to furnished and unfurnished accommodation, the SBC is also prepared to rely on estimates of what registered rents would be. These should be treated with some scepticism unless the SBC can prove both that a rent officer or rent tribunal has supplied the information and has inspected the premises before doing so; in practice this cannot happen since inspections only occur if an application is made for a rent determination. Thus the SBC practice of presenting SBATs with oral accounts of estimates obtained by telephone from rent officers and rent tribunal clerks should be challenged as inaccurate guesswork (unless supported by appropriate 'comparables') and as ultra vires (see Ellis's case above).

If a local authority, in calculating a rent rebate or allowance, has exercised its discretion to treat the claimant's rent as reduced (see ch 11(A)(2)(a)(ii)), the SBC cannot subsequently rent-stop the claimant at a lower figure (Housing Finance Act 1972, Sch 9, para 6).

(iii) Owner-occupiers   The SBC will not treat a home-owner's housing costs as unreasonable except in so far as the accommodation may be unreasonable for the claimant and then only if he is likely to be in receipt of SB for more than six months (Handbook, para 56).

When is accommodation unreasonable for a claimant? The Handbook instances 'overhousing' and living in 'excessively luxurious accommodation' or 'an unduly expensive neighbourhood' (Handbook, paras 55-6). Such considerations, if used to justify a rent-stop, should be carefully scrutinized in the light of local housing opportunities and the family and other circumstances of the claimant.

What the Handbook does not disclose is the true basis of SBC rent-stop policy—the rent ceilings adopted for areas. Rents over the local ceiling are automatically 'stopped' unless permission to exceed the ceiling in a particular case is obtained from a DHSS regional office. This leads to absurd differences between cases, since the size and amenities of accommodation are disregarded in the arbitrary application of rent ceilings, although the Act directs attention to the 'circumstances' of the claimant (SBA 1966, Sch 2, para 13(1)). The same ceilings, often equally unrealistic, may be applied to home-owners (see 'Poverty', no. 30, pp. 33-4).

If the SBC decides a rent is unreasonable, the local office discusses this with the claimant and takes account of how long he has lived in the accommodation, the availability of cheaper accommodation, his likely period in receipt of SB, his age, health and other personal circumstances, disregarded income and capital (see (C) below), charitable payments to meet rent, and the possibility of non-dependants in the household meeting more than their proportionate share of the rent (see (e) above) (Handbook, paras 57-8). If there are no other resources to meet the full rent, if this cannot be reduced immediately and it 'is not so high that it would be out of the question to meet it', the full rent may be met temporarily (Handbook, para 59).

The SBC will often, however, encourage rent-stopped claimants to move or apply for a registered rent. The former course of action is often unrealistic and an appeal should then be considered; the latter course should remove the rent-stop either by lowering the rent or, if the rent is approved or increased, by proving that the rent-stop was wrongly applied (in which case the previously 'stopped' portion of the rent should be claimed in arrears).

Appeals against the rent-stop must be carefully presented, since SBC policy arguments, such as the assertion that public funds must not be used to subsidize 'luxurious accommodation', have a strong appeal to many SBAT members who have little experience of the worse sectors of the housing market.

As a result of the Finer Committee's consideration of the rent-stop (Cmnd 5629, paras 6.97-102), the SBC announced in early 1975 that single parents are less likely to be rent-stopped since they experience greater difficulties in finding suitable accommodation.

(4)   Requirements of Special Categories of Claimants

The requirements of most claimants are assessed by the formula: scale rates plus attendance requirements (if any) plus rent. However separate provision is made by the SBA 1966 for four categories of claimants and by SBC policy for a fifth.

(a) Claimants in Part III accommodation   A claimant living in accommodation provided by a local authority under Part III of the National Assistance Act 1948 (see ch (8)(A)(2)) is deemed to have as requirements the statutory minimum rates of payment for accommodation and personal requirements prescribed by statutory instrument under that Act (SBA 1966, Sch 2, para 15). The current rates are shown in table 5. The sum of £2.00 for personal requirements is to be increased by the amount of any NI attendance allowance (see ch 2(B)(6)) or II constant attendance allowance (see ch 3(A)(3)) to which a claimant is entitled.

(b) Claimants or dependants in hospital   The requirements of a claimant who is a hospital in-patient is 'such amount, if any, as may be appropriate, having regard to all the circumstances' (SBA 1966, Sch 2, para 16). A patient with no dependants is usually accorded £2.00 per week and an allowance for rent and other 'outside commitments' (Handbook, para 145).

If either a married claimant or his wife enters hospital and is being paid SB on admission, it continues unchanged for eight weeks, when it is reduced by £2.00 (Handbook, para 141); unless a NI benefit is also in payment, in which case that benefit is reduced and the SB remains constant. In either case, a claimant who cannot manage after the deduction should appeal, or seek an increase of SB (as an ECA: see (5) below). After two years in hospital, the SBC no longer regard a patient as a member of a household and treat him or her as a single claimant.

In the case of a child in hospital, the SBC reduces the scale rate figure appropriate to his or her age to £2.00 after twelve weeks (Handbook, para 143). If this is insufficient an ECA (see (5) below) can be claimed, and the SBC's welfare duty stressed if such a claim meets resistance (SBA 1966, s3(1)).

(c) Boarders   A claimant who pays an all-in charge for board and lodging is deemed to have requirements of 'such amount as may be appropriate', which must not be less than the amount which would be applicable if he qualified for the normal scale rate requirements and attendance requirements, if any (SBA 1966, Sch 2, para 17). Within this very wide discretion SBC policy is typically rigid: a simple formula providing for the lodging charge in full (though a 'lodgings-stop' closely akin to the rent-stop is sometimes applied: Handbook paras 117-21), plus an allowance of £2.70 per week (£3.05 in long-term cases) for personal expenses. It must be remembered that this sum (and the 'lodgings-stop') are mere creations of the 'A' Code; in law both the SBC and SBATs have a discretion to pay 'such amount as may be appropriate', which clearly means the amount appropriate to each case.

(d) Prisoners   The requirements of a claimant in prison or other legal custody are nil, except for any dependants (SBA 1966, Sch 2, para 18). In practice the SBC regards a prisoner's wife as a claimant and assesses her as a single person. The SBC will make ENPs (see (D) below) to visit a prisoner or to help prisoners on short leave. Claims from discharged or paroled prisoners are treated in the normal way (Handbook, paras 150-9).

(e) Single parents under eighteen   Following the recommendation of the Finer Committee (Cmnd 5629, para 5.255), the SBC increases the scale rate requirements of a lone non-householder parent under eighteen to the rate for single non-householders over eighteen (see table 4), under the power to increase SB in exceptional circumstances (SBA 1966, Sch 2, para 4(1)(a)).

(5)   Exceptional Circumstances Additions

Any claimant's requirements may be increased by discretionary additions 'where there are exceptional circumstances' (SBA 1966, Sch 2, para 4(1)(a)). The Handbook specifies domestic assistance, special diets and high heating or laundry costs as the most usual items for which the SBC makes provision under this power, and it adheres to policy rules in regard to each of them; but other examples of special expenses are listed (Handbook, para 74) and claimants should claim ECAs whenever they are faced with recurring expenditure they cannot meet out of their basic benefit.

In the case of some items, such as domestic assistance, the SBC calculates an ECA on the basis of actual cost, which would be the most satisfactory basis on which to decide all claims for ECAs. However, in relation to some expenses, it is almost impossible to secure an ECA in excess of the SBC's own prescribed amounts, without resorting to an appeal. Thus the SBC permits an addition of £0·50 per week for special diets of any kind (regardless of the food or illness concerned), with the exception of £1·12 per week for those suffering from diabetes, peptic ulcers and certain other conditions (Handbook, para 69). Similarly, high heating costs are met by ECAs of £0.55, £1.10 or £1.65 per week depending on the state of health of the claimant or a dependant and the difficulty of heating the accommodation (Handbook, paras 70-1). An ECA of £1.60 per week is made for a person using central heating who is obliged as a result to spend more on heating than he would otherwise (Handbook, para 72). Laundry costs in excess of £0·10 per week are 'taken into consideration' in certain circumstances (Handbook, para 73).

It is important to note that qualification for an ECA does not automatically effect an increase in the calculation of requirements for all claimants. Those entitled to be assessed, on the scale rates, at rate A do receive the full benefit of ECAs. Those on rate B only receive the balance (if any) of an ECA after the sum of £0.50 has been set off against it; those on rate C after a set-off of £0.75 per week. The reason for this is the dubious belief that long-term and pensioner claimants receive the higher scale requirements because their expenditure on such items as heating or special diet is greater than those of other claimants; thus to grant an ECA in full might be to pay twice for the same item. Such a policy fails to appreciate, for example, the difference between sick and healthy pensioners.

After judicial disapproval of this set-off at a time when it had no greater authority than the 'A' Code (R v Greater Birmingham Appeal Tribunal, ex p Simper [1973] 2 All ER 461) it has been enshrined in legislation (National Insurance and Supplementary Benefit Act 1973, Sch 4, para 4), and now applies by law to all ECAs except those for heating expenses, discretionary increases in the flat-rate non-householder rent addition of £1.00 per week, or expenditure relating to children whose requirements are aggregated with the claimant's for SB purposes.

(C)   Resources

The treatment of resources is simpler than the assessment of requirements in three respects. First, whereas requirements are calculated by applying legal provisions to the circumstances of the claimant, the reverse is true of resources—the claimant's actual resources form the basis of calculation according to the statutory rules (SBA 1966, Sch 2, Pt III). Second, there are no special categories of claimants. And third, much less is left to the SBC's discretion. Resources taken into account are totalled and set-off against requirements, the balance being the SB payable.

'Resources' include both income and capital. A claimant need not be in possession or enjoyment of an asset for it to be included in his resources. Thus sums held on discretionary trusts for a claimant may (but need not) be treated as part of his resources (SBA 1966, Sch 2, para 28). Resources may also include 'notional' resources, such as income received in respect of a certain period but spent before the expiry of that period (R v Preston SBAT, ex p Moore, 'The Times', 5 March 1975, CA, in which a student had, by the beginning of a vacation, exhausted a grant supposed to cover the vacation as well as the term; the court approved payment of ECAs (see (B)(5) above) in such cases).

Subject to other provisions a claimant is only deemed to own an asset if he is absolutely entitled in possession to the whole beneficial interest; if the claimant and others are beneficially entitled, they are treated as entitled to equal shares, unless it appears they are not so entitled, in which case they are treated as entitled to 'such shares as appears to be just' (SBA 1966, Sch 2, para 29).

Resources are treated in one of three ways: wholly taken into account; wholly disregarded; or partly disregarded, the rest being taken into account.

(1)   Wholly Taken into Account
The following resources are wholly taken into account (SBA 1966, Sch 2, para 24(2)-(7)).

(a) All benefits under the NI, II, FA or FIS legislation, and all war and service pensions and allowances, except those mentioned below as wholly or partly disregarded (the consequent 'loss' of a NI attendance allowance is compensated by the addition of attendance requirements: see (B)(2) above).

(b) Maintenance payments, whether voluntary or under a court order, to a claimant or dependant made by a person liable to maintain the recipient under s22 of the SBA 1966 (see (H)(1) below).

(c)   Capital exceeding £1,200 in value (see (4) below).

(2)   Wholly Disregarded
The following resources must be wholly disregarded by law.

(a) The capital value of the dwelling in which a claimant resides (SBA 1966, Sch 2, para 19).

(b) NI death grant, maternity grant (see ch 2 (B)(7)(12)), Victoria or George Cross annuities (SBA 1966, Sch 2, para 20).

(c) All capital resources (other than a dwelling occupied by a claimant) and income from such capital together amounting to £1,200 or less (SBA 1966, Sch 2, para 21; see (4) below).

(d) The earnings of a child or person receiving full-time education whose resources are aggregated with those of the claimant (SBA 1966, Sch 2, para 23(1A)).

In addition, the SBC under a discretionary power to treat resources not specified in Schedule 2 as reduced 'by such amount (if any) as may be reasonable in the circumstances' (SBA 1966, Sch 2, para 26) wholly disregards the following resources.

(e) Personal possessions such as furniture and jewellery.

(f) The capital value of a business upon which a claimant normally relies for his livelihood (Handbook, para 27).

(g) 'Payments made by friends, relatives or charities for items not specifically covered by SB'; examples given in the Handbook are payments for holidays or to meet mortgage capital repayments. Occasional gifts in kind are also ignored even if of items covered, in the SBC's view, by SB (see (B)(1) above); 'but regular and substantial provision in kind is normally taken into account' (Handbook, para 26).

(h) Education maintenance allowances paid by a local authority (see ch 7(B)(3)).

(3) Partial Disregards

The following resources are disregarded by the amounts stated, the remainder being taken into account.

(a) A £2.00 disregard of the net weekly earnings of the claimant if he is required to register for work as a condition of receipt of SB (see (F)(1) below).

(b) A £4.00 disregard of the net weekly earnings of a claimant not required to register for work or of any adult dependant (SBA 1966, Sch 2, para 23(1)).

These disregards operate whenever the claimant or a dependant has earnings (in the case of a claimant, of course, they can only be earnings from part-time work while unemployed, since full-time work is a total bar to receipt of SB). Net weekly earnings for SB purposes are gross salary or wages minus any statutory deductions or expenses reasonably incurred in connection with employment (SBA 1966, Sch 2, para 7 and SI 1966/1065, reg 4). Thus income tax deductions, NI and pension scheme contributions, fares to and from work, meals at work, the provision of tools or overalls by an employee, trade union subscriptions and the cost of child-minding if that is necessary to enable a claimant or dependant to work, are all deductible. Where net weekly earnings cannot be calculated from pay slips or other records, the SBC may calculate or estimate as it thinks appropriate, in which case it is wise to check the SBC's estimate.

As well as these partial earnings disregarded (if any), there is a further maximum disregard of £4.00 of the following forms of income.

(c) II death benefit and parent's and relative's pensions (see ch 3(5) (d)(e)), the difference between NI widow's pension and the higher war and service pensions and II death benefit pensions for widows and widowers (see ch 3(5)(a)(b)); £0.38 of any war or service pension or II death benefit allowance or increase of NI widow's allowance, widowed mother's allowance or child's special allowance for a first or second child (see ch 2(B)(13)(a), ch 3(A)(5)(c)); and £0.28 of any such allowance or increase for a third or subsequent child (SBA 1966, Sch 2, para 24(3)-(6)).

(d) £1.00 of an occupational pension or periodical sum paid in respect of redundancy (SBA 1966, Sch 2, para 25).

(e) Any other income except earnings and capital over £1,200. This disregard can only operate when the total amount (if any) disregarded under (c) and (d) above does not come to £4.00; and the total amount disregarded under (c), (d) and (e) cannot exceed £4.00 (SBA 1966, Sch 2, para 24(1)). This disregard can apply, for example, to payments from private sources treated as income by the SBC (see (2)(g) above), income tax refunds or other payments resulting from a trade dispute (see (G)(2) below), and any resources not specified in schedule 2 but treated as income by the SBC under its discretionary power (SBA 1966, Sch 2, para 26).

(4)   Capital
The treatment of capital and income therefrom requires further explanation; such resources are totally disregarded if they amount to less than £1,200. Any excess over £1,200 is 'converted' to an assumed income by the operation of a crude tariff: £0.25 per week is assumed for each complete £50 (SBA 1966, Sch 2, para 22). A claimant with savings of £1,300 is therefore assumed to have an income of £0.50 per week from capital. This rate of assumed income represents a far higher income than could be gained from investment of capital. The Handbook explains, as the reason for this, that large capital resources must be used for day-to-day living expenses since, if reduced or exhausted, SB entitlement will increase (Handbook, para 31). While it may appear equitable not to 'subsidize the wealthy', the victims in practice of the tariff are those claimants, particularly pensioners, who after saving against retirement or other events, find themselves penalized for their prudence. In a few cases, there may be a solution—for example, a long-term claimant living in rented accommodation who had sufficient resources could buy outright a house, the value of which must be disregarded.

We have now discussed the manner in which weekly SB is calculated for most claimants (there are further considerations in the case of some unemployed claimants and all claimants affected by trade disputes: see (F)(2)-(6), (G)(1)-(2) below). As well as such weekly benefit, there are two further types of payment, unrelated to the requirements/resources equation: ENPs and payments in urgent cases.

(D)   Exceptional Needs Payments

The SBC has the power to make lump-sum payments 'where it appears reasonable in all the circumstances' to meet 'exceptional need' (SBA 1966, s7). This power is additional to the obligation to pay weekly SB to a claimant whose resources do not meet his requirements; indeed ENPs can be made to persons who do not qualify for weekly SB ('Poverty' no. 29, p.34). SBC policy on ENPs can be discerned in some detail from the Handbook (paras 85-114) and a special ENPs report.

The SBC interprets 'exceptional need' as 'essential need'. No need which is not essential is met; provision must be necessary to avoid hardship (Handbook, paras 87-8; ENPs Report, para 7). However the SBC, in relation to ENPs, interprets 'in all the circumstances' in a personal sense—needs and potential hardship are measured in relation to individual claimants and not by a general yardstick for all claimants. Accordingly, no fixed sums are laid down by the SBC for particular items (compare its policy on ECAs: see (B)(5) above).

But the 'personal' approach of the SBC may not always strike the claimant as generous. Great emphasis is placed on the exceptional nature of ENPs to justify policies of not asking claimants whether they have needs which might qualify for payment (ENPs Report, para 11); of only providing enough for the purchase of second-hand-items where possible (ENPs Report, para 8(2)); and of reluctance to meet costs which should be borne by weekly SB, despite the absence of any statutory indication of how that should be spent. There is also a reluctance to make ENPs to claimants with a 'record' of claims for or payments of ENPs: records which are frequently cited at appeals, regardless of whether an appeal concerns ENPs or not. None the less, the number and amount of ENPs have steadily increased in recent years and it is not SBC policy to reverse or halt this trend (ENPs Report, para 9). The categories of needs which may qualify for ENPs are not closed (ENPs Report, para 10), though the SBC offers detailed examples of the needs most commonly met or which it may be prepared to meet (Handbook, paras 91-114; ENPs Report, paras 14-28 and App 1).

Despite the policy that ENPs should not provide for items deemed by the SBC as covered by the scale-rates (see (B)(1) above), the largest single category of ENPs is for clothing and footwear (ENPs Report, para 5), which the SBC recognizes long-term claimants cannot afford to replace out of weekly benefit. Local offices are provided with a standard list of clothing and bedding (Form B040: reproduced in ENPs Report, App 2), and this is used as a guide when dealing with claims for these items. The SBC warns against using this as a check-list but claimants lacking items on it should claim ENPs in order to obtain them, and cite the list on appeal if payments are refused.

A similar list of items of furniture and household equipment is contained in the ENPs Report (App 1, paras 9-10). SBC policy permits ENPs to provide new bedding, curtains, and lino (but not carpet!), but claimants with furniture needs are often referred to the second-hand store of a local authority social services department or voluntary organization. This can lead to understandable resentment among claimants, who prefer applying for ENPs to the receipt of charity, but who are not in a position to grumble (and fear the label of 'scrounger' if they claim ENPs or grumble too often!). Perhaps the best way to avoid a referral to charity is, as Lynes suggests, to request the help of social workers by asking them to refuse to supply from local authority stores, thus forcing the SBC to decide a claim (Lynes, 1974. p.97). On the recommendation of the Finer Committee (Cmnd 5629, para 6-39), the SBC has directed its staff, in awarding ENPs, to appreciate the particular problems of one-parent families in furnishing a home.

Other items which the SBC are prepared to meet by way of ENPs are fares for employment interviews or to visit hospital patients; necessary removal expenses; redecoration (though again the SBC tries to enlist private charity to keep the costs down); fireguards where children or infirm persons may be at risk; the installation of telephones if needed as a 'lifeline' and not provided by a local authority under the Chronically Sick and Disabled Persons Act 1970; and funeral expenses if, again, no other souce of public funds is available (ENPs Report, App 1).

SBC policy does not permit payments of ENPs for amenities, let alone luxuries, since to do so would raise the living standards of SB recipients above that of many persons in work on low incomes. So holidays, for example, will never be countenanced, though with strong support from his doctor, an invalid claimant might receive an ENP if a convalescent holiday was vital.

It is accepted by the SBC that fuel debts and rent arrears, which should have been met at the proper time out of weekly SB, may require ENPs (Handbook, paras 105-6; ENPs Report, paras 19-24). Although this infringes the policy of stressing 'essential' need, it conforms to that of avoiding hardship by use of ENPs—though the SBC stresses that use of ENPs to clear debts is very exceptional, and countenances the possibility of hardship taking its own course: 'where the household consists only of adults in good health, it may be right to let the disconnecting of the fuel supply take its course' (ENPs Report, para

39). Even with regard to healthy adults, such a policy is hard to reconcile with the SBC's welfare duty (SBA 1966, s3(1)).

In deciding ENP claims, the SBC has a discretion to have regard to resources disregarded in the calculation of weekly SB (SBA 1966, Sch2, para 6). It is SBC policy to ignore any income so disregarded (ENPs Report, para 3(2)), so this provision only affects the claimant with capital, of which £1,200 is disregarded for weekly SB purposes (see (C) (4) above). For ENP purposes, however, the SBC takes account of capital over £150 (ENPs Report, para 13), though this is not done in cases where refusal of an ENP would result in a reduction of capital to less than £150 (Lynes, 1974, p.87); and this rule of policy does not affect capital assets such as homes, furniture or businesses which are still disregarded in relation to ENPs. Since this is a mere policy rule, an appeal should always be considered where refusal of an ENP on the grounds that such capital should be used seems unreasonable—for example, if investments cannot be realized in time to meet the need in question. It is important to bear in mind that evey diminution of capital over £1,200 effects an increase in weekly SB, whereas a reduction below £1,200 has no effect.

In cases where a claimant appears to resort regularly to ENPs for items supposedly within the scale rates, the SBC considers a temporary reduction of weekly SB to offset lump-sum payments. This can only be justified legally by reliance on the SBC's general power to reduce a supplementary allowance in exceptional circumstances (SBA 1966, Sch 2, para 4(1)(b)), and this use of that power is of dubious legality (Lynes, 1974, p.94). Since no such power exists in relation to supplementary pension, such 'loans' to pensioners are certainly unlawful.

(E)   Payments in Urgent Cases

The SBC is empowered to make a payment 'in an urgent case' regardless of the normal exclusions of full-time employment or schooling or involvement in a trade-dispute (see (A)(1)above, (G)(1) below), regardless of the conditions which may be attached to SB for unemployed claimants, and disregarding, if appropriate, the computing of financial elegibility (SBA 1966, s13(1)). This power can be invoked if a claimant who will require regular SB is penniless at the time of his initial claim; if a flood or fire has left the claimant without food or other essentials; if a pay-packet has been lost or stolen; or if a claimant is unavoidably prevented from going to work and as a result is temporarily unable to manage (Handbook, para 115). Where a s13 payment is made to a person in full-time work, the SBC has the power to decide that all or part of the payment may be recovered by the Secretary of State for Social Services, if 'satisfied that the circumstances are such that recovery would be equitable' (SBA 1966, s13(2)). This would appear to permit the use of s13 payments as loans to persons in work. An appeal against a repayment requirement is specifically provided for and should be exercised (SBA 1966, s18(1)(c)). Even if the appeal fails, it may buy a little time in which to save for the repayment.

It is SBC policy not to provide s13 payments for the replacement of essential clothing and household belongings if a claimant can provide these himself out of savings over £150 (Handbook, para 115). Like all SBC policy, this has no legal force and can be appealed against; though in the situations for which s13 is designed, payment after a successful appeal may be too late.

(F)   Unemployed Claimants

Most unemployed claimants will be entitled initially to NI unemployment benefit (see ch 2(B)(1)) and will only require SB to 'top up' their income to the SB level. Those without unemployment benefit must rely entirely on SB while out of work. All the rules discussed below apply to all unemployed claimants, with the exception of the penalty reserved for those disqualified for unemployment benefit (see (3) below).

(1)   Registration for Employment
The SBC can make the right of any claimant to a supplementary allowance (not pension) conditional upon registering for work at an employment exchange (careers office if under eighteen) (SBA 1966, s11). In many cases this will not affect claimants since they would register when claiming unemployment benefit or to find new employment. But there are three consequences of this condition which can affect SB entitlement.

First, some claimants (such as students) may be placed in an awkward position if subsequently offered work by the employment exchange: to accept may be impractical or impossible, to refuse may incur disqualification for unemployment benefit (see ch 2(B)(1)(b)(iv) (v)) and a consequential reduction of SB (see (3) below).

Second, the wage-stop and the 40 per cent rule can only be applied to registered claimants (see (2)(3) below). Third, only unregistered long-term recipients of supplementary allowance qualify for the higher rate B scale rate requirements (see (B)(1) above) after two years. Therefore, it may be crucial for a claimant to avoid the registration requirement.

There are no statutory criteria for the use of this power, but the SBC's policy is clearly outlined in the Handbook (para 7): the rule 'is normally applied to anyone who is capable of work'. It seems reasonable to give the phrase 'capable of work' the same meaning as it has in the context of unemployment benefit (see ch 2(B)(1)(a)); so a claimant not entitled to that benefit because he is not capable of work should not be required to register as a condition of receipt of SB, and an appeal against the requirement (specifically provided for: SBA 1966, s18(1)(c)) could be supported by the NI Commissioners' decisions on this point. This view is reinforced by the SBC policy of not requiring claimants who are incapable of work to register (Handbook, para 8); so a claimant entitled to sickness or invalidity benefit (see ch 2(B)(2)(3)) should be exempt from registration (as should claimants who would be so entitled but for a deficient NI contribution record).

The SBC also exempts from registration lone parents with dependent children under sixteen at home; and blind claimants not accustomed to working outside the home (Handbook, para 8). It is also prepared, 'depending on all the circumstances of the case' to waive the requirement or demand registration for only part-time work for other claimants including those who have to stay home to care for sick relatives; women widowed in late middle age with no experience of employment, and 'where there is evidence of some ill-health'; and, in certain circumstances, those on training or educational courses (Handbook, para 9). In all such cases a waiver of registration should be sought initially, since many claimants in these categories are likely to be long-term recipients of SB, for whom the wage-stop and the inability to proceed to rate B scale-rate requirements after two years will work hardship.

If required to register, a claimant must 'sign on' weekly at the employment exchange; but those within ten years of retirement and unemployed for two years, or those severely handicapped mentally or physically and unemployed for one year, may be permitted to sign on quarterly (Handbook, para 196) (though handicapped claimants should always seek a waiver of the registration requirement). The Handbook warns if anyone fails to register when required, 'supplementary allowance may be withheld' (para 10). When this happens, advisers should check to ensure there are no good reasons for not signing, and if hardship will be caused, appeal and pending the hearing claim a s13 payment (see (E) above). Withholding benefit is only permissible 'where there are exceptional circumstances' (SBA 1966, Sch 2, para 4(1)(b)); an SBAT might not deem failure to sign on sufficiently exceptional to warrant cutting off SB.

Appeals against the imposition of registration must be well documented—doctors' letters and other evidence of disabilities should be produced to tribunals, and any factors preventing a claimant from working clearly stressed.

(2)   The Wage-Stop

The SBC is empowered to reduce the SB payable to an unemployed claimant so that it does not exceed his net weekly earnings were he in full-time work in his usual occupation (SBA 1966, Sch 2, para 5(2)). This is known as the 'wage-stop'. The principle behind the rule is that it is wrong to give an unemployed claimant a higher income than he enjoyed in work; a sorry admission that many workers receive incomes below SB level. Despite SBC denials that the wage-stop is a work-incentive rule (Handbook, para 78; Wage-Stop Report, para 4), there can be little doubt that is has that effect, and that it forms a disincentive to employers to pay wages above the poverty line. That the wage-stop is controversial was recognized by the publication in 1967 by the SBC of a special report, which sets out SBC policy in some detail, though there have been some changes since 1967.

The wage-stop can only be applied to claimants required to register for work (see (1) above), or where 'by reason only of temporary circumstances the imposition of that condition would be innappropriate' (SBA 1966, Sch 2, para 5 (1)). The latter provision may be used to wage-stop a low-paid worker who is sick for a short period (Handbook, para 81) or temporarily laid off otherwise than through a trade-dispute. But in most cases registration is a pre-condition of the wage-stop and the first consideration in challenging the wage-stop must be the possibility of challenging registration.

The net weekly earnings to the level of which a wage-stopped claimant's SB must be reduced are calculated as for the purposes of assessing resources (see (C)(3) above); but in addition the claimant's FIS (if any), or the FIS to which he would be entitled if in work, must be included as part of his net weekly earnings (Family Income Supplements Act 1970, s13(2); for entitlement to FIS, see ch 5(B)(1)). In calculating the wage-stopped SB payable, the SBC must also have regard to any income received by a claimant by reason of being unemployed (e.g. earnings from a temporary part-time job); together with his SB and any unemployment benefit, these must not exceed the wage-stop level (SBA 1966, Sch 2, para 5(2) (3)).

If a claimant has detailed evidence of recent wages such as pay-slips, the SBC will base net weekly earnings on these. It is important to check the SBC's calculations (on Form W3(WS)) with the claimant, ensuring that any regular overtime or bonuses have been taken into account. In deducting from the gross earnings figure for wage-stop purposes, it is SBC policy only to allow for statutory deductions and travelling expenses (if any—so if a claimant usually walks or cycles to work, these should not arise). Other items which can and should be deducted when calculating resources (e.g. meals at work, wear and tear on tools and overalls) are not deducted for wage-stop purposes, being offset 'by additional expenses when the man is at home and looking for work' (Wage-Stop Report, para 29).

When evidence of recent earnings is not available, the SBC is empowered to estimate a claimant's normal earning capacity (SBA 1966, Sch 2, para 7 and SI 1966/1065, reg 4(2)). The SBC does this by using the current wages of local authority manual workers as fixed by the National Joint Council for Local Authorities (Manual Workers)—the 'NJC rates'. The Wage-Stop Report (para 27) implies this is done for all such claimants, whereas the Handbook (para 80) apparently reserves the NJC rates method for labourers. Since the Handbook is the later statement of policy, and since the NJC is only concerned with labourer and light labourer employees of local authorities, the application of NJC rates should be challenged in any case where a claimant does not fall in these categories (unless it would benefit a claimant to be so assessed) and net earnings in the claimant's actual occupation submitted on appeal. If a classification is successfully challenged resulting in an increase of SB, arrears should be claimed. It is also advisable to check with the employment exchange that the claimant's proper classification has been recorded.

The SBC allows the possibility of using higher rates than NJC rates in regions where prevailing rates of pay are 'clearly substantially higher' (Wage-Stop Report, para 27). So advisers should always inquire of the local authority and trade unions as to the current rates of wages in a locality, and present evidence from these sources on appeal. Similarly, whereas the SBC usually takes the basic NJC rates (including the minimum earnings guarantee laid down by the NJC) but ignoring overtime payments at higher rates stipulated by the NJC, advisers should ensure that claimants' wage-stop levels are in line with local average overtime payments; again, evidence from the town hall and trade unions should be submitted on appeal (and, as with all evidence in wage-stop appeals, directed principally at the Trades Council member of the SBAT).

In fact, the SBC policy of using the NJC rates to fix the wage-stopped SB of all labourers who cannot produce evidence of recent earnings is probably unlawful, for two reasons. First, it is a misinterpretation of the regulations on which the SBC relies as authority for the practice (SI 1966/1065, reg 4(2)), which permits the SBC to estimate earnings 'having regard to all the circumstances of the case'; as so often happens, SBC policy appears to abuse the discretion given by statute by ignoring the discretion to treat cases individually and determining decisions, in effect, in advance: a discretion exercised the same way every time arguably ceases to be a discretion.

Second, 'it is improper for an authority to delegate wide discretionary powers to another authority over which it is incapable of exercising direct control, unless it is expressly empowered so to delegate' (de Smith, 1973, p.269). In other words, the SBC's policy effectively permits the NJC to determine the SB paid to a whole class of wage-stopped claimants. In other contexts, such a surrender of discretion by one authority to another has been held ultra vires (Ellis v Dubowski [1921] All ER 272). Although tribunals may not appreciate such finer points of law, they could ground an application for certiorari (see ch 1(C)(1)).

A claimant who is out of work through sickness is not wage-stopped 'if it is clear at the outset that the man is unlikely to be fit for work within three months' (Handbook, para 81). In such cases, a doctor's letter accompanying an initial claim for SB may save subsequent negotiation and appeal. Where the duration of the sickness is likely to be less than three months or is unknown at the outset, claimants are wage-stopped and the wage-stop is subsequently lifted after three months. This is mere SB policy, and should be resisted if it causes hardship. In all cases where the wage-stop is lifted, arrears of SB (the difference between wage-stop benefit and full entitlement) should be paid.

If a man enters prison for less than three months, the SB payable to his wife, if higher than his wage-stopped entitlement were he unemployed, is restricted to the level of his normal net earnings. This is done under the SBC's general power to reduce benefit 'where there are exceptional circumstances' (SBA 1966, Sch 2, para 4(1)(b)).

The SBC claims to review earnings rates continuously with a view to increasing wage-stopped SB (Wage-Stop Report, para 31). Since in practice this takes some time, a claimant who learns of a wage increase in his normal occupation should claim an increase of SB, with appropriate arrears, backdated to the date of the increase in earnings.

Whenever the wage-stop is applied, advisers must seek to maximise the use by claimants of ENPs (see (D) above). Claiming ECAs (see (B)(5) above) is, however, of little practical use since they are subjected to the wage-stop, being part of the calculation of a claimant's requirements. Although it could be argued that since ECAs are awarded 'where there are exceptional circumstances' (SBA 1966, Sch 2, para 4(1)(a)), the wage-stop should not extend to them since it applies 'unless there are exceptional circumstances' (SBA 1966, Sch 2, para 5(1)(a)): to grant an increase of requirements is to recognize exceptional circumstances (carried a step further, this reasoning suggests the wage-stop cannot be imposed at all if an ECA has been awarded in the calculation of requirements).

A similar problem arises in the case of a wage-stopped claimant whose family includes a person who entitles the claimant to the inclusion of attendance requirements in the calculation of his SB (see (B)(2) above). In some cases, such an inclusion could be sufficient to bring the claimant's SB over his normal earnings level—but for the attendance requirements, he would not be wage-stopped. Yet the avowed purpose of introducing attendance requirements was to ensure that SB recipients received the equivalent of NI attendance allowance which they would receive if not on SB. This could be achieved if the SBC considered such cases as 'exceptional circumstances' and thus did not impose the wage-stop (SBA 1966, Sch 2, para 5(1)(a)).

SBC staff are instructed to bring to the attention of wage-stopped claimants the possibility of claiming other means-tested benefits, in particular rent rebates or allowances and rate rebates (see ch 11(A),(B)). A wage-stopped claimant with a family who returns to work on low wages should apply for FIS (see ch 5(B)).

(3)   The 40 per cent Rule

NI unemployment benefit can be refused for up to six weeks on certain disqualifying grounds (see ch 2(B)(1)(b)). Such disqualified claimants will need to claim SB as their sole source of income for the period of disqualification; but they will find that in so doing their sins are visited upon them again. For the calculation of the requirements of these claimants must include a 40 per cent reduction of their scale-rate requirements; though this does not include the scale-rate sums for dependent children and, in the case of married claimants, the reduction is only 40 per cent of the difference between the scale-rate requirements for a husband and wife and those for a single householder, the difference being rounded down to a multiple of £0.05 (SBA 1966, Sch 2, para 11(1)).

This mandatory reduction can also apply to those who have not claimed unemployment benefit or do not yet know the outcome of such a claim, or have been refused unemployment benefit for another reason, such as a deficient contribution record (SBA 1966, Sch 2, para 11(2)). In these cases the 40 per cent penalty is imposed if the SBC is of the opinion that a claim for unemployment benefit (if made, decided or refused for another reason) would result in a disqualification (the 'opinion' is in practice that of the employment exchange). Any such 'opinion' not in keeping with the NI rules and the NI Commissioner's decisions should be appealed against, and the discrepancy explained. The 40 per cent rule only applies to claimants required to register for employment (SBA 1966, Sch 2, para 11(1)).

In any case where this penalty is invoked, it may only remain in force for the duration of the unemployment benefit disqualification, if that is the cause of the penalty, which cannot be longer than six weeks. So if an appeal against such a disqualification (to a NI Local Tribunal or Commissioner) results in a reduction of the disqualification period, this should be reflected in the SB penalty and arrears of SB paid to the claimant, and similarly if the disqualification itself is overruled on appeal. Those penalized by the 40 per cent rule on the strength of an 'opinion' could point out on appeal (to a SBAT) that the SBC and the tribunals have a discretion to penalize for less than six weeks. The 40 per cent penalty should never last beyond six weeks.

Like the wage-stop, the 40 per cent rule may leave its victims more than usually short of money. The SBC recognizes this to some extent by instructions in the 'A' Code to consider increasing the reduced benefit under its general discretionary power (SBA 1966, Sch 2, para 4(1)(a)) in certain hardship situations such as sickness, rent arrears or pregnancy (Handbook, para 200). However this apparent concern for claimants' welfare is restricted to those penalized for the full six weeks; and 'unless the circumstances are very exceptional' a deduction of £0.75 per week is still made so that industrial misdemeanours 'should not be a matter of indifference' (Handbook, para 200). Claimants subjected to the 40 per cent rule should make maximum use of ECAs and ENPs; despite this unwelcoming approach to hardship of the SBC, SBATs may be more sympathetic.

(4)   Refusal of SB
The SBC asserts the right in certain circumstances to refuse or withdraw SB totally to unemployed claimants. The Handbook is sketchy in its treatment of this, but the Fisher Report has revealed the precise criteria employed by the SBC (Cmnd 5228, para 259).

In all cases there must be:

(a) an unemployment benefit disqualification or 'opinion' (see (3) above) and

(b) no appeal outstanding against the disqualification or opinion; and in addition one of the following conditions must be satisfied in all respects: either

(c) a specific job is immediately available for the claimant, which is suitable for him, having regard to any handicaps from which he may suffer; or

(d) the claimant has been voluntarily unemployed at least three times in the last six months; there are abundant suitable job opportunities in the area and the claimant could obtain work in his occupation without difficulty; he has no mental disability, and no dependent children; if married his wife has been seen by an officer of the DHSS, is in good health, under forty, fit for work and likely to obtain it; the claimant has no social handicap which would make it particularly difficult to find work; he has no dependants or other persons who might suffer hardship if SB were refused or withdrawn; and refusal or withdrawal is authorized by an officer of the Higher Executive grade.

Since an appeal against a disqualification or opinion makes the procedure inapplicable, it is clearly worth lodging an appeal regardless of the prospects of success. Any cases where SB is refused or stopped must be checked to ensure the SBC has complied with its own conditions; if not an appeal must be lodged. Pending appeal, and in any case where hardship is caused, claims for s13 payments must be made (see (E) above).

The Fisher Report, while revealing this procedure in detail, passed no comment on its legality. It is indeed a doubtful interpretation of the power to reduce or withdraw SB (SBA 1966, Sch 2, para 4(1)(b)) in 'exceptional circumstances' which covers every case which fulfils the SBC's conditions. But it is almost unquestionably unlawful to refuse SB ab initio to a claimant who fulfils the conditions of entitlement—whose requirements exceed his resources. The 1966 Act nowhere authorizes refusal to meet claims which reveal entitlement, and in the light of the SBC's welfare duty (SBA 1966, s3(1)) there seems no scope for implying such a power.

(5)   Withdrawal of SB
In areas of good job opportunities, single, fit, unskilled claimants under forty-five and registered for employment are liable to be summoned for interview with an Unemployment Review Officer after receiving benefit for four weeks. These officers discuss with claimants their difficulties in finding work and, if satisfied that no serious attempt to find work has been made, may withdraw SB. This is known as the four-week rule. Mere failure to attend the interview may also result in withdrawal of benefit (Handbook, para 203). In the same areas, this procedure is applied to other fit claimants under forty-five after thirteen weeks, to unfit claimants and those between forty-five and sixty (fifty-five in the case of women) after six months, and to claimants over that age after a year.

SB can only be withheld in 'exceptional circumstances' (SBA 1966, Sch 2, para 4(1)b)). Since benefit has already been awarded in the cases to which this procedure is applied, the SBC must have grounds for reviewing its initial decision in order to withdraw it. The only applicable power of review in such cases is a change of circumstances (see (I) below) giving rise to 'exceptional circumstances' meriting withdrawal. But withdrawals are made in practice on the ground that circumstances have not changed. The legality of such withdrawals is, therefore, dubious.

An appeal should always be made and emergency payment of SB (see (E) above) sought pending a hearing. At the hearing any efforts to find work should be described, any factors impeding the search for employment stressed, particularly if they question the claimant's fitness, and any failure by the SBC to observe its own procedures mentioned.

(6)   Re-establishment Centres
These centres, provided by the SBC 'for the re-establishment of persons in need thereof through lack of regular occupation or of instruction or training' (SBA 1966, Sch 4, para 1), are normally attended voluntarily by long-term unemployed claimants 'in response to opportunities offered by local offices' (Handbook, para 210). But a SBAT can, on receiving a report from the SBC and after a hearing, direct that a supplementary

allowance only be payable on condition of attendance at a centre for a period specified by the tribunal (SBA 1966, s12 (1)). A precondition of a SBC report must be failure by a claimant to maintain himself or his dependants—a duty placed on all spouses and parents by s22 of the 1966 Act (see (H)(1) below).

A claimant subjected to this condition has the right to apply to a tribunal if there has been a change of circumstances with a view to revocation of the condition (SBA 1966, s12 (5)). This is an important right since there is no limit to the period of attendance which a tribunal may impose.

In deciding on a SBC report or an application for revocation, the tribunal, as always, has complete discretion in law. At such hearings, any personal difficulties in attending and any favourable points in a claimant's employment record must be stressed. Committal to a centre is a drastic measure, not to be lightly imposed, and SBC policy reflects this view (Handbook, para 210).

If a tribunal direction is in force, the SBC may require the claimant to attend instead 'such course of instruction or training approved by the Minister . . . as the Commission may specify' and to 'comply with the rules there in force' (SBA 1966, s12(2)). Appeal against such a requirement is specifically provided for (SBA 1966, s18(1)(c)). The SBC is empowered to make arrangements with other government departments or voluntary organizations for the maintenance of persons subject to a tribunal direction in centres provided by those bodies for purposes similar to those of re-establishment centres, such as the Industrial Rehabilitation Units of the Department of Employment (SBA 1966, s12(4)).

While subject to a direction, a claimant may, instead of receiving SB, be maintained by the SBC in a re-establishment or similar centre, but he is still entitled to 'such payments (if any) for meeting his personal requirements or the requirements of any dependant of his as they (the SBC) think fit' (SBA 1966, s12(3)). While it may be in the claimant's interest not to be responsible for all his financial affairs while attending a centre or course of training, he can, if dissatisfied with these arrangements for payment of benefit, appeal against them under the general right to appeal as to the 'right to or amount of any benefit' (SBA 1966, s18(1)(a)).

The 1966 Act gives neither the SBC nor the SBATs the power to compel attendance at a re-establishment centre; the only power is to make payments of benefit conditional on attendance. A claimant is free to leave a centre at any time, the only incentive to stay being the certain loss of SB if he leaves.

(7) Prosecution
The last resort to which the SBC may feel driven in dealing with an

unemployed claimant is prosecution. Persistent refusal or neglect to maintain oneself or one's dependants is a summary offence (SBA 1966, s30(1)), if as a result of such refusal or neglect either SB is paid to meet the requirements of the defendant or his dependants or board and lodging in a reception centre (see ch 8(A)(1)(b)) is provided for him. The maximum sentence is three months' imprisonment or a fine of £100 or both.

This is the criminal sanction for the enforcement of the duty placed on a man, for the purposes of the 1966 Act, to maintain himself, his wife and his children (SBA 1966, s22(1)(a)), and is more often used where the refusal or neglect relates to dependants than to the claimant himself (see (H)(4) below). Prosecutions in the latter category are rare—64 in 1971 out of 85 cases considered for proceedings (Cmnd 5228, para 442). The Fisher Report declined to comment on evidence that only those so inadequate as to be unable to avoid prosecution by a minimum amount of work were prosecuted; but equally it rejected suggestions that prosecution of the unemployed was under-used: 'Its primary value may be as a threat' (Cmnd 5228, para 445).

(8)   Returning to Work

The bar on payments of SB to persons in full-time work does not apply in the first fifteen days of an employment. Thus a formerly unemployed claimant may continue to receive SB for the first two weeks in a new job.

Assessment is based on the normal calculation of requirements and resources, so to qualify a claimant must receive wages which do not, under the resources calculations (see (C) above), amount to more than his requirements. In assessing his resources, the SBC disregards only £1 of a claimant's wages (if any) instead of the usual £2. This is done under the discretionary powers to reduce SB (SBA 1966, Sch 2, para 4,(1)(b)), and is probably unlawful since that power is only exercisable 'where there are exceptional circumstances' and taking employment is hardly exceptional, particularly in view of the measures designed to encourage unemployed claimants to seek work.

The SBC also puts pressure on claimants returning to work to seek a 'sub' from their new employers before it considers a claim, but this should be resisted since its effect may be to put the claimant out of pocket at a later date, when he has to repay the sub but can no longer avail himself of this fifteen-day rule—though in one case a tribunal invoked s13 (see (E) above) to overcome this obstacle (Lynes, 1974, p.185).

A claimant should ensure that the calculation of his requirements includes allowance, in the form of ECAs (see (B)(5) above) for expenditure not incurred in the previous period of unemployment, such as fares to work, trade union subscriptions, and the higher cost (if any) of meals at work. And a claim for ENPs (see (D) above) to meet such items as tools or overalls, if an employee has to provide these for himself, should be considered.

There is a similar provision for claimants returning to work after a trade-dispute, but it is important not to confuse the two categories of unemployed and trade-dispute cases, since, in the latter case, the SB may be recouped out of wages (see (G)(4) below).

(G) Claimants Affected by Trade-Disputes

As with NI unemployment benefit (see ch 2(B)(1)(b)(i)), involvement in a trade-dispute produces penalties for SB claimants. There are special rules relating to the assessment of both requirements and resources; and while there is provision for the payment of SB in the first fifteen days after a dispute ends, this is offset by recovery provisions. There is no power to prosecute a person for refusal or neglect to maintain himself or his dependants 'by reason only of anything done or omitted in furtherance of a trade-dispute' (SBA 1966, s30(2)).

(1) Requirements

A person affected by a trade-dispute is disqualified personally, in that he is excluded from the calculation of requirements (SBA 1966, s10(1)); thus a single claimant is not entitled, and if a claimant's dependant is affected by a trade-dispute, that dependant's requirements are ignored. But a claimant with dependants, being himself affected by a trade-dispute, will be assessed as normal except that instead of being accorded the husband and wife scale-rate requirements, the highest non-householder rate is substituted (see table 4).

When is a claimant involved in or affected by a trade-dispute for this purpose? The provisions of the 1966 Act are modelled on those for unemployment benefit (SSA 1975, s19(1)). Thus disqualification attaches to a claimant who 'by reason of a stoppage of work due to a trade-dispute at his place of employment is without employment for any period during which the stoppage continues'; if during a stoppage a disqualified claimant becomes 'bona fide employed elsewhere in the occupation which he usually follows or regularly engaged in some other occupation', the disqualification lapses (SBA 1966, s10(1)), though, of course, the total disqualification of being in full-time employment then applies, subject to the fifteen-day rule (see (F)(8) above), which if applicable does not carry the recovery possibility discussed below (see (4) below). Apart from such cases of re-employment elsewhere, the disqualification can only be avoided if the claimant proves he is not 'participating in or financing or directly interested in' the trade-dispute and that he does not belong to a grade or class of workers, members of which are so involved (SBA 1966, s10(2)).

Appeals on the question of disregarding requirements under s10 lie to the NI Local Tribunals (SBA 1966, s18(2)), thus giving the possibility of further appeal to the NI Commissioners, and recourse can be made to the Commissioners' Decisions on questions of trade-disputes. Where there are simultaneous claims for unemployment benefit and SB, a successful appeal against the trade-dispute disqualification for unemployment benefit must also lead to payment in full of SB and arrears.

(2)   Resources

The resources of a claimant disqualified under s10 but entitled to SB for dependants are assessed as usual (see (C) above), except that any income tax refunds and strike pay which he receives or could receive on demand, as a result of being without employment during a trade-dispute are taken into account, even if not actually claimed or received, subject to the general £4 disregard (see (C)(3) above). Tax refunds resulting from periods of sickness or unemployment are not so treated; so if a period of sickness coincides with a trade-dispute, no account should be taken of tax refunds since the claimant would not be at work were there no dispute (SBA 1966, Sch 2, para 25A).

(3)   ENPs and s13 Payments

If a claimant has dependants, ENPs (see (D) above) for items which cannot be met out of weekly SB but might be met out of normal wages should be claimed, stressing the hardship resulting not merely from loss of wages but from lower SB payments than would be received in the case of a family whose breadwinner was out of work for other reasons.

A single claimant, although involved in a trade-dispute, can claim s13 payments (see (E) above), and these may be his only source of money in the absence of strike pay. The SBC is specifically empowered to disregard s10 in deciding s13 claims, so strikers without money for rent or food should stress this in applying.

As might be expected, the SBC adopts a standard policy on the administration of s13 in trade-dispute situations.

If a striker could, by using recent wages and other income, restrain his spending to £6.50 a week or less no payment is made; otherwise a s13 payment is only made to bring income up to £5 per week if the striker is in lodgings or a hostel and is threatened with eviction or is in private accommodation with no other source of assistance or lives with relations who are themselves receiving SB or an income near SB level (Lynes, 1974, pp. 127-8; Handbook, para 168). If a claimant needs more than this limit to meet urgent needs, the SBC is able to pay more, and arguably bound to do so since s13 implies that claims are to be treated individually and failure to do this may be a breach of the SBC's welfare duty (SBA 1966, s3(1)), or a misuse of discretion. Negotiation over s13 payments must, of course, be with the local office if they are to have any effect, since unless the trade-dispute is a protracted one, an appeal victory will be a hollow one.

The SBC has been known to use s13 to offer advances to single strikers rather than payments as such. This is unlawful since s13 payments can only be recovered from claimants in full-time work (SBA 1966, s13(2)). It has also been known to demand written undertakings to repay such monies; these are equally invalid and should not be countenanced by claimants.

(4)   Returning to Work

A disqualified claimant returning to work at the end of a trade-dispute is entitled to SB for the first fifteen days after the dispute: however the SBC has powers to recover benefit paid during this period through a somewhat elaborate procedure (Social Security Act 1971, s2(1)(2)).

If a claimant who has been disqualified during a dispute returns to work and his requirements exceed his resources then the SBC must pay him benefit, but must also determine his 'protected earnings' figure; this is arrived at by assessing his requirements as for weekly SB (see (B) above), adding £3.00 and deducting any Family Allowance (SSA 1971, s2(4)(5); for entitlement to Family Allowance, see ch 5(A)(1)). Notice in writing of the protected earnings figure and the amount of SB paid must be given to the claimant and the Secretary of State for Social Services (SSA 1971, s2(4)). Any later increase of SB resulting from a review of or a successful appeal against the initial decision has the effect of a further notice to the Secretary of State, though the protected earnings figure must remain the same (SSA 1971, Sch 1, para 8).

Unless the claimant has already repaid the SB (which he is under no obligation to do), the Secretary of State must then serve a 'deduction notice' on the claimant's employer which notifies the employer of the sum (which is the SB paid less any repayments already made) to be recovered by deductions from the claimant's wages, and of the protected earnings figure (SSA 1971, Sch 1, para 2(1)-(3)). The notice requires an employer to deduct on pay-days during the currency of the notice the excess (if any) of earnings over the protected earnings figure, if that excess amounts to, or is less than one-tenth of the recoverable benefit; if it amounts to more, the employer may with the claimant's written consent deduct a larger amount, so long as the claimant's final take-home pay is not below the protected earnings figure. The deduction must be made from 'available earnings': those earnings remaining after all normal deductions have been made (SSA 1971, Sch 1, para 1(1)).

An employer may not make deductions if an employee satisfies him that he has not obtained the SB to which a deduction notice relates, and the employer must then, on pain of a £20 fine, inform the Secretary of State that no deduction has been made; nor may an employer deduct an amount which is more than the outstanding balance (SSA 1971, Sch 1, para 4(4)(5)).

A deduction notice is valid from the date of service on an employer until the claimant dies, leaves his employment, repays the benefit (including repayments under earlier valid notices), or until fourteen weeks from service have elapsed (SSA 1971, Sch 1, para 3(1)). On the occurrence of any of these events (except leaving the employment) the notice lapses and no further recovery can be made by this method. If a claimant changes employment, a fresh deduction notice may be served on his new employer, though unlike the first notice this is not mandatory (SSA 1971, Sch 1, para 5).

An employer does not commit a criminal offence if he contravenes the deduction requirements; but an employer who fails to make deductions where excess earnings are available is liable to recovery of the sums in question from himself by the Secretary of State, and these are deemed repayments by the employee (SSA 1971, Sch 1, para 6(2)).

The SSA 1971 makes no provision for appeals against the decision that benefit is recoverable, the amount to be recovered, or the protected earnings figure. However the first two issues at least, and possibly the third as well, are covered by the right to appeal against 'the right to or amount of any benefit' (SBA 1966, s18(1)(a)), and a failure to hear an appeal could be challenged by mandamus (see ch 1(C)(2)).

Since the tribunals can only make decisions within the power of the SBC, they cannot remove the application of the recovery provisions unless it is proved that they have been applied in an inappropriate case—to a claimant who was not or should not have been disqualified during a trade-dispute. Although an obstacle, an unsuccessful appeal against disqualification is not a bar to appeal against recovery on the grounds that s10 was incorrectly invoked. The former appeal will have been heard by a NI Local Tribunal, the latter will be heard by a SBAT, and the two have been known to deliver conflicting decisions.

If the issue of recovery itself cannot be challenged, or is unsuccessfully challenged, the SBC's calculations may still be questioned on appeal; this may serve to raise the protected earnings figure.

The Secretary of State has the power to cancel a deduction notice before recovery is completed and, once this is done, no further notice relating to the SB in question may be served (SSA 1971, Sch 1, para 3(2)-(3)). In cases where deduction is causing genuine hardship, therefore, a request for cancellation, although not specifically provided for, can be made since otherwise this power would seem redundant. Again, a refusal could be challenged under the general right of appeal (SBA 1966, s18(1)(a)).

The Secretary of State also has a residual power to recover by other means (see ch 6(C)(5)(b)) benefit paid in the fifteen days after a trade-dispute if this procedure is 'not practicable' (SSA 1971, Sch 1, para 7(1)). This power extends to sums outstanding after partial recovery by the deduction notice procedure.

(H)   Single Spouses and Unmarried Mothers

We have already seen that unmarried but cohabiting couples are treated as married for SB purposes, causing problems if the SBC suspects a single woman of cohabitation (see (A)(2) above). Here we consider the other provisions of the 1966 Act and aspects of SBC policy and procedures relating to separated spouses, unmarried mothers and their children.

(1)   Liability to Maintain
The statutory liability to maintain has already been discussed in the context of unemployed claimants (see (F)(6)(7) above). A man is liable to maintain his wife and children, including illegitimate children of whom he has been adjudged the putative father; a woman is liable to maintain her husband and her children, including illegitimate children (SBA 1966, s22(1)). A spouse's duty to maintain the other spouse ceases on divorce but not so the duty to maintain children (Handbook, para 175). A husband's liability cannot be avoided by the provision of inadequate maintenance under a separation agreement or an undertaking by a wife on separation not to seek maintenance in the courts (NAB v Prisk [1954] 1 All ER 400; Stopher v NAB, and NAB v Parkes [1955] 1 All ER 700). All the policies of the SBC relating to 'liable relatives' stem from these duties; since husbands and wives are under these duties, the SBC has a responsibility to see the duties observed and thus minimize payment of SB to the dependants of those failing to maintain. Apart from information in the Handbook (Ch 8), SBC policy is contained in the 'Liable Relative Code' (part of the 'A' Code), but important sections of this have been published: (1974) LAG BUL. 14, from which the excerpts below are taken.

The discussion which follows centres for obvious reasons on the position of unsupported wives or mothers seeking SB and husbands or fathers sought by the SBC to ensure compliance with their duty to maintain. But, in the less common situation of a separated husband claiming SB when, as is even less common, his wife could maintain him or her children if they are living with him, the same principles apply.

(2)   The SBC's Powers
If SB is paid to meet the requirements of a separated woman and/or her children, the SBC may take proceedings in the magistrates' court by way of complaint against her husband (SBA 1966, s23(1)(2)). The magistrates must 'have regard to all the circumstances of the case and, in particular, to

the (husband's) resources', discounting, if the complaint concerns SB paid in a period before the complaint, any increase in the husband's resources since that period. The magistrates may then at their discretion order the husband to pay to the Secretary of State or the claimant wife (or another person if in the wife's interest) a sum fixed by the court, usually weekly (SBA 1966, s23(2)-(4)). The order made by the magistrates should not have the effect of reducing the husband below SB level (Ashley v Ashley [1965] 3 All ER, 557, 559; Attwood v Attwood [1968] 3 All ER 385, 388; Williams v Williams [1974] 3 All ER 377, 383). If the wife deserted the husband or has committed adultery, the magistrates may decline to make an order (NAB v Wilkinson [1952] 2 All ER 255). If payment to the Secretary of State is ordered, the SBC may be party to any subsequent proceedings for enforcement, revocation or variation of the order (SBA 1966, s23(4)). Unlike a woman's own right to seek maintenance in the magistrates' court which is time-barred after six months (Magistrates' Courts Act 1952, s104; Matrimonial Proceedings (Magistrates' Courts) Act 1960, s12), this right of the SBC may be exercised whenever the preconditions of wife's claim and husband's breach of duty exists.

The SBC has similar powers if SB is paid to meet the requirements of an illegitimate child. If no affiliation order (i.e. an order for the payment of money by the putative father: Oldfield v NAB [1960] 1 All ER 524) is in force, the SBC may, within three years of any payment of SB, apply for an order (SBA 1966, s24(1)(2); Affiliation Proceedings Act 1957, s1). The SBC can apply for an order even though the mother is no longer entitled to do so (NAB v Mitchell [1955] 3 All ER 291; NAB v Tugby [1951] 1 All ER 509) or even if the mother has previously applied unsuccessfully for an order (Clapham v NAB [1961] 2 All ER 50). The proceedings are as on a mother's application except that the court must in addition hear any evidence produced by the SBC; and any payment ordered by the court to be made may be paid to the Secretary of State, in which case the SBC may be party to any proceedings to enforce, vary or revoke the order (SBA 1966, s24(3)(4)). If a mother herself takes affiliation proceedings, the SBC may apply at the hearing for payment to be made to the Secretary of State; and an order made payable in the first place to the mother or the SBC can on subsequent application be varied and made payable to the SBC or the mother respectively, or to another person with custody of the child in question (SBA 1966, s24(5)(6)). An order made in favour of the SBC need not, therefore, be revoked by the magistrates if SB in respect of the child ceases (Payne v Critchley [1962] 1 All ER 619). The SBC may apply for variation of an order even if the mother has died and no person has custody of the child, or if the child is not in the mother's care and she is not contributing to his maintenance (SBA 1966, s24(7)), provided there has at some point in time been a payment of SB for the requirements of the child.

(3)   Procedures

When a claim for SB results from a separation, the SBC 'tries to contact the husband as soon as possible to find out why he is failing to maintain his dependants' (Handbook, para 179). Such inquiries (which, if a man has 'disappeared', are rigorous, including searches of the central NI records in Newcastle) culminate in a request to the man to fulfil his statutory duty. If he offers to contribute towards maintenance of his dependants, this is 'invariably accepted' if amounting to the SB in payment to his dependants or more, or if less than this but 'reasonable having regard to the man's statement of his circumstances which he will be expected to substantiate' (Handbook, para 180).

An offer is judged reasonable by the following formula devised by the SBC and published by the Finer Committee: from the man's net income are deducted the appropriate SB scale-rate requirements for himself and any dependants in a 'new family', his actual housing costs, and the greater of £5 or one quarter of his net earnings; an offer in the region of the amount arrived at by this calculation is usually considered reasonable (Cmnd 5629, paras 4.187-90). A man contacted by the SBC should make it fully aware of his present commitments.

If a husband's offer equals or exceeds the SB in payment, he is asked to pay directly to his wife (Handbook, para 181). If, as often happens, a husband defaults on voluntary payments, his wife must re-apply immediately for benefit. If a husband's offer falls short of the SB paid to his wife, his contribution is usually made to the SBC, which pays SB in full to the wife (Handbook, para 181).

If a husband refuses to make an offer or defaults after voluntary payments have been arranged, either the wife can seek maintenance in the magistrates' court on one of several grounds (MP(MC)A 1960, s1(1)), a right she can exercise regardless of the stage reached by the SBC in its procedures, or the SBC can use its own powers of complaint (see (2) above).

The SBC's official policy is to allow separated wives to choose for themselves whether or not to seek maintenance orders through the magistrates' courts. At most, the SBC states it will
'advise a wife about taking her own proceedings wherever possible, because:

(1) the possibility of reconciliation will receive proper consideration when she is brought into direct contact with the court officials;

(2) if she takes proceedings and the court makes an order it may be for a sum greater than the current rate of supplementary benefit;

(3) an order made in her favour will not lapse if she no longer needs SB, if for example she goes out to work' (Handbook, para 183).

There is no evidence that women who go to court at the SBC's bidding enjoy particular prospects of reconciliation and magistrates' courts rarely order maintenance at more than SB level. So only the third of these reasons carries much weight, a view endorsed by the Finer Committee (Cmnd 5629, paras 4. 198-201). To many women, the inducement of this third reason may understandably be outweighed by other considerations. The Finer Committee concluded that this SBC policy 'is a form of intervention in the matrimonial situation which does much more harm than good' (Cmnd 5629, para 4. 202).

The fairly extensive unofficial practice of DHSS officers of forcing women to go to court is wrong, both in law and SBC policy. This is usually effected by threatening to reduce or even withdraw benefit unless a woman takes legal action. Where this is done because the SBC cannot trace a liable relative and suspects the claimant knows but is concealing his whereabouts, one can perhaps sympathize; but in practice there is often no such justification and the practice is moreover unlawful. Such threats could only be implemented by invoking the discretion to reduce or withdraw a supplementary allowance (SBA 1966, Sch 2, para 4(1)(b)), but a broken marriage cannot constitute the 'exceptional circumstances' necessary to justify such action, nor would it be in keeping with the SBC's welfare duty (SBA 1966, s3(1)). If the SBC wishes to plead non-disclosure by a woman of her husband's whereabouts as an exceptional circumstance, it must also shoulder the burden of proving this before a SBAT, which may explain why such threats are rarely implemented—unless they succeed in their aim. When a claimant is threatened in this way, the local office should be referred to its copy of the Liable Relative Code which prohibits officers from making such threats and instructs them, where a wife is reluctant, to invoke the SBC's own powers to proceed. If this does not put an end to the threats, the office should be asked to put its decision in writing so the claimant can appeal.

There are three situations in which, despite the general policy of encouraging women to seek their own orders, the Code instructs DHSS officers not to do so:

(a) the wife is in desertion or has committed adultery (since these are bars to a wife's complaint: Naylor v Naylor [1961] 2 All ER 129; MP(MC)A 1960, s2(3)(b));

(b) divorce proceedings have begun or a High Court order already exists (since the magistrates can refuse maintenance if the High Court could more conveniently deal with the matter: MP(MC)A 1960, s5);

(c) if a wife's complaint to the magistrates' court would be time-barred.

In four other situations DHSS officers may only encourage women to obtain orders after authorization from SBC headquarters:

(a) the separation is by agreement;

(b) the services of a solicitor will be needed;

(c) the husband is not in a position to make any payment;

(d) the husband and wife are living in the same house but not cohabiting.

The SBC is presumably reluctant because, in (a), it is unwilling to worsen cordial relations between spouses; in (b) because it would be unfair to make a claimant incur legal costs (though 'Legal Aid is usually available for this purpose': Handbook, para 117; see ch 13(A)(2)); in (c) because nothing will be gained; and in (d) because reconciliation may still be possible or because children may not be aware of their parents' differences and legal proceedings would adversely affect them.

If a woman will not proceed herself then the SBC has to consider use of its own powers (see (2) above) to ensure the husband's compliance with his duty to maintain. In eight situations the Liable Relative Code specifically directs SBC staff to use these powers:

(a) the wife is unwilling to apply for her own order;

(b) the wife has agreed not to sue for maintenance (such agreements are void in law (Matrimonial Causes Act 1973, s34(1)(a)) and not binding on a wife, far less the SBC: NAB v Parkes [1955] 1 All ER 700);

(c) the SBC is taking criminal proceedings against the husband (see (4) below);

(d) a divorce petition has been filed but there is no application for maintenance pending suit;

(e) maintenance for children only is sought because the wife is in desertion or has committed adultery;

(f) SB is no longer in payment to the wife, but the SBC wishes to recover benefit paid prior to the proceedings;

(g) the SBC wishes to recover SB paid to a wife before she obtained an order in her favour;

(h) the SBC holds information crucial to the success of the wife's proceedings (such as evidence of a husband's cohabitation if a wife chose to make a complaint of adultery).

Several of these situations naturally relate to those described above in which the SBC does not encourage or is reluctant to encourage women to proceed themselves. Others are clearly designed to allow enforcement of the husband's duty to maintain where his wife has no further interest in the matter (situations (f) and (g) above). Situation (h) is presumably designed to avoid SBC officers 'taking sides' by having to give evidence for one spouse against the other; though a woman could choose to proceed herself and, if she could identify the SBC evidence sufficiently, compel its production by witness summons (Magistrates' Courts Act 1952, s77).

This procedure for separated wives applies equally to unmarried mothers. The same process of SBC inquiries, voluntary payment or legal action is undertaken. Alleged putative fathers should be wary of SBC interviews, since any acknowledgment of fatherhood, particularly through payments, might be cogent evidence of paternity in subsequent affiliation proceedings. For obvious reasons, the unmarried mother may be unwilling to give the SBC information about the father of her child, and the improper pressure to go to court will be the more distressing.

In three situations, the Liable Relative Code sanctions use by the SBC of its powers to seek an affiliation order:

(a) the mother's application is time-barred (Affiliation Proceedings Act 1957, s2; Affiliation Proceedings (Amendment) Act 1972, s2; for the SBC, time runs for three years from any payment of SB: SBA 1966, s24(2));

(b) the mother is living with her husband who is receiving SB which includes the requirements of the illegitimate child;

(c) the mother is unwilling to proceed herself.

In the second of these situations, it would clearly endanger a satisfactory family situation to pressure the mother to seek an order, though for the SBC to pursue the putative father could conceivably have the same effect.

Apart from drawing the SBC's attention to its own instructions there is no way of preventing it from taking its own legal action to seek either maintenance or affiliation orders if it so decides. While it can choose not to proceed, the SBC clearly feels under an obligation to recoup benefit from a liable relative if possible, though it is not under a statutory duty to do so. If a woman does not want past history raked up or personal matters aired in court in an SBC-instigated case, she may have a negotiating lever if her evidence is crucial to the SBC's case; though the SBC can seek to compel her evidence by witness summons. A further problem is that any reluctance by a woman either to go to court herself or to testify against her husband may suggest to the SBC that a separation has been 'rigged' in order to obtain SB: the practice known as 'fictitious desertion' and much frowned on by the Fisher Committee (Cmnd 5228, paras 346-7). If the SBC incorrectly suspects fictitious desertion and SB is withdrawn, reluctance to go to court should never be allowed to sway a SBAT against restoring benefit.

A woman with a maintenance order against her husband can avoid the problems resulting from sporadic compliance or from non-compliance by her husband, by diverting payment to the SBC. This procedure requires both the consent of the woman and that of the clerk to the justices (who usually complies, although it seems that some clerks only divert payments when in arrears, a practice now discouraged: Home Office Circular 8/1974). A woman claimant should never be pressured into such an arrangement under threat of reduced or withdrawn benefit. The advantages of the diversion procedure are the convenience of income provided by a book of orders encashable at a post-office, thus avoiding journeys to the court office; and no worries about non-payment, the SBC being responsible for enforcement of the order against the husband. A woman can withdraw her consent to diversion at any time.

A divorced woman can similarly 'sign over' an order for financial provision, but will first need to register her order in the magistrates' court.

Whether maintenance or affiliation orders are made in favour of women or the SBC itself, the SBC seeks to ensure compliance by liable relatives through 'inquiries into (their) circumstances from time to time' (Handbook, para 188). It may, as a result of its inquiries or on receiving information from claimants, consider seeking enforcement or variation of an order or may advise a claimant to do so.

(4)   Prosecution
Prosecution of those who persistently refuse or neglect to maintain themselves has been discussed earlier (see (F)(7) above). Prosecutions under the same provision (SBA 1966, s30(1)) are also considered 'in cases where all other efforts to obtain maintenance from a liable relative have failed'. Usually the SBC only prosecutes 'where the wife's claim is the direct consequence of her husband's failure to maintain and he cannot be traced' and civil proceedings will thus be ineffective and prosecution will enable his arrest by warrant (Handbook, paras 178, 189). In most cases, it seems unlikely that prosecution will have more effect than civil action, though a probation order might in the long term encourage a recalcitrant husband to maintain his dependants.

(5)   Social Work Agencies
The SBC recognizes that its actions in cases of separated families may jeopardize possible reconciliation, but feels 'bound to avoid a situation in which financial pressure on the wife forces her to agree to a reconciliation on almost any terms the husband cares to make' (Handbook, para 194). In this connection, the Handbook refers to liaison with the Probation Service and Marriage Guidance Counsellors. Since the SBC makes this marginal recognition of the possible dangers inherent in its intervention and the need for co-operation with social work agencies, it may be that a social worker dealing with the matrimonial problems of a client who is a claimant or liable relative will be best able to impress the SBC in negotiation over decisions which endanger his client's interests. The duty of the SBC to promote the welfare of those affected by its work (SBA 1966, s3(1)) should never be subordinated to its zeal in tracing or calling to account liable relatives.

(6)   General Provisions
If a lone parent is in full-time employment there can of course be no entitlement to SB (except to s13 payments: see (E) above), but there may be entitlement to FIS (see ch 5(B)(1)). Family problems, and the absence of the breadwinner in particular, should put advisers on inquiry as to the need to claim ECAs or ENPs (see (B)(5), (D) above).

(I) Procedure, Payment and Appeals

Supplementary allowances for claimants also in receipt of NI unemployment benefit is claimed (on Form B1) at employment exchanges and paid there. Other claimants for allowances must claim (on Form SB1) at the local office of the DHSS, as must pensioners. Payment is usually made either by weekly giro order (always used in respect of claimants required to register for work: see (F)(1) above) or by a book of orders, covering thirteen or twenty-six weeks, encashable weekly at a post office. Such orders represent the sum of SB and any weekly NI benefits. Occasionally, payments over the counter at local offices may be made in the form of a giro order or even cash (e.g. s13 payments: see (E) above) if, in an urgent case, there would not be time for the claimant to cash a giro order the same day. Weekly SB calculated at less than £0.10 is not payable (SBA 1966, Sch 2, para 2(1)).

In 'exceptional circumstances' the SBC is empowered to meet all or part of a claimant's SB by the provision of goods or services (SBA 1966, s14). This power is used, for example, to give vouchers for hostels or meals to claimants with no fixed abode or in emergency situations (Handbook, paras 221, 236). Payment can also be made, in whole or in part, to a person other than the claimant if the claimant so requests or if the SBC considers this necessary to protect the claimant's interests or those of his dependants (SBA 1966, s17(3)). This power may be exercised, for example, if a claimant has a history of rent arrears, by payment of rent direct to a landlord; or by payment of all SB to a relative or social worker entrusted with assisting a claimant to budget. Following the Finer Committee recommendation (Cmnd 5629, para 6.106), direct rent payments to landlords of lone parents, if requested by a landlord, tenant or social worker, are only refused on the authority of a senior DHSS officer.

A postal claim is dealt with by a home visit, at which the claimant will be expected to produce evidence of his resources (e.g. pay-slips, bank books) and requirements (e.g. his rent book). If a claim is made in person at a local office, it is advisable to take all relevant evidence, since it may make an immediate decision possible. Benefit is usually only payable from the date of claim but any payment can in 'exceptional circumstances' be backdated to any earlier date determined by the SBC (SI 1966/1067, reg 6(3)). Refusal to backdate a claim to the date requested by the claimant can ground an appeal, since it affects 'the amount of any benefit' (SBA 1966, s18(1)(a)).

If any or all of a claim is not met, a claimant has the right to appeal to a SBAT (SBA 1966, s18(1)). These tribunals are composed of a chairman and two members, one drawn from a panel of persons nominated by Trades Councils. All are appointed by the Secretary of State and none have legal qualifications.

An appeal must be brought within twenty-one days by written notice to a DHSS local office, though a chairman may allow a late appeal 'for good cause' (SI 1971/680, reg 5). More than a week's notice of a hearing is rarely given. With the notice an appellant receives copies of his appeal, a written submission by the SBC and the assessment of his SB (details of an assessment can be obtained in any case by requesting Form A 124 from the local office). The procedure is determined by the chairman and although usually very informal, skilled representation is advisable since the tribunals often experience difficulty in distinguishing SBC policy from law and since the SBC's presenting officers often put their cases forcefully. Purely legal argument is often hard to explain. The parties retire after the hearing and decisions are normally sent by post. The decisions must give reasons (SI 1971/680, reg 12) but these are sometimes unilluminating and minority decisions are not recorded or indicated. Travelling expenses and compensation for loss of working time are paid to appellants, witnesses and representatives (SI 1971/680, reg 13).

There is no further appeal, but a tribunal decision can be questioned by way of the prerogative orders (see ch (1)(C)), though the Court of Appeal has stated that the courts should only entertain applications for certiorari in cases where a court decision will 'lay down the broad guidelines for tribunals' or where SBATs have exceeded their jurisdiction or acted contrary to natural justice (R v Preston SBAT, ex p Moore, 'The Times', 5 March 1975, CA). An appeal, however, is not always the last resort. The SBC has the power to review a decision of itself or a SBAT in any of the following circumstances: if the decision was made in ignorance of, or based on a mistake as to, a material fact; if there has been a relevant change of circumstances since the initial decision was made (only possible either if the change occurs in the year preceding the request for review and the review will result in an increase of benefit or if a decrease of more than £0.20 in benefit would result); or if the initial decision was based on a mistake of law (SI 1966/1065, reg 5). If a review results in a different but still unsatisfactory decision, an appeal against the new decision may be made; equally, if the SBC refuses to review its prior decision, an appeal against the refusal can be made (SBA 1966, s18(1)).

In practice, the SBC reviews all decisions in respect of which an appeal is lodged, and if a new decision is made the appeal lapses. So a claimant who is still dissatisfied must appeal against the new decision (Coleman, 1972). In some cases, the SBC informally offers to increase the benefit decided initially in return for the claimant dropping his appeal; but a proper decision should always be insisted on so that further appeals can be considered.

References

'Social Insurance and Allied Services', Report by Sir W. Beveridge, Cmd 6404 (1942).

Atkinson, A. B. (1969), 'Poverty in Britain and the Reform of Social Security', Cambridge University Press.

'Supplementary Benefits Handbook', 4th ed., HMSO (1974).

Lister, R. (1973), 'As Man and Wife? A Study of the Cohabitation Rule', CPAG, London.

'Cohabitation', Report by the SBC to the Secretary of State for Social Services, HMSO (1971).

'Report of the Committee on Abuse of Social Security Benefits', Chairman: the Hon. Sir Henry Fisher, Cmnd 5228 (1973).

'Report of the Committee on One-parent Families', Chairman: the Hon. Sir Morris Finer, Cmnd 5629 (1974).

Lynes, T. (1974), 'Penguin Guide to Supplementary Benefits', 2nd ed., Penguin, Harmondsworth.

'Exceptional Needs Payments', Report by the SBC, HMSO (1973).

'Administration of the Wage-Stop', Report by the SBC to the Minister of Social Security, HMSO (1967).

de Smith, S. A. (1973), 'Judicial Review of Administrative Action', 3rd ed., Stevens, London.

Coleman, R. J. (1972), 'Supplementary Benefits and Administrative Review of Administrative Action', CPAG, London.

Chapter 5

**Family Allowances and
Family Income Supplements**

Poverty studies have invariably demonstrated a connection between size of family and the existence and degree of poverty. This chapter is concerned with Family Allowances, the principal legislative attack on family poverty (apart from additions to other benefits in respect of dependants), and Family Income Supplements, a far more recent assault on the same problem. However, their avowed aim is almost their only common factor. The means by which they seek to achieve this aim represent starkly conflicting philosophies of poor relief—those of universal benefits and the means-test (see ch 1(A)).

(A) Family Allowances

A universal scheme of child allowances was viewed by Beveridge as a necessary pre-condition of the system of social security proposed in his report (Cmd 6404, paras 410-25). In fact, pressures for such a scheme date from the 1920s, and the earliest effort to enact such a measure is credited to William Pitt, whose bill to introduce allowances for children in 1796 failed when Parliament preferred to debate grouse shooting (George, 1968, p. 187). Between the wars demographic and even eugenic arguments were forwarded in favour of allowances, but these receded with the decline in fears that the population was dwindling and are now obsolete in an age when over-population is the greater anxiety.

FA is a weekly payment, avowedly 'for the benefit of the family as a whole' (FAA 1965, s1), made to families with two or more children. It is not related to contributions and there is no means-test for qualification. The cost falls entirely on the Exchequer (FAA 1965, s16). The allowance is £1.50 for each of the second and subsequent children. In 1942, Beveridge recommended 8s.(£0.40), but the FAA 1945 provided only 5s.(£0.25) on the ground that other benefits (in kind, such as welfare milk and free school meals) covered the difference. Such other benefits are now defunct as universal benefits and only available to the poorest on a means-test basis (see ch 7). As late as April 1975, when the present rate was introduced, the allowance was only £0.90 for the second child and £1.00 for each subsequent child. Moreover, FA is clawed back from many recipients through income tax, though taxpayers also have the benefit of income tax child allowances (Income and Corporation Taxes Act 1970, ss24, 219(1)(b)). FA is also treated as a resource for SB purposes and as part of 'gross income' in calculating FIS (see ch 4(C)(1) and (B)(2) below).

(1) Entitlement
The principal ground of entitlement is the existence of a family 'which includes two or more children' (FAA 1965, s1). The first child of a family has never qualified parents for FA, it being somewhat curiously assumed from Beveridge onwards that most couples can better afford the expense of their first child than their subsequent children. FA paid in respect of a child ceases on the child reaching school leaving age (sixteen years) or, in the case of those continuing education or apprenticeship beyond that age, reaching the age of nineteen (FAA 1965, s2). An 'apprentice' must be in 'full-time training' and not earning more than £2 a week (FAA 1965, s19(1)). The burden of proving that a child is an apprentice (or presumably, by analogy, that a child over sixteen is still in education) lies on the claimant (R (F) 12/61).

For FA purposes, the term 'family' covers three situations:

(a) a man and wife living together, any child(ren) of both or either of them, and any child(ren) maintained by them;

(b) a single man with any such child(ren);

(c) a single woman with any such child(ren) (FAA 1965, s3(1)).

Thus no difference in entitlement exists between a married couple, unmarried couple, or single parent. In situation (a), FA belongs to the wife, although either husband or wife may receive the allowance (FAA 1965, s4(1)(a) and (2)). On the complaint of either spouse or the Secretary of State for Social Services or a local authority that one spouse is not 'a proper recipient of allowances for their family', a magistrates' court can order that the other spouse be the sole recipient (FAA 1965, s4(3)). In situations (b) and (c), FA belongs to the man or woman respectively (FAA 1965, s4(1)(b) and (c)).

For a child to be included in the family of a claimant, it must be established that the child is living with the claimant, or alternatively that the claimant contributes at least £1.50 per week to the cost of providing for the child (FAA 1965, s3(2) and Sch, para 1). An adopted or legitimated child is treated no differently from others (FAA 1965, s17(3) and (4)), nor is a step-child if his parents' marriage ended by death (FAA 1965, s17(2)). An illegitimate child is not treated as the issue of his father (FAA 1965, s17(5)).

Temporary absence of a child from the family, or temporary

interruption of or reduction in providing for a child, does not result in disentitlement (FAA 1965, s17(7)). 'Temporary absence, interruption or reduction' includes, in the case of a parent claimant, hospitalization of a child for any length of time, absence at school for up to twelve weeks, or any other absence of up to four weeks. In the case of a non-parent claimant any absence except at school is only 'temporary' for up to four weeks. 'Absence' does not include any absence not intended to be temporary (SI 1969/212, regs 11–14; Hill v MPNI [1955] 2 All ER 890, 896).

Several other categories of children are also excluded from a claimant's family for FA purposes: those who are subject to a care order under the Children and Young Persons Act 1969; those in respect of whom local authorities have passed resolutions assuming parental rights (Children Act 1948, s2(1)—cancellation of a resolution only restores FA entitlement from the date of cancellation (R(F) 3/62)); those in the care and possession of prospective adoptive parents (this exclusion only lasts for twelve weeks from giving notice of intention to apply for an adoption order); and those children in respect of whom a NI guardians allowance (see ch 2(B)(9)) is in payment (FAA 1965, s11).

The question whether a child is 'living with' a claimant is not settled conclusively by residence under the same roof, but in such cases it requires 'very clear and cogent evidence of the absence of the normal (parent-child) relationship' to defeat the 'very strong presumption' which this situation creates (R (G) 4/62, in which an invalid mother who had not relinquished parental control of her illegitimate child to her own mother could still count the child as living with her; the same applies where a lone mother goes out to work full-time–R(F) 3/63, R(F) 1/71).

'Providing for a child' (the alternative requirement to 'living with') means 'making available for the child food, clothing, lodging, education and all other things reasonably required for the child's benefit having regard to all the circumstances' (FAA 1965, s18(1)). Provision must be at the claimant's own expense (so a payment by a third party direct to the person having care of a child is not a contribution by a claimant–R(F) 2/62); and provision in kind is treated as equal to its money value (FAA 1965, s18(2)). Since a contribution to provision must only equal £1.50 per week, few claimants with serious claims to maintaining a child can be faulted on this ground. The Commissioners have held that sporadic contributions are to be treated as contributions to provision in the weeks when they are actually paid (R(F) 8/61, R(F) 10/61, R(F) 11/61, R(F) 1/73), and that contributions must reach the person who is maintaining the child (R(F) 9/61).

Complications and disputes can arise in the case of separated or divorced couples, or in the situation where a child does not live with his parents, since in either case there may be two 'competing' families which satisfy either or both of the 'living with' or 'contribution' conditions. Where a father and mother have 'competing claims', the child in question is treated as being exclusively in the family of one only either by agreement between the parents or, in default of agreement, by the discretionary decision of the Secretary of State (in practice a DHSS official of the FA branch in Newcastle) (FAA 1965, s3(3) and Sch, para 2). As with 'Minister's questions' under the NI legislation (see ch 2(C)(1)), these decisions may be reconsidered and varied. Since none are published no general principles are discernible, though it appears from the authors' experience in dealing with such cases that residence with a parent or custody granted by a court points the way in the exercise of this discretion.

Where either or both parents have a 'competing claim' with a non-parental family, the Act decrees that the blood (or adoptive) tie takes precedence (FAA 1965, s3(3) and Sch, para 2).

FA can only be paid in Great Britain (FAA 1965, s20(5)). Further, either the mother or father, in the case of spouses living together, must be a British subject born in the United Kingdom or resident in Great Britain for a total of one year in the two years preceding a claim. Subjects of other countries only qualify for FA by residence for a total of two years in the preceding four years. In the case of a single parent he or she must satisfy one of these nationality or residence requirements (FAA 1965, s20(1) and SI 1969/212, regs 2-6). A man or his wife, if living together, or a single claimant must be in Great Britain in order to qualify for FA, as must a child in order to be treated as a member of the family for FA purposes (FAA 1965, s20(2)(3)). Temporary absence from Great Britain by parents or children results in cessation of FA only in certain prescribed circumstances (FAA 1965, s20(4) and SI 1969/212, regs 7-10A).

(2)   Claims, Payments and Appeals

FA is claimed by completing form FAM 2 which must be sent or taken to the local office of the DHSS together with a birth certificate for each child mentioned on the claim form. Decisions on entitlement are not made by local offices but by the FA branch of the DHSS in Newcastle. As a result of this centralized decision-making perhaps, there is a greater uniformity in FA decisions than in any other area of social security practice. Visits or postal inquiries to claimants are rare, except in the case of 'competing claims' discussed above. When a claim succeeds, the claimant is notified direct from Newcastle and instructed to collect at a post office (selected by the claimant when completing the claim form) a book of orders encashable at that post office. The orders are dated at weekly intervals and each may be cashed on or up to twelve months after the date (a Tuesday) on its face. After twelve months the right to payment is extinguished (R(F) 5/63), even if a claimant has never received the notification that an order book is available for collection (R(F) 1/64).

A claim for FA may be backdated by up to six months, if the claimant was entitled to FA at an earlier date within that period (FAA 1965, s6(2)); but no claim can be met for a time falling more than six months before the date of claim, even if a claimant delays making a claim as a result of official misinformation (R(F) 3/61).

The payment of allowances continues uninterrupted and without further inquiries by the DHSS, though a claimant must on the expiry of an order book, complete a declaration specifying the children in his or her family. In the case of spouses living together, payment continues after the death of either of them (FAA 1965, s6(3)). FA is only terminated or reduced when a condition of entitlement lapses—usually when a qualifying child reaches the age of sixteen. If entitlement to FA ceases but subsequently re-arises, a fresh claim must be made (R(F) 8/61). (The detailed regulations governing claims and payments are contained in SI 1970/1524.)

Apart from the centralized decision-making, the procedure for determining FA claims and for appeals follows that for NI benefits (FAA 1965, s5). Appeal thus lies from an insurance officer's decision to a NI Local Appeal Tribunal, with a further appeal to a NI Commissioner (see ch 2(C)(3)). The power of the Secretary of State to decide 'competing claims' between parents has been discussed (see (1) above). No appeal lies from these decisions, but an insurance officer, tribunal or Commissioner can refer such decisions to the Secretary of State for review.

As in NI cases an insurance officer may review a previous decision (see ch 2(C)(4)), subject to the usual appeal rights of the claimant. (The detailed regulations governing procedure as it applies to FA are contained in SI 1967/1572.)

(B)   Family Income Supplements

The Conservative government of 1970-4 promised on election an increase in the rates of FA. This pledge was translated, by the Family Income Supplements Act 1970, into a far different scheme of things. By contrast to FA, FIS is a means-tested benefit, more akin to SB than FA both in principle and in operation. It is restricted to a relatively small group of potential claimants—extremely low-paid workers and their families.

The principles of the FIS scheme are simple. The 1970 Act, as amended, prescribes certain amounts and provides for a family to receive FIS if its gross income falls below the appropriate prescribed amount. Within the small group it assists, FIS has the merit of taking account, unlike FA, of the first child of a family. Like FA the cost of FIS is met entirely by the Exchequer (FISA 1970, s15). The scheme is operated by the SBC (FISA 1970, s6(1)); appeals are heard by SBATs (FISA 1970, s7(3); see ch 4(I)). Unlike SB little is left to the SBC's discretion, and the SB Handbook gives no guidance as to the way the SBC makes such discretionary decisions as it is entrusted with.

The take-up rate for FIS is widely felt to be poor (Coates and Silburn, 1973, p.17). The present government has indicated that repeal of the 1970 Act is under consideration.

(1)   Entitlement

FIS is paid to a family if its gross income falls short of the prescribed amounts (FISA 1970, s1(2)). The first condition of entitlement is thus a family as defined by the 1970 Act. The low-paid worker without a family is outside the scheme.

A 'family' for FIS purposes consists of a man or a single woman in full-time work, a wife or a woman who 'lives with (a man) as his wife', and any child(ren) whose requirements are provided for, in whole or in part, by any of these persons (FISA 1970, s1(1)). A 'child' means a person under sixteen (FISA 1970, s17(1)) or child over sixteen but still at school (SI 1971/226, reg 9). The only exclusion is of foster-children boarded out by a local authority or approved voluntary body (SI 1971/226, reg 6).

As with FA, there is the possibility of 'competing claims' in respect of some children. If these claims cannot be settled by agreement, the SBC has a blanket discretion to decide whose family such children are to be included in (SI 1971/226, reg 7). An appeal should always be considered if the blood or adoptive tie, a court order for custody, or (as between two non-parental families) residence is not accorded precedence. Analogies in FA law and practice could form a helpful submission to a tribunal (see (A)(1) above). Once included in a family, a person may not be included in another family for FIS purposes, regardless of any change in circumstances (FISA 1970, s8(1)), though changes can be reflected periodically since it is usually necessary to re-apply for FIS every year (see (3) below).

The second condition of entitlement is the need for the man or single woman in a family to be 'engaged, and normally engaged, in remunerative full-time work' (FISA 1970, s1(1)(a)). To qualify on this ground, a man or woman must normally work not less than thirty hours a week (SI 1971/226, reg 5). It is not clear whether this means at least thirty hours every week or an average of thirty hours a week, though the latter seems the more sensible interpretation and the former, if applied by the SBC, should be appealed against if it leads to disqualification.

What constitutes 'remunerative full-time work' is not clear. The regulations governing calculation of resources indicate that it may extend beyond employment or self-employment (see (2) below).

The third condition of entitlement is residence in Great Britain (FISA

1970, s1(2)). There are two limbs to this qualification. First a family must be 'ordinarily resident in the United Kingdom'; and second, at least one adult member of the family must be resident in Great Britain (SI 1971/226, reg 8). Thus a man with a family in Northern Ireland working in Great Britain may qualify for FIS.

The fourth and final condition of entitlement is a gross income sufficiently below the appropriate prescribed amount (see (2) below).

A family unable to satisfy any of these four conditions is disqualified for FIS. In addition, there is one disqualification: FIS is not payable for any period during which a person otherwise entitled to receive FIS refuses or neglects to maintain any other member of his family with the result that SB is paid in respect of that other person (FISA 1970, s8(2) and SI 1971/226, reg 4(1)). The effect of this provision is, however, mitigated in the case of a man and woman both of whom are entitled to receive FIS. If either of them refuses or neglects to maintain a member of their family, only the 'guilty' party is disqualified and the 'innocent' party can continue to receive FIS (SI 1971/226, reg 4(2)). These provisions are of course of little significance in the most common situation to which they apply—desertion by a man of his wife and children. Unless the wife can go out to work, she will have to claim SB, and her FIS will be included in her resources in calculating SB (see ch 4(C)(1)).

Unlike FA, maintaining children is not a condition of entitlement. Thus if children are taken into care or leave the family home, their parents are still eligible for FIS.

(2)   Calculation

The FIS paid to a successful claimant is half the difference between gross income and the 'prescribed amount' appropriate to his family (FISA 1970, s1(2)). The detailed calculation resembles a simplified version of that governing the award of SB (see ch 4(B)(C)). The 'prescribed amounts' take the place of the scale rate requirements, and gross income that of resources.

The prescribed amounts are varied (upwards) periodically: the current rates are £31.50 for a family with one child, which is increased by £3.50 for each subsequent child. Number of children is the only factor governing the prescribed amount for a particular family (FISA 1970, s2(1)). Unlike SB, rent and exceptional circumstances are of no account.

The gross income of a family is the aggregate of the 'normal gross income' (i.e. income before any deductions, and not take-home pay) of its adult members (FISA 1970, s4(1)).

'Normal gross income' is calculated, in the case of the weekly-paid, by reference to the average pay for the five weeks preceding a claim for FIS, or, in the case of those paid monthly, the average pay for the preceding two months (SI 1971/336, reg 2(2)). However the SBC is given a very wide discretion to take the average pay 'over such other period or periods as may appear appropriate' and the regulations indicate that this should be done in any of the following cases:

(a) where a person has been working abnormally long or short hours, or

(b) has only recently begun work, or

(c) a person's earnings fluctuate seasonally, or

(d) a person works otherwise than under a contract of service (e.g. the self-employed) (SI 1971/226, reg 2(2)).

Clearly the exercise of this discretion could cause hardship, for example, if a person has recently lost the opportunity of regular overtime but this is not apparent to or is discounted by the SBC. It is therefore important to bring such matters to the SBC's attention (by sending a covering letter with the claim form), and to appeal if they are ignored.

In the case of a person remunerated by salary, wages or fees the gross income is the gross amount paid; in the case of the self-employed person, the gross income is the net profit derived from his occupation (SI 1971/226, reg 2(3)).

If any or all gross income does not consist of 'earnings from a gainful occupation', the SBC has once more complete discretion to select the basis of calculation. This provision would appear to allow certain categories of claimants to receive FIS, such as students with families or persons taking Department of Employment training courses. The question of whether such categories of claimants are 'engaged in remunerative full-time work', however, must also be decided in such cases. (An appeal tribunal has ruled that an applicant on a Department of Employment course is eligible, apparently accepting the submission that 'full-time work' need not be full-time employment: (1974) LAG BUL 16.)

This discretion also allows the SBC to deal with such income as payments by boarders, rent from sub-tenants, affiliation and maintenance payments, and FA. According to Lynes, income from boarders is usually treated by the SBC as one-fifth net profit and this fifth is taken into account. Rent from sub-tenants is taken into account in full, subject to a deduction of £0.50 in the case of an unfurnished and £1.00 in the case of a furnished tenancy. Maintenance and affiliation payments received are averaged over 'whatever period seems reasonable . . . generally not less than six months' (Lynes, 1974, p.194). FA is always taken into account in full. It must be stressed that these are mere rules of policy and any claimant who finds their effect results in hardship should appeal, preferably producing evidence of the actual income from e.g. sub-letting.

The following forms of income are not included in the calculation of 'normal gross income':

(a) the whole of any NI attendance allowance (see ch 2(B)(6)), II

constant attendance allowance (see ch 3(A)(3)), or war disablement
pension constant attendance allowance;

    (b) the whole of any boarding-out payments in respect of a foster-child;

    (c) the whole of any FIS in payment;

    (d) the whole of any SB (see ch 4);

    (e) up to £2.00 per week of any war disablement pension (apart from a
constant attendance allowance—see (a) above);

    (f) the whole of any rent allowance under the Housing Finance Act
1972 (see ch 11(A)) (SI 1971/226, reg 2(5)).

When the 'normal gross income' has been computed thus, FIS is
calculated by halving the difference between the 'normal gross income'
and the appropriate 'prescribed amount' (FISA 1970, s3(1)). The sum
arrived at by this final calculation is the FIS payable, subject to a
maximum of £5.50 for one- or two-child families and £7.00 for larger
families (FISA 1970, s3(1)), and a minimum of £0.11 (FISA 1970, s3(2)).
If the sum arrived at is not a multiple of £0.10, it is rounded up to the
nearest multiple (FISA 1970, s3(3)).

(3) Procedure, Payment and Appeals

FIS is claimed by completing form FIS 1 which must be sent to the DHSS
FIS branch in Blackpool which processes all claims. If a family includes a
man and a woman both must sign the form unless it would be
unreasonable to require this (FISA 1970, s5(2) and SI 1971/227, reg
2(6)). FIS cannot be backdated more than three months and then only if
delay in claiming can be blamed on the post or if the claimant can prove
the delay was no fault of his (SI 1971/227, reg 2(1A)). Therefore it is wise
to claim as soon as possible entitlement arises even if supporting evidence
(such as recent pay slips) cannot be sent with the claim form. Though this
delays the calculation and payment of FIS, it ensures ultimate payment
from the earliest possible date. A defective claim, if re-submitted
correctly within a month, is treated as made on the date of original
submission (SI 1971/227, reg 2(3)).

Entitlement to FIS is decided centrally in Blackpool and queries are
usually dealt with by post. Payment is made by the issue of books
containing orders encashable weekly at a post office from the Tuesday
date on their face for the twelve months following that date (SI
1971/227, reg 4,5). The twelve month period may be extended by a
written request for payment if there was 'good cause' for not seeking
payment earlier (SI 1971/227, reg 5(2)). As with SB, a person can be
appointed to receive FIS on behalf of a person 'unable to act' (SI
1971/227, reg 6(1)).

FIS is usually awarded for a period of a year (FISA 1970, s6(3)).
Thereafter a new claim is required and this can be made during the period
from four weeks before to four weeks after the end of the year without

any pause in entitlement (SI 1971/227, reg 2(7) and SI 1971/226, reg 3(2)). If the SBC is satisfied that FIS is payable but uncertain of the exact rate, it may for a minimum of four weeks pay FIS at a rate lower than that ultimately arrived at (SI 1971/226, reg 3(1)). Curiously there is no provision allowing for the difference, if any, to be backdated; but the SBC's review powers could be invoked to secure this (see below).

It is also curious that although a claim, made after a revision in the prescribed amounts has been made but not come into force, can be met as of the date the new amounts come into force, the one year period still runs from the date of claim (SI 1971/226, reg 3(3)).

Once awarded, payment of FIS is not affected by any change of circumstances during the one year period (FISA 1970, s6(3)), though it may in one situation only be limited to a man or a woman when originally made payable to either (see (1) above). Entitlement does not cease on the death of the person or persons in receipt of FIS if a suitable adult requests to be appointed to exercise the rights of the deceased recipient(s) (SI 1971/227, reg 7(2)). An undecided claim, however, lapses with the death of the claimant(s) (SI 1971/226, reg 7(1)).

As with SB, the SBC has the power to review an award of FIS. This may be done if the SBC is satisfied that its original decision was based on a mistake of law; that it was made in ignorance of or based on a mistake of a material fact; or that FIS should not be paid on account of the 'SB disqualification' (see (1) above) (SI 1971/226, reg 11). Payment of FIS may be suspended pending the outcome of a review (SI 1971/227, reg 8).

Appeals against SBC decisions or reviewed decisions lie to the SBATs. Despite the existence of separate procedural rules for FIS appeals (SI 1971/662), the procedure (and indeed the rules themselves) are as for SB appeals (see ch 4(I)).

References

'Social Insurance and Allied Services', Report by Sir W. Beveridge, Cmd 6404 (1942).

George, V. (1968), 'Social Security: Beveridge and After', Routledge & Kegan Paul, London.

Coates, K. and Silburn, R. (1973), 'Poverty: The Forgotten Englishman', Penguin, Harmondsworth.

Lynes, T. (1974), 'Penguin Guide to Supplementary Benefits', 2nd ed., Penguin, Harmondsworth.

Chapter 6

Overpayment and Other Provisions

This chapter deals with provisions contained, with some variations, in all the principal social security legislation covered by chapters 2-5 and governing the inalienability of benefits, overlapping benefits, overpayment, offences and the recovery of overpaid benefit. These provisions attempt to ensure that benefits are only paid to those entitled and that the issue of public monies to those in need is not abused.

(A) Inalienability

The principal acts governing social security benefits contain near identical provisions making void any assignment of or charge on benefits including agreements to assign or charge (Social Security Act 1975, s87(1); Supplementary Benefit Act 1966, s20; Family Allowances Act 1965, s10(1); Family Income Supplements Act 1970, s9). The same provisions prevent benefits passing to the trustee of a bankrupt claimant or other person acting on behalf of creditors (though a similarly worded provision elsewhere has been held to permit an order in bankruptcy proceedings for the payment of a pension to a trustee for creditors' benefit—Re Garrett [1930] All ER 139).

(B) Overlapping Benefits

With slight variations the NI, II and SB statutes contain provisions designed to avoid duplication of benefit (SSA 1975, s85(1)(a),(2); SBA 1966, s16(1)). The detailed NI and II provisions are contained in regulations which provide for adjustment of benefits where a claimant qualifies for two or more NI or II benefits at once or for a NI or II benefit and another 'pension or allowance payable out of public funds' except FA (SI 1972/604; SI 1973/1478; SI 1964/504, Part VII).

The SB provision is somewhat different. If a claimant is paid SB for a period during which he is entitled to but not in receipt of a NI benefit (except death grant) or an II, FA or FIS benefit, these latter benefits may subsequently be reduced, at the discretion of the DHSS, by the amount by which the SB paid exceeds the SB which would have been paid had the other benefit been in payment.

Disputes concerning overlapping payments centre on questions either of entitlement (which have been discussed in relation to each benefit) or of arithmetic. A claimant dissatisfied with a decision should appeal to allow a tribunal to consider his entitlement or the calculation of benefits. The Commissioners' Decisions give several examples of the resolution of overlapping benefit questions under the NI and II schemes (e.g. CS 166/49, R(G) 7/54). It is important to note that the SB provision is discretionary, and this allows claimants' welfare to be taken into account.

(C) Overpayments

The term 'overpayment' embraces cases of official error, reversal on appeal of a decision favourable to a claimant, innocent mistakes by claimants and deliberate fraud. All the social security statutes create offences confined to the last category and provide for recovery of overpayments generally.

(1) Offences
Earlier chapters have discussed offences relating to specific aspects of a particular scheme of benefits, such as NI contributions (see ch 2(A)(2)) and failure to maintain under the SB scheme (see ch 4(F)(7),(H)(4)). We are concerned here with offences relating to obtaining and receiving benefits.

(a) General law offences   It is an offence to obtain by deception property belonging to another with the intention of permanently depriving the other of it, and an offence dishonestly to obtain a 'pecuniary advantage' by deception (Theft Act 1968, ss15(1), 16(1)). These offences, which carry maximum sentences of ten and five years' imprisonment respectively, appear to be rarely charged in social security cases, though the Fisher Report recommended consideration of a Theft Act charge in all cases of social security abuse (Cmnd 5228, para 432).

To forge an order for payment of a benefit or present a forged order for payment or obtain benefit by producing forged documents all constitute offences carrying a maximum of fourteen years' imprisonment (Forgery Act 1913, ss2(2)(a), 6,7(a)).

(b) Social security law offences   These offences fall into three categories: false information; improper receipt of benefit; and non-compliance with statutory requirements.

(i) False information   Provisions making an offence of supplying false information with a view to obtaining benefit are inserted in all the principal social security Acts, though the exact manner of falsehoods covered varies.

In relation to NI or II benefits a 'false statement or false misrepresentation' or the production of 'any document or information false in a material particular' are all itemized (SSA 1975, s146(3)(c)). Knowingly to use any of these to obtain benefit is punishable by a £400 fine, three months' imprisonment or both. The FISA 1970 creates an almost identical offence (FISA 1970, s11).

In relation to FA it is an offence to furnish information known to be false, to furnish false information 'recklessly' or to withhold 'material information' with intent to obtain FA for oneself or another (FAA 1965, s9(a)). It is unclear whether the 'withholding' limb of this offence requires knowledge (mens rea) on the claimant's part. The offence carries a £50 fine, three months' imprisonment or both.

It is an offence to make any statement or representation known to be false either to obtain SB or to avoid or reduce any liability under the SBA 1966 (SBA 1966, s29). The maximum sentences are a £100 fine and/or three months; mens rea is required (Moore v Branton, 'The Times', 8 May 1974). This offence as worded apparently covers false statements by SBC officers intended to reduce the SBC's liability to pay SB to claimants. Nothing was no doubt further from the draftsman's mind and it illustrates the unfortunate differences between the statutes. The Fisher Committee called for a common formula clearly requiring mens rea (Cmnd 5228, para 430). At present the situation is extremely unclear; for example is a false document permissible in a SB claim or caught by the phrase 'false representation'?

In relation to the appropriate benefits, non-disclosure of cohabitation, earnings or capital or working while claiming could all ground prosecutions under these provisions. There is a little evidence that magistrates are not concerned to discover whether the acts or omissions in question (such as cohabitation) are proved, but only whether false information was supplied, as if the former were unrelated to the latter (Lister, 1973, pp.32-6; H. Hodge (1973) LAG BUL. 97, 99).

(ii) Improper receipt of benefit   The FAA 1965 makes an offence of receiving FA for oneself or another knowing it to be 'not properly payable, or not properly receivable' by the recipient (FAA 1965, s9(b)). The maximum sentence is £50, three months' imprisonment or both. Mens rea is clearly required (R v Curr [1967] 1 All ER 478, CA). There are no comparable offences regarding other benefits.

(iii) Non-compliance with statutory requirements   The NI, II and FA Acts and regulations make offences of contravention of or failure to comply with the requirements of regulations to furnish such certificates, other documents or information as may be required by the Secretary of State (in practice a DHSS officer); and of failure to notify changes of circumstances 'affecting the right' to FA or which the claimant might 'reasonably expect to affect' his right to NI or II benefits (yet another unnecessary discrepancy in wording) (SSA 1975, s146(5) and SI 1971/707, regs 13, 16, SI 1964/73, regs 5, 26; FAA 1965, s13(3) and SI 1970/1524, reg 9). For the NI and II offences the maximum penalty is a £50 fine plus a further £10 for every day the offence continues after conviction. The FA offence carries a simple £10 maximum fine. There are no comparable offences regarding SB or FIS.

These offences complement those in the false information category (see (i) above). Thus a claimant who 'added' a non-existent child to a FA claim could be prosecuted for furnishing false information (FAA 1965, s9(a)), whereas the claimant who does not inform the DHSS that a child has left school and continues to draw FA in respect of the child has failed to notify a change 'affecting the right' to FA (FAA 1965, s13(3)).

(2)   Detection

Although the police and the post office (in relation to giro order offences) conduct some social security fraud prosecutions, most of the detective work as well as prosecuting is carried out by the DHSS (D of Em in relation to unemployment benefit). Overpayments may come to notice through official action, such as checking a claimant's information (e.g. that he is unemployed) or through information from other sources, including informers (often anonymous) and information supplied belatedly by claimants. Normally suspect cases are checked locally by a 'fraud officer' who tries to verify facts and if necessary interviews claimants.

In a NI, II or FA case the matter is also referred to an Insurance Officer to reconsider entitlement and consider whether the overpayment is recoverable (see (5)(a)(i) below). In cases requiring difficult or time-consuming detective work (such as observation of cohabitation suspects) NI Inspectors or (in SB cases) Special Investigators are employed. (NI Inspectors are principally concerned with policing the contribution side of the NI scheme; they have limited powers of entry (SSA 1975, s144(2)(3)); Stott v Hefferon [1974] 3 All ER 673) but not arrest; Special Investigators have no powers even of entry.) If and when an offence appears evident, an officer challenges the claimant with the facts and asks for a statement. (The 'AX' Code instructs Special Investigators to caution suspects; it seems they sometimes ignore this—Lister, 1973, p.18.) In SB cases Special Investigators are known to remove order books from suspects, although the Fisher Report disapproved of the practice (Cmnd 5228, para 340).

(3) Prosecution
The decision to prosecute is particularly difficult where the suspect is poor and possibly further disadvantaged in some respect. According to the Fisher Report, the criteria considered in deciding to prosecute or not are adequacy of evidence, the claimant's welfare, the sum involved, and any voluntary disclosure by the claimant or official mishandling of the case. The number of prosecutions is low compared with the figures of known or suspected fraud: in 1971, 11,320 cases were closed without consideration of prosecution and, of 15,819 considered for proceedings, 7,873 were prosecuted producing 7,130 convictions (Cmnd 5228, paras 433-41).

Unlike most summary offences, proceedings for social security offences may be started within three months from the date on which sufficient evidence to justify a prosecution comes to official notice, or within twelve months of the commission of the offence, whichever period finishes later (SSA 1975, s147(3); SBA 1966, s33(3)(b); FISA 1970, s12(2); FAA 1965, s14(4)). NI Inspectors and other authorized DHSS or D of Em officers usually conduct prosecutions.

In NI and II cases, prosecutions or actions for recovery of overpaid benefit (see (5)(b)(ii) below) must be adjourned if a Minister's question is reviewed or taken on appeal to the High Court (see ch 2(C)(1)) or until the time for such an appeal expires; otherwise decisions on Minister's questions are conclusive for the purpose of such prosecutions or actions (SSA 1975, s148(1)(3)).

(4) Sentence
The maximum sentences have been indicated, though these are rarely invoked; indeed, there is some feeling (not least among DHSS investigators) that sentences are remarkably low, but this must be viewed in the light of the ability of social security recipients to pay fines and the fact that prison sentences for social security offences may be suspended (Criminal Justice Act 1967, s39(3)).

(5) Recovery of Overpaid Benefit
(a) The requirement to repay   It is not every overpayment of benefit which leads to recovery of the overpaid sums. There are different procedures for determining whether repayment is due, and if so how much is involved, in relation to SB, FIS and other benefits.

(i) NI, II and FA   Whether any overpayment of benefit has been made is a question for an Insurance Officer. If he decides there has been an overpayment and consequently alters the rate of future benefit or stops benefit this constitutes a review of the initial award and may be appealed against. Additionally, the Insurance Officer has to decide whether the claimant or any person on his behalf has used 'due care and diligence' to avoid overpayment, since recovery is only permissible if this is not so; this also applies to benefits reduced or stopped as the result of an appellate decision (SSA 1975, s119(1)(2); FAA 1965, s8(1)). This decision can also be appealed against.

The test of 'due care and diligence' is objective; it is not a test of a claimant's honesty but of whether he has taken sufficient steps to avoid overpayment (R(U) 6/70). Ignorance of the law being no excuse, a claimant in doubt should make inquiries of the local office (R(U) 6/70; R(P) 1/70). Even if a claimant believes, for example, that she is not cohabiting when in law she is (see ch 2(B)(8)(d)), failure to report cohabitation shows a lack of due care and diligence (R(G) 2/72; but cf. Moore v Branton, 'The Times', 8 May 1974). Where someone acts on a claimant's behalf, the test applies equally to him (R(U) 7/64). But a claimant who can prove he was unaware that someone made a claim in his name is not required to repay (R(S) 2/70); and merely signing a form giving incorrect information is not conclusive evidence of lack of care (R(U) 6/70).

Where a prosecution has been initiated it may be advantageous to seek an adjournment pending an appeal to a tribunal or Commissioner. Adjournment of an appeal pending the outcome of a prosecution must be decided in the interests of fairness to the claimant (R(S) 2/70).

(ii) SB   Overpaid SB can be recovered if any person fraudulently or otherwise misrepresents or fails to disclose a material fact leading to overpayment (SBA 1966, s26(1)). The question whether any sum or what amount is recoverable must be referred by the Secretary of State to a SBAT (SBA 1966, s26(2)). In the authors' experience such a reference may only result if a claimant lodges an appeal against a decision to request repayment. If only the amount of the overpayment is in question, it is advisable to see whether the claimant received his full entitlement including all possible ECAs (see ch 4(B)(5)), since the tribunal can increase benefit retrospectively and set it off against the sum demanded. More generally, any delay or oppressive behaviour by the SBC should be mentioned before the SBAT and the SBC's welfare duty stressed (SBA 1966, s3(1)).

(iii) FIS   Overpayments are recoverable if it can be proved that the benefit in question was not due to the recipient and that he did not disclose 'all material facts' (FISA 1970, s8(3) and SI 1971/226, reg 10). Since FIS has been awarded, the burden of proving these allegations should rest with the SBC. There is no automatic reference to a SBAT but an appeal is clearly contemplated by the Act and regulations. Unlike SB overpayments, which are recoverable even if the claimant acted in all innocence, under the FIS provisions (like those for NI, II and FA) recovery of an overpayment hinges on proof of an act or omission by the claimant and, although the provisions are differently worded, the Commissioners' Decisions may offer some guidance in appealing (see (i) above).

(b) Methods of recovery

(i) From the claimant's pocket   The normal procedure for recovery of overpaid benefit is for the claimant to be sent a written document, stipulating the amount and requesting either a lump sum payment or payment by instalments, which the claimant is requested to sign. This should never be done if the matter is still pending consideration by a tribunal, nor should oral requests for repayment be entertained. In practice a lump sum payment is demanded where the claimant has the means to pay immediately; in the case of SB claimants, the relative value of slow depletion of capital by instalment repayments and the possibility of increased SB resulting from immediate depletion by a lump sum repayment must be balanced (see ch 4(C)(4)). There is no appeal against the manner of repayment chosen but a satisfactory method should be negotiated whenever possible; in SB and FIS cases the SBC's welfare duty can again be stressed to avoid oppressive demands (SBA 1966, s3(1)). A NI tribunal cannot order a particular method of repayment (R(G) 7/51).

The obligation to pay does not end with a claimant's death, and his estate remains liable for the repayment (Law Reform (Miscellaneous Provisions) Act 1934, s1; Secretary of State for Social Services v Solly, 'The Times', 29 June 1974, CA). A personal representative, however, has all the appeal rights of the deceased claimant (Law Reform etc. Act 1934, s1).

(ii) Civil Proceedings   While not denying the Secretary of State the right to use any other method of recovery, provision is made for recovery of overpaid SB and FIS summarily as civil debts within three years (for SB) or one year (for FA) of the matter arising (SBA 1966, s33(2)(3)(a); FAA 1965, s8(4)). In summary proceedings for recovery of overpaid SB a certificate signed by a SBAT clerk is conclusive evidence of a tribunal decision on an overpayment reference (see (a)(ii) above) and that decision in turn is 'conclusive for all purposes' (SBA 1966, s26(2)).

(iii) Set-off against other benefits   The recovery of overpaid benefit is also possible by way of set-off against other benefits which are correctly payable: a convenient form of debt-collection for the DHSS but a possible cause of hardship to claimants (SSA 1975, s86; SBA 1966, s26(4); FAA 1965, s8(3); FISA 1970, s8(4)). Where SB is reduced by the use of set-off, an appeal may be made since 'the amount of any benefit' is in question (SBA 1966, s18(1)(a)). While it may be fruitless to contest the amount overpaid at this appeal, it may produce an extension of the set-off period and consequently a smaller decrease in weekly SB in cases of hardship.

References

'Report of the Committee on Abuse of Social Security Benefits', Chairman: the Hon. Sir Henry Fisher, Cmnd 5228 (1973).

Lister, R. (1973), 'As Man and Wife?' A study of the Cohabitation Rule', CPAG, London.

Chapter 7 **Other Benefits**

Chapters 2-6 have dealt only with the national schemes of income maintenance. This chapter is concerned with a range of benefits, all means-tested or needs-tested, which are not part of the general schemes but none the less provide sources or savings of money for certain classes of claimants. Apart from some health services benefits, all are administered by local authorities and variations between areas exist which prevent consideration in as much detail as the national schemes. The existence of precise means-tests also avoids larger areas of administrative discretion in decision-making and, perhaps related to this, no provision is made for appeals: the only way of challenging decisions is the prerogative orders which are singularly ill-suited for the purpose (see ch 1(C)).

Three forms of means-tested benefits are described in detail elsewhere: rent rebates and allowances (see ch 11(A)), rate rebates (see ch 11(B)), and legal aid, advice and assistance (see ch 13(A)).

(A) Health Services and Welfare Benefits

The Beveridge Report emphasized the need for a comprehensive health service which was realized in 1946 and embodied the principle of services 'free of charge' (Cmd 6404, paras 426-39); National Health Service Act 1946, s1(2)). Even the 1946 Act, however, contained exceptions to this principle and subsequent legislation has increased the size and range of charges, affording exception only to certain categories; 'free of charge' has become 'free only to some'.

(1) Prescription Charges
The standard charge (currently £0.20) paid to a chemist or hospital pharmacy for provision of drugs or appliances prescribed by a doctor or dentist is waived in the case of:

(a) persons under sixteen, men aged sixty-five or over, women aged sixty or over;

(b) expectant mothers and mothers with children under one year;

(c) those suffering from certain conditions (specified in SI 1968/759, reg 7(1)(d));

(d) war or service disablement pensioners if the prescribed items relate to their pensionable disablements;

(e) SB and FIS recipients;

(f) persons exempted on grounds of low income;

(g) holders of pre-payment certificates (SI 1968/759, reg 7).

A person claiming exemption must sign the declaration on the back of each prescription form. Those in category (a) need do no more. Those in categories (b) and (c) must hold an exemption certificate provided by an Area Health Authority. Those in categories (e) and (f) must hold a similar certificate provided by the local DHSS office; exemption on income grounds is assessed by local DHSS offices using an amended form of the SB means-test (see ch 4(B)(C)) which allows mortgage capital repayments and hire-purchase commitments to be included as requirements (SI 1968/759, reg 7(1)(f)(ii)). If a claimant's income is £1.50 more than his resources by this amended formula, no payment is made unless the charges in question amount to more than £1.50. Those with higher incomes may receive exemption from part of a charge over £1.50.

Those in category (g) must have obtained a pre-payment certificate from an Area Health Authority. These are available to anyone for a charge of £2 for six months or £3.50 for a year and are only worth obtaining by those not exempted under (a)–(f) and likely to require more than ten drugs or appliances in a six month period.

Anyone in categories (a)–(f) (except service disablement pensioners) is also entitled to a refund of prescription charges paid on production of a receipt from the chemist at a local DHSS office (SI 1968/759, reg 8).

(2)   Dental and Optical Charges
As with prescription charges, several categories are exempt from charges for dental treatment, dentures or glasses provided under the NHS. No charge may be made for any of these supplied to children under sixteen or over sixteen but still at school; nor for dental treatment or dentures supplied to expectant mothers or mothers with children under one year; nor for dental treatment supplied to anyone under twenty-one (NHSA 1952, s2(4); NHSA 1961, s1(3)(4)). The following categories are also exempt from charges and entitled to a refund of charges paid for the replacement or repair of appliances and drugs and medicines supplied by a hospital, dentist or optician:

(a) recipients of FIS or welfare foods (see below);

(b) persons holding exemption certificates;

(c) persons with low incomes qualifying under the amended SB means-test for medical charges (see (1) above) (SI 1974/1377).

(3)   Welfare Milk and Foods

A statutory scheme provides for the supply of free welfare milk and food to those designated as 'beneficiaries' (Emergency Laws (Re-enactments and Repeals) Act 1964, s4; SI 1971/457). Beneficiaries comprise:

(a) an expectant or nursing mother who either already has two children under five years and one month or is in a 'family in special circumstances' (a family receiving SB or FIS or whose requirements exceed its resources when calculated by the amended SB means-test for medical expenses (see (1) above), with the addition to requirements of the standard price of one pint of milk per day and the cost of welfare foods);

(b) the third and subsequent children under five years and one month in any family regardless of income;

(c) all children under five years and one month in a 'family in special circumstances';

(d) a handicapped child (not in (b) or (c)), under sixteen and unable to attend school (SI 1971/457, regs 2,3).

All beneficiaries are entitled to seven pints of milk or a packet of dried milk per week free of charge, except a mother nursing her baby (although the mother may consume the milk to which the baby is entitled). A child beneficiary under one year fed mainly on dried milk is entitled to an additional quantity of dried milk, the amount depending on his age at the time of application. A child over five years and one month who has not started school continues to receive free milk until he does (SI 1971/457, reg 4 and Sch 1).

'Welfare foods' is the statutory term for vitamin drops and tablets available free of charge to beneficiaries in categories (a), (b) and (c) (SI 1971/457, reg 5 and Sch 2).

Welfare milk and vitamins are obtained in exchange for tokens issued by the DHSS when a claim form is completed, though in practice SB and FIS recipients usually receive tokens automatically. Entitlement lasts for beneficiaries in families in special circumstances as long as they receive SB or FIS or, in other cases, for up to twelve months regardless of changes in income (SI 1971/457, reg 3(2A)).

(4)   Local Authority Health Services

Local health authorities are required to provide health services for mother and children (NHSA 1946, s22) and a home help service for those who require it, which may include the provision of laundry facilities (Health Service and Public Health Act 1968, s23). LHAs may, but are not obliged, to make a charge for residential accommodation, day-nurseries, childminders, food and articles provided to mothers and children, home-help and laundry services; the standard formula permits 'such charges (if any) as the local authority consider reasonable, having regard to means'. Thus if a LHA exercise its discretion to charge, it must institute a means-test and those who qualify will receive these services free or for less than the full charge. Inquiries should be made to the public health department of a local authority.

(B)   Educational Benefits

Local education authorities are empowered to provide payments or exemption from payments in regard to several aspects of education. All such benefits are means-tested, some with local variations. Inquiries and claims should be made to the education department of a local authority.

(1)   School Meals
LEAs must provide meals for all school children attending their schools and milk for primary school children (Education Act 1944, s49; Public Expenditure and Receipts Act 1968, s3 and SI 1969/483, regs 3-5). Milk is free of charge but LEAs must charge parents £0.15 for every meal provided, but can remit the charge 'in the case of any parent who satisfies them that he is unable to pay without hardship'. SB recipients are deemed to fall into this category; otherwise entitlement to remission of the charge rests on the size of 'net income'—take-home pay less certain disregards and deductible expenses specified by regulations. Depending on the size of a claimant's family, the lower his net income the more children in respect of whom he need not pay the meal charge (SI 1968/483, reg 10 and Sch 1).

(2)   School Clothing
LEAs are empowered to provide clothing for children who are 'unable by reason of the inadequacy or unsuitability of (their) clothing to take full advantage of the education provided', to ensure they are 'sufficiently and suitably clad' (Education (Miscellaneous Provisions) Act 1948, s5 (2)); and to recover from parents the cost of the clothing or such lesser sum as they are 'without financial hardship' able to pay (E(MP)A 1948, s5 (6); SI 1948/2222, reg 3). No standard means-test is prescribed and LEAs are free to determine their own.

(3)   Maintenance Allowances
LEAs have several powers to contribute to the expense of keeping a child at school, including the specific power to provide maintenance allowances for children remaining at school beyond the upper limit of compulsory schooling, i.e. sixteen (EA 1944, s8(1); EA 1964, s2; SR & O 1945/666). These allowances are paid to parents qualifying by a means-test prescribed by the local authority.

(4)   Student Grants
The Secretary of State for Education and LEAs are empowered to grant awards for persons over compulsory school age attending higher education and other courses in this country and elsewhere; except for post-graduate students and those over twenty-five, the amount of the award depends on a parental means-test (EA 1962, ss1-4; EA 1975; SI 1963/1223). Parents who are assessed as being able to pay a 'parental contribution' are expected but not legally bound to pay the contribution to their children. The assessment and allocation of awards is made by LEAs to students whose homes are in their areas. The amount of the awards and the means-test are standard.

In vacations, students are eligible for SB (see ch 4). Students with families may be eligible for FIS (see ch 5(B)).

(C)   Transport

(1)   Travel Concessions
Many local authorities providing transport services offer free or concessionary fares to certain categories of passengers, most frequently to old-age pensioners. In 1955 a scheme for pensioners was disallowed at the instance of a ratepayer (Prescott v Birmingham Corp [1955] 3 All ER 698,CA). Current schemes were swiftly legitimated by statute and since 1964 local authorities have been free to operate concessions for pensioners, children under sixteen, older children in full-time education (for travel between school and home) and blind persons (Public Service Vehicle (Travel Concessions) Act 1955, s1; Travel Concessions Act 1964, s1). A typical arrangement is the provision of a pass for pensioners who establish entitlement by producing a pension order book. Inquiries should be made to the office of a local passenger transport executive.

(2)   School Transport
LEAs must provide necessary transport to enable attendance of pupils at their schools and in the absence of such arrangements may pay all or part of reasonable travelling expenses (EA 1944, s55). If a child lives more than three miles from school the LEA must provide transport over the whole distance (Surrey CC v Minister of Education [1953] 1 All ER 705); some authorities make no arrangements for shorter distances; otherwise the usual arrangement is the provision of a special bus service or of passes enabling children to use normal services. Inquiries should be made to local authority education departments.

A parent charged with the offence of his child failing to attend school has a defence if he can prove that the school in question is beyond walking distance and that no suitable arrangements have been made by the LEA

(EA 1944, s39(1)(2)(c)).

(3)   Attendance at Hospitals
A person attending a hospital or clinic or other NHS service is entitled to be paid his travelling expenses if 'the payment of such expenses by the patient would involve hardship'; the travelling expenses of a companion may also be paid unless the age, health or other circumstances of the patient make it unnecessary for him to be accompanied (NHSA 1946, s3(3); SI 1950/1222, reg 3). Entitlement is decided by the SBC using the amended SB means-test for medical expenses (see (A)(1) above).

(D)   Children and Young Persons Act 1963

Local authorities have a duty 'to make available such advice, guidance and assistance as may promote the welfare of children by diminishing the need to receive children into care or to bring children before a juvenile court, and any provisions made may include provision for assistance in kind, or, in exceptional circumstances, in cash' (CYPA 1963, s1(1)). As research in the late 1960s discovered (Heywood and Allen, 1971), this very broad power is interpreted with wide variations by local authority social service departments: some departments allocating manpower to administer these provisions, some laying down written policy guidelines, some making large financial allocations, some taking few of these steps. It is advisable therefore to make general inquiries of a local authority in order to be able to advise those who may require s1 assistance.
    A further problem is that of possible overlap with the SBC's power to make 'exceptional' or 'emergency' payments (see ch 4(B)(5), (D), (E)); through local authorities are not obliged to provide services under s1 which duplicate facilities available under other acts (CYPA 1963, s1(3)). It is not unknown for families in need to be 'shuttle-cocked' between social service departments and SBC offices for some time before money is forthcoming from either source. A Home Office Circular gives some guidance; in particular it encourages liaison between local authorities and the SBC and instructs authorities to consult the SBC before assistance in cash or kind is given except in cases of emergency or where the head of the household is in full-time work (HO Circular 204/1963, para 10). This does not avoid possible confusion in emergency cases since the employment bar to SB does not apply to emergency payments by the SBC. Regular assistance in cash or kind under s1 may be treated by the SBC as resources (see ch 4(C)(2)(g)).
    Clearly the absence of children precludes assistance under s1; on the other hand, although the assistance given must be designed to avoid taking children into care or juvenile court proceedings, it need not be confined to

the immediate needs of children; help given to parents or a family as a whole may avoid the need to take into care. The Home Office Circular instances the provision of bedding, kitchen equipment, fuel and the payment of rent arrears and bills for gas, water or electricity (Circular 204/1963, App, para 5). A later D of En Circular envisages the use of s1 to provide rent guarantees for both private and public sector tenants threatened with eviction (D of En Circular 18/74, App, paras 4(iv),5). Although assistance in cash is only available 'in exceptional circumstances' this is also subject to varying local interpretation. Hopefully no local authority would withhold cash in a genuine emergency. (A family which is homeless or threatened with eviction can be assisted to find accommodation by either housing or social services departments: see ch 8(A)(2).)

An adviser wishing to pursue the possibility of s1 assistance for a family should contact his local authority social services department as soon as possible (there is usually a social worker on duty outside normal hours) and arrange a meeting between a social worker and the family.

References

'Social Insurance and Allied Services', Report by Sir W. Beveridge, Cmd 6404 (1942).
Heywood, J.S. and Allen, B.K. (1971), 'Financial Help in Social Work', Manchester University Press.

Part II **Accommodation**

Chapter 8 **The Provision of Emergency Accommodation**

(A) Provision by the State

Homelessness is endemic, but increasing. The number of applications for local authority temporary accommodation rose from 18,000 in 1968 to 33,000 in 1973: but it is well known that many applicants are turned away (three-quarters of those applying in 1973 were unsuccessful), having to rely on the kindness of relatives or friends where possible, and often living in fear that their children may be taken into care.

Even where such accommodation is available, it is often of poor quality (see 'The Grief Report', Ch 7); alternatively, the accommodation offered may seem unduly extravagant (it can easily cost £50 per week to keep a family with two children in bed and breakfast accommodation in the London area: but such accommodation is far from being 'a holiday on the rates': see 'Bed and Breakfast', p.26 and Ch 3).

The main candidates for emergency accommodation appear to be people on the streets because of the decline in cheap rented property, former prisoners and mental patients, and the old. The numbers failing to secure accommodation and sleeping rough appear to be increasing alarmingly (in London alone there was a five-fold increase between 1965 and 1972), so that it is important to consider the scope of the existing legislation, and the means of enforcement. Leaving aside the various voluntary bodies (e.g. the Salvation Army and Christian Action: for full details see Matthews, 1974), responsibility for emergency accommodation falls on the Supplementary Benefits Commission and local authorities. Apart from the various formal methods of compelling these bodies to act (detailed below), informal pressure on local councillors and MPs can be useful.

(1) Provision by the Supplementary Benefits Commission
The SBC has responsibility for providing re-establishment centres and reception centres under the Supplementary Benefit Act 1966, s34 and Sch 4. The addresses of these centres are listed in the Supplementary Benefits Handbook.

(a) Re-establishment centres   The SBC may provide re-establishment centres (under the SBA 1966, Sch 4, para 1) to re-train people for employment; their purpose is not primarily to provide accommodation, and indeed only four of the fourteen centres in 1972 were residential. Further, there is no provision at any centre for family accommodation.

Where a claimant resides in such a centre following a SBAT direction, the SBC may in consequence withhold his supplementary allowance, permitting him such payments for personal requirements as it thinks fit (SBA 1966, s12(3): see ch 4(F)(6)).

The Act refers to these centres in purely permissive terms, but a disappointed claimant may in theory threaten to bring an action for mandamus (see ch 1(C)), since the SBC has a duty to exercise its functions 'in such manner as shall best promote the welfare of persons affected by the exercise thereof' (SBA 1966, s3).

(b) Reception centres   The SBC has a duty to 'make provision whereby persons without a settled way of living may be influenced to lead a more settled life', and to 'provide and maintain centres . . . known as reception centres, for the provision of temporary board and lodging for such persons' (SBA 1966, Sch 4, para 2). The SBC may require local authorities to run reception centres on its behalf, and in 1972 there were sixteen reception centres run by the SBC and three run by local authorities on its behalf.

Since, as will be seen, local authority accommodation is in practice normally reserved for homeless families, the single homeless can only resort to reception centres or voluntary bodies. The applicant may either be referred to a reception centre by the SBC's officers, or go to the centre on his own accord.

If a person 'persistently resorts to reception centres when capable of maintaining himself' the SBC can direct that he shall remain in a designated reception centre for a specified period, not exceeding forty-eight hours, and while there he must do such suitable work at the centre as the SBC may require, on pain of fine or imprisonment (SBA 1966, Sch 4, para 3); thus 'though it may do so but feebly and rarely, the ghost of the workhouse still walks' (Harding Boulton, 1972, p.159).

Once admitted, the applicant may be required to pay such sums for his board and lodging as the SBC decides (SBA 1966, s34(3)).

There is a duty to give accommodation, which is in theory enforceable against the SBC by order of mandamus (see ch 1(C)), but it appears that the duty may be satisfied once the SBC has 'made provision' as far as reasonably possible, even though the accommodation is now full (see (2)(c)(ii)below).

(2)   Provision by the Local Authorities
(a) General   Prior to 1974, local authorities considered that their

responsibilities for emergency accommodation were to be found in the National Assistance Act 1948, Pt III, and the provision of accommodation under this Act was made a social services function by the Local Authority Social Services Act 1970, s2(1) and Sch 1. Thus while the housing authority would deal with general housing matters, the social services authority would deal with emergency accommodation. However, in D of En Circular 18/1974 this division of function was disapproved of: 'the prevention and relief of homelessness is a function of local government as a whole, and not of either housing authorities or social services authorities alone' (para 13). The primary responsibility for emergency accommodation was however directed to be shifted from social services authorities to housing authorities (paras 18 and 19). The role of social services authorities will eventually be mainly in helping to prevent homelessness and providing supporting services, including social work help, to people in housing difficulties (para 22); but social services authorities will still be responsible under the NAA 1948 for providing residential accommodation for the elderly and infirm (para 30), and temporary accommodation to deal with 'sudden large scale emergencies and disasters beyond the resources of the housing authority' (para 27). It is thus necessary to separate local authorities' housing responsibilities from their social services responsibilities.

In view of the 1974 Circular, the initial application should be made to the housing department: if no help is offered, application should then be made to the social services department. Outside office hours, the social services department will have a duty officer available for emergencies, whose telephone number can be obtained from the local police station.

(b) Housing responsibilities   Under the 1974 Circular (para 26), the new responsibilities on housing authorities for emergency accommodation are to be found, not in the NAA 1948, but in the general provisions of the Housing Act 1957, Pt V. Section 91 of this Act provides that it shall be the duty of every local authority to consider housing conditions in its district and the need for further housing accommodation, and as often as occasion arises, or within three months after notice from the Secretary of State, to prepare and submit proposals for the provision of new houses.

The persons covered   The 1974 Circular stated that 'all those who have no roof, or who appear likely to lose their shelter within a month' should be helped, but that where resources are scarce, first claim must be given to certain 'Priority Groups', i.e. 'families with dependent children living with them, or in care; and adult families or people living alone who either become homeless in an emergency such as fire or flooding or are vulnerable because of old age, disability, pregnancy or other special reasons' (paras 8-10). For persons within these Priority Groups, the authority should accept responsibility at least seven days before they are actually homeless and tell them that it will secure accommodation for them (para 11). Moreover, the reason for homelessness, whether eviction, housing stress, or even lack of foresight, must be disregarded (para 37).

The authority responsible   Responsibility lies with the authority where the need exists, and persons should not be sent back to the authority where they previously lived unless it has been established with that authority that it has accommodation for them (para 37).

The type and duration of accommodation   The range of possibilities open to authorities is dealt with in the Appendix to the 1974 Circular. They are urged to make maximum use of their own short-life property acquired for redevelopment, to prevent privately owned property from being kept needlessly empty, and even to co-operate with 'reliable squatter organizations' (doubtless on the 'if-you-can't beat 'em, join 'em', principle). Pre-fabs, mobile homes and caravans are not encouraged. The accommodation should 'enable a family to be housed together' and be 'self-contained'; lodgings, guest houses or hotels should only be used 'as a last resort' (and will then be a social services responsibility); the receiving into care of the children of a homeless family is ruled out save in exceptional cases; and the husband should not normally be excluded from the accommodation.

The question of the duration of the accommodation is not specifically dealt with in the Circular but, at least in the case of Priority Groups, it seems that the accommodation should last as long as the need, without arbitrary limits.

The perennial problem of whether homeless families should be allowed to jump the queue for permanent local authority housing is dealt with later (see ch 10(A)(1)(c)).

Payment for the accommodation   By the HA 1957, s111, the authority may make such reasonable charges as it may determine (see ch 10(C)).

Enforcement   It is argued below (see (c)(ii)) that in the exercise of their functions under the NAA 1948, Pt III, social services authorities are under an express duty to obey Government Circulars. In the case of housing authorities under the HA 1957, no such statutory duty can be spelled out, but it is still possible to maintain that the Housing Act impliedly obliges authorities to have regard to Circulars, this obligation being theoretically enforceable in court by mandamus on behalf of a homeless family (Associated Provincial Picture Houses Ltd v Wednesbury Corp [1947] 2 All ER 680, 682, CA).

Alternatively, it is possible to ask the Secretary of State to serve notice on a defaulting authority requiring it to submit proposals for the provision of new houses (see HA 1957, s91 (above)), though this would hardly help the individual homeless family.

The default powers in the Housing Act 1957 (ss171-6) permitting the

Secretary of State to intervene where an authority had failed to carry out its functions (including Pt V functions) were repealed by the Local Government Act 1972.

Thus the shift to housing authorities of primary responsibility for helping the homeless seems to have diminished the chances of enforcement by the individual homeless family (compare the remedies below: (c)).

(c) Social services responsibilities   Before 1 April 1974 social services authorities were under a limited duty to provide both residential and temporary accommodation under the NAA 1948, s21 (known as 'Part III accommodation'); however, by a significant amendment in the Local Government Act 1972 (unsportingly concealed in Schedule 23), the former duty was apparently replaced by a mere power as from 1 April 1974: thus s21(1) of the 1948 Act now provides that: '. . . a local authority may with the approval of the Secretary of State, and to such extent as he may direct shall, make arrangements for providing—

(a) residential accommodation for persons who by reason of age, infirmity or any other circumstances are in need of care and attention which is not otherwise available to them;

(b) temporary accommodation for persons who are in urgent need thereof, being need arising in circumstances which could not reasonably have been foreseen or in such other circumstances as the authority may in any particular case determine.'

Thus there is now only a duty to act if the Secretary of State so directs, but he in fact issued a Directive (ref D/N 120/8) to all social services authorities on 11 February 1974 stating that after 1 April 1974 they should provide residential and temporary accommodation for the persons referred to in s21(1)(a) and (b): this Directive therefore restores the s21 duty, although it contemplates the duty as being only temporary pending the transfer of responsibilities to housing authorities (see (a) above).

(i) Residential accommodation   The 1974 Circular (see (a)above) does not affect the responsibility of social services authorities for residential accommodation under s21(1)(a) (set out above), but there are normally long waiting lists.

The persons covered   Section 21(1)(a) 'will not include sick persons needing treatment in hospital . . . but will comprise a wide range of elderly, infirm, disabled or subnormal people who are unable to look after themselves in their own homes and cannot obtain from relatives, friends or others the care and attention they require' (MOH Circular 87/1948, para 14). But if help is given or offered to the applicant other than by the local authority, the applicant loses the chance of admission to a local authority home, for the necessary help is 'otherwise available': the applicant should therefore curb any tendency towards kindness on the part of 'relatives, friends or others'.

The authority responsible   The relevant local authority is normally the one in whose area the applicant is ordinarily resident, save that if he has no settled residence or is in urgent need and ordinarily resident elsewhere, the authority in whose area he is found has responsibility (NAA 1948, s24).

The type and duration of accommodation   The accommodation 'will be a substitute for a normal home, and must meet all reasonable needs of the residents' (Circular 87/1948, para 16). It will presumably last until either the need ends or the necessary help becomes 'otherwise available'.

Payment for the accommodation   Accommodation 'is to be available to those in need of it irrespective of their means' (Circular 87/1948, para 19). However, the residents must normally pay for it in accordance with a standard rate fixed by the authority, reducible in cases of hardship (NAA 1948, s22). For the position of supplementary benefit claimants, see ch 4(B)(4)(a).

Enforcement   As we have seen, the old duty to provide residential accommodation has been restored by Directive, and there are two main lines of attack. First, under the NAA 1948, s25 (as amended), where the SBC is satisfied that a person in the area of the local authority is in urgent need of Pt III accommodation (which would include residential accommodation in an urgent case), it may require the authority to provide that accommodation: thus the SBC should be asked to make a s25 order, and if it fails to do so in a suitable case an application could be made to court for an order of mandamus on the ground that the SBC has a duty to exercise its functions 'in such manner as shall best promote the welfare of persons affected by the exercise thereof' (SBA 1966, s3). In March 1973 notice of motion for mandamus in this situation was served on the SBC to force it to make a s25 order against Bristol corporation for the temporary accommodation of a homeless family (see (ii) below), and the accommodation was granted without the need for trial.

Second, by the NAA 1948, s36, where the Secretary of State (for Health and Social Security) is of opinion that a local authority has failed to discharge any of its functions regarding Pt III accommodation, he may order the authority to discharge its functions as he directs: thus the Secretary of State may be asked to make a s36 order, though mandamus will not lie against him since there is no duty to act.

It has been suggested that ss25 and 36 afford the only relief open to a disappointed applicant, since Parliament did not intend that he should be able to sue the local authority directly (LB of Southwark v Williams [1971] 2 All ER 175, 178, CA). But it is still possible to argue that a third remedy may be available, directly against the authority by way of mandamus (see ch 1(C)) to force it to do its duty (see e.g. R v LB of Hillingdon, ex p Royco Homes Ltd [1974] 2 All ER 643, CA); this is considered further at (ii) below.

(ii) Temporary accommodation

The persons covered   The exact scope of s21(1)(b) (set out above) is not clear. In view of the 1974 Directive (see above), it is still important to distinguish between the two limbs of s21(1)(b). By the first limb, there is a duty to provide temporary accommodation in cases of 'urgent need . . . being need arising in circumstances which could not reasonably have been foreseen', and problems arise in eviction cases: is there a duty to accommodate, or is eviction through e.g. non-payment of rent quite foreseeable? The Ministry in 1948 regarded the duty as extending to eviction, and not just to cases such as fire or flood (Circular 87/1948, para 15), and it has been successfully argued that there is a duty in eviction cases since the 'unforeseeable circumstances' are the fact that no alternative accommodation could be found rather than the eviction itself ((1973) LAG BUL. 281). By the second limb, there is, even after the 1974 Directive, prima facie merely a discretion to act 'in such other circumstances as the authority may in any particular case determine'. Thus it is still important to establish that the circumstances fall within the first limb of s21(1)(b), since it will be easier to force action out of the authority in such a case (see below).

It was suggested in LB of Southwark v Williams (see (i) above) that s21(1)(b) is restricted to emergency cases such as fire or flood, and that homelessness of itself, unaccompanied by some separate disaster, is not within it. But that view is incompatible with the inclusion of eviction in the old 'duty' cases by the 1948 Circular (see above); and even if it be correct that the first limb of s21(1)(b) (which was alone considered in Williams's case) is restricted to emergencies like fires or floods, this cannot apply to the second limb: indeed another Ministry Circular has urged that the 'discretion given in Section 21 . . . as to the admission of families in foreseeable circumstances should be . . . widely used without artificial discrimination' (MHLG Circular 58/1966, para 10). However, as noted above (at(a)), the 1974 Circular and Directive contemplate that eventually social services authorities should only act under s21(1)(b) in cases of sudden emergencies and disasters.

Although the Act refers to 'persons', not families, in practice priority is given to homeless families with children: 'couples without children will normally be expected to find accommodation for themselves' (Circular 58/1966, para 10; and see the 1974 Circular on 'Priority Groups' ((b) above)). But even families with children have no guarantee of accommodation: there has been a disturbing tendency (disapproved of by the 1974 Circular) to 'offer' to take a homeless family's children into care instead, resulting in the family being frightened into dropping its application for accommodation; such practice contravenes the Children and Young Persons Act 1963, s1, which puts local authorities under a duty to take measures to reduce the need to take children into care. Clearly the single homeless seeking accommodation are treated even less favourably. Further, Circular 87/1948 stated (para 15) that s21(1)(b) 'does not . . . apply to persons without a settled way of life', since provision is made for them in reception centres: but in many areas there are no convenient reception centres, so is this not 'artificial discrimination'?

The authority responsible   The relevant authority is the one in whose area the person 'is', there being no question here of ordinary residence: NAA 1948, s24. Thus the common practice of dumping families 'over the border' (see 'The Grief Report', Ch 5) is illegal.

The type and duration of accommodation   Circular 87/1948 laid down, by way of masterly understatement, that 'persons given temporary accommodation . . . may not need a full range of services' (para 16). However, bed and breakfast accommodation was disapproved of in the 1974 Circular (see (b) above), and is clearly not authorized by the NAA 1948, since the accommodation must be in premises managed by a local authority (s21(4)), or in premises managed by a 'voluntary organization' (s26(1)), which is defined as 'a body the activities of which are carried on otherwise than for profit' (s64); see further 'Bed and Breakfast', App 2. Circular 58/1966 stated (para 8) that four types of accommodation are normally used: emergency centres (for unforeseen disasters), short term reception units (mainly for migrants), family units (for self-contained family use), and rehabilitation units (for families needing help in learning to manage their affairs). The same Circular recommended that 'families should remain in temporary accommodation no longer than can be avoided', but that 'permanent accommodation need not necessarily be provided . . . in council property' (para 6); further, 'the primary aim is to enable husband, wife and children to remain together' (para 9), and length of stay 'should be related to need' (para 10).

A later MHLG Circular (62/1967) elaborated on the position, referring to 'the need to avoid as far as possible the removal of families from their normal area of residence and employment' (para 11), and stating that 'once a family have been given temporary accommodation because they are homeless, they should not, except for special reasons, be compelled to leave unless they have satisfactory alternative accommodation' (para 13); the practice of setting an arbitrary time limit on residence was condemned, and at the other extreme it was recommended that 'families should not be forced to stay in temporary accommodation indefinitely without the offer of some sort of more permanent accommodation' (para 14).

Payment for the accommodation   As with residential accommodation, although temporary accommodation is to be available to those in need irrespective of means (Circular 87/1948, para 19), they must normally pay at the rate fixed by the authority (NAA 1948, s22). For the position of supplementary benefit claimants, see ch 4(B)(4)(a).

Social services departments forced to use bed and breakfast type accommodation can meet the cost under the Children and Young Persons Act 1963, s1, or the Local Government Act 1972, s137 (see 'Bed and Breakfast', App 2).

Enforcement   Similar problems of enforcement arise as in the case of residential accommodation. Thus the SBC can be asked (or forced) to make an order under the NAA 1948, s25, and the Secretary of State can be asked to make an order under s36 (see (i) above). The third possible remedy previously mentioned (see (i) above), namely mandamus against the local authority directly, is also relevant here, even in 'foreseeable circumstances' cases (see above). We have seen that various Circulars have given guidance on temporary accommodation to authorities. Now, the Local Authority Social Services Act 1970, s7, provides that: 'Local authorities shall, in the exercise of their social services functions, including the exercise of any discretion conferred by any relevant enactment, act under the general guidance of the Secretary of State'; and 'functions' with regard to Pt III accommodation include 'powers': NAA 1948, s64. It is therefore possible to argue that in exercising their duties and powers under the whole of s21(1) social services authorities are under a duty to follow the guidance of the Circulars. This approach finds support in Associated Provincial Picture Houses Ltd v Wednesbury Corp [1947] 2 All ER 680, 682, CA, was held to constitute a 'triable issue' in interlocutory proceedings in Bristol Corp v Stockford 1973 (Goff J, unreported), and is further developed in 'The Grief Report' at pp. 13-17. The argument will be particularly important in cases of foreseeable homelessness under s21(1)(b), where as we have seen there is no duty to act imposed by the 1974 Directive itself.

However, a possible limit to mandamus here was indicated in R v Bristol Corp, ex p Hendy [1974] 1 All ER 1047, 1051, CA: although this case (see ch 10(A)(2)) was not concerned with Pt III accommodation, Scarman LJ though that mandamus will not lie against an authority which is doing all it 'honestly and honourably can' to meet the statutory obligation and failure arises out of circumstances over which it has no control.

(3) Conclusion

The rules relating to emergency accommodation form an unharmonious hotchpot. Many of the responsibilities of local authorities are laid down in various Circulars and the important 1974 Directive, rather than in statutes, with consequent difficulties of enforcement. Also, there is a danger that under the 1974 Circular the homeless may find themselves in a state of limbo between housing and social services authorities, neither being prepared to accept responsibility. The Secretary of State announced in 1974 a wide review of provision for the homeless, to take account of regional variations and to 'avoid a legalistic approach to what are essentially human problems'.

(B)   The Squatting Movement

The concept of 'squatters' rights' is not novel: the law has long recognized that a person taking 'adverse possession' of another's land will extinguish the latter's title after twelve years. Recently, however, occupation rights of a more transient nature have been asserted in the fight against homelessness by 'people who, in the modern vernacular, and I use it without desiring to give offence, are referred to as squatters' (R v Robinson [1970] 3 All ER 369, 370, CA).

When the modern squatters' movement was born in 1968, the law was ill-equipped to deal with it, so that some owners—including local authorities—employed 'eviction experts' to winkle out squatters illegally (see Bailey, 1973). Subsequently however the courts have found some reasonably effective teeth, and 'if squatters are going to frustrate the law by treading a path through its technicalities, they must tread very carefully indeed' (Bailey, 1973, p.131). London squatting groups have however received the consent of certain local boroughs to the rehousing of families in short-life properties.

Not surprisingly, the judges have (with some exceptions) taken a stern view of unauthorized squatting: 'If homelessness were once admitted as a defence to trespass, no one's house could be safe . . . So the courts must, for the sake of law and order, take a firm stand. They must refuse to admit the plea of necessity to . . . the homeless; and trust that their distress will be relieved by the charitable and the good' (LB of Southwark v Williams [1971] 2 All ER 175, 179, CA). Yet it is still pertinent to ask, on behalf of those homeless families finding the 'charitable and the good' thin on the ground, what the relevant legal sanctions are and whether it is possible to avoid them.

We shall separate the squatter's position prior to and in process of entry from his position once in occupation.

(1) The Squatter's Position prior to and in Process of Entry
The act of unauthorized entry on the owner's property will always be a civil wrong, the tort of trespass; and even if no criminal offence is contemplated in connection with the entry, if two or more squatters simply agree to the trespass, they thereby commit the crime of conspiracy to trespass (Kamara v D P P [1973] 2 All ER 1242, HL); if they also agree to commit any criminal offence in connection with the trespass, they are

guilty of the crime of conspiracy to commit that offence as well.

The obvious crime that may result from one or more squatters gaining entry is forcible entry, contrary to the Statutes of Forcible Entry which date from 1381. The 1381 Act states that entry on land should be made 'not with strong hand, nor with multitude of people, but only in peaceable and easy manner'. Although there must be someone in prior possession of the land before squatters can be guilty of this offence, even the owner of empty property will have sufficient 'possession' to satisfy this requirement. However, mere trespass will not suffice for the commission of the offence, since there must be some show of force by the squatters 'calculated to deter the rightful owner from sending them away' (Milner v Maclean [1825] 2 Car & P 17). The force may be directed against either the occupier or the property, so that once again it does not matter if the property is empty and the offence will be committed if it is damaged on entry (Hemmings v Stoke Poges Golf Club Ltd [1920] 1 KB 720, 734, CA). Thus if squatters break down doors or windows or force locks in order to enter, they will be guilty of forcible entry, but not if they gain access by opening a door with a key or crawling through an open window, or by a trick (see 'Russell on Crime', 1964, p.286).

Some other possible crimes particularly applicable to the squatters' entry are: assault on the occupier; unlawful assembly (i.e. where three or more persons meet together to support each other in carrying out a purpose which is likely to involve violence, even if that purpose is never carried out: thus squatters should behave with decorum at all times); riotous assembly (i.e. where three or more persons, having a common purpose, commence that common purpose with intent to help one another by force if necessary against anyone who may oppose them, and they display force or violence so as to cause alarm: thus squatters should not be prepared to resist anyone obstructing them); and damage to property contrary to the Criminal Damage Act 1971 (this Act creates the offences of intentionally or recklessly destroying or damaging another's property, threatening another to destroy or damage property, and possessing anything with intent to destroy or damage property, without lawful excuse; further, under the Powers of Criminal Courts Act 1973, s35, the court may on conviction require the offender to pay compensation). This is not an exhaustive list: squatters may be prosecuted for offences less closely connected with the act of entry, e.g. if they were sanguine enough to announce that their activities were directed towards the wider aim of revolution, they might be guilty of sedition!

In gaining entry, then, the 'model' squatter should act alone (thus avoiding any charge of conspiracy, unlawful assembly or riotous assembly), he should not damage the building when entering, and should not carry any incriminating objects. He will thereby avoid any criminal liability. But he will be civilly liable to the owner for trespass: no damage need be shown, but if none has been done it will be a waste of the owner's money to sue.

(2)   The Squatter's Position after Entry

(a) Criminal offences by the squatter   Several of the offences already referred to can obviously be committed following entry, as well as in pursuance of it. But the squatter should particularly beware after entry of committing the crime of forcible detainer contrary to the Forcible Entry Act 1429. The offence can be committed even though the original entry was 'peaceable' (R v Mountford [1971] 2 All ER 81, CA) and consists of detaining possession by force: as to 'force', 'accumulating an unusual number of people or unusual weapons, or making other preparations of such a kind which indicate in themselves that any attempt to enter will be opposed by force may amount to the use of force in detaining the premises even though the owner is deterred and never makes the attempt at all' (R v Robinson [1970] 3 All ER 369, 372, CA). The test, then, is basically the same as for forcible entry: is the owner likely to be deterred by the show of force from evicting the squatters? Clearly the mere refusal to depart will not suffice for forcible detainer, nor will simply turning the key in a lock even if this caused the owner to break down the door to get in (R v Robinson, at p. 373); and as to barricades, 'so much would depend on the facts in each individual case, particularly on the degree of barricading, the time and effort which had been spent on it, and the effect of the barricades generally' (R v Robinson, at p. 373). Thus to avoid conviction for this offence the squatters need to ensure that they occupy in small numbers, accumulate no suspicious materials, and in protecting their occupation do not exceed the bare precautions of locking and bolting doors etc (but see Law Commission Working Paper No.54 ('Offences of Entering and Remaining on Property', 1974), which would make it an offence, being unlawfully on property, to fail to leave after being ordered to do so by the owner). The use of gas or electricity may be theft, if unauthorized (see (e) below).

There is also the danger of prosecution for offences against the Housing and Public Health Acts (see ch 12): thus squatters should not overcrowd or cause insanitary conditions, nor enter a vacated building after a demolition order (Housing Act 1957, s22(4): see ch 12(A)(4)(b)(ii)). However, in 'deserving cases' the local authority may be persuaded to make a control order (see ch 12(C)(2)(c)(iv)) on a house in multiple occupation by squatters, thus protecting them (in London, at least one authority has done this).

It is sometimes even possible for a local authority to prosecute squatters under the planning legislation, since the use as two or more separate dwellinghouses of a building previously used as a single dwellinghouse is a 'material change of use' requiring planning permission:

Town and Country Planning Act 1971, ss22, 87 and 89.

(b) Can the owner recover possession by self-help?   Before 1973, squatters considered that they were protected from private eviction since the Forcible Entry Acts applied even to the owner (e.g. Bailey, 1973, p.65). Those holding this view were in for a shock, however, when the Court of Appeal stated in McPhail v Persons Unknown [1973] 3 All ER 393 that the owner need not resort to court if squatters refuse to go quietly, but may himself re-enter and use reasonable force to evict the squatters without being guilty of forcible entry or liable in damages: the squatters, being trespassers, never gain possession (as opposed to occupation) unless the owner acquiesces in their presence, and the Forcible Entry Acts only apply to the eviction of persons in possession; thus the evicting owner, who retains 'possession' throughout, will only be liable to the squatters if he uses unreasonable force (in which case he is guilty of assault, though not of forcible entry).

There were existing cases to support this view (Scott v Mathew Brown [1884] 51 LT 746, Browne v Dawson [1840] 12 Ad & E 624), but they merely established that trespassers cannot gain possession as against the true owner simply by entry. If, as is usual, the trespassers entrench themselves by locking themselves in, it is difficult to resist the conclusion that they have taken possession, and even McPhail's case recognized that trespassers can gain possession if the owner 'acquiesces' in their presence. The very court order that an owner normally seeks is that he 'do recover possession', implying that possession is in the defendants, and if the owner really retains possession all along, it seems that the squatters cannot be guilty of forcible detainer. Local authorities regard squatters as 'occupiers' for the purposes of the rating, housing and public health legislation; and the view that trespassers can never gain possession without the owner's acquiescence cannot be reconciled with the provisions in the Limitation Act 1939 (ss4, 5 and 10) allowing the acquisition of title to land after twelve years' adverse possession, for which purpose 'a squatter has a title based on his own possession' (Megarry and Wade, 1966, p.1006).

McPhail's case was primarily concerned with the separate issue of suspension of possession orders against squatters (see (c) below), so that these difficulties regarding 'possession' were not fully canvassed. An owner relying on this decision and maintaining that since he never acquiesced in the trespassers' presence he can regain his property by forcible self-help, may find he has acted too rashly. The true answer to the crucial question of whether squatters are in 'possession' should depend, not primarily on the owner's 'acquiescence', but on the extent of the squatters' action, i.e. whether they have in fact made it clear that they have excluded the owner regardless of his non-acquiescence. Since the mere act of trespass will not suffice (without acquiescence by the owner), 'an owner who reacts swiftly to the invasion of his premises will not normally offend against the statutes . . . the ejection of the trespasser can amount to no more than forcible detainer by the party entitled, which is justifiable' (Dashwood, Davies and Trice (1971) Crim LR 317, 325); but delay on the owner's part may mean the gaining of possession by the squatters and consequent forfeiture of the owner's right to self-help. An owner guilty of forcible entry would not however be civilly liable to squatters unless he used unreasonable force; for no civil remedy lies for breach of the Statutes of Forcible Entry where the defendant had a right of entry against the plaintiff, and the subsequent expulsion of the squatters would be justifiable (Hemmings v Stoke Poges Golf Club Ltd [1920] 1 KB 720, CA).

(c) Possession orders   Assuming that our landowner has decided that discretion is the better part of valour and uses the courts rather than self-help, he can employ the new procedure for recovery of possession of land from trespassers introduced in 1970 by Order 113 of the Rules of the Supreme Court and Order 26 of the County Court Rules (as to the defects of the previous procedure, see e.g. Manchester Corp v Connolly [1970] 1 All ER 961, CA). For historical reasons, actions to recover land are part of tort law (Bramwell v Bramwell [1942] 1 All ER 137, 138, CA); and it is clear that, although the defence of necessity is occasionally recognized in tort law, it will not avail a squatter: LB of Southwark v Williams [1971] 2 All ER 175, CA ('necessity can very easily become simply a mask for anarchy' (p.181)). The objects of the 1970 orders were to circumvent the owner's difficulty where he cannot identify the squatters, and to expedite the obtaining of the final possession order.

This new procedure covers both squatters entering without the owner's consent and former licensees whose licences have been ended (Bristol Corp v Persons Unknown [1974] 1 All ER 593; GLC v Jenkins [1975] 1 All ER 354, CA). Under it, the owner can issue a special form of summons not naming the parties, where he is 'unable, after taking reasonable steps, to identify every person occupying the land for the purpose of making him a defendant': but if he does not make reasonable inquiries to identify every squatter before issuing this summons (and the inquiries have to be set out in the affidavit), the summons will be dismissed (Re 9 Orpen Road [1971] 1 All ER 944). The originating summons and copy affidavit (High Court) or originating application and copy affidavit (county court) must be served on any identified squatters: those who are unidentified can be served by fixing the copy documents to 'the main door or other conspicuous part of the premises'. Save in urgent cases, there must be not less than seven clear days (including Saturdays and Sundays) between the service of the documents and the hearing: and the fact that the owner wants possession to complete a sale does not make it an urgent case (Mercy v Persons Unknown, 'The Times', 5 June 1974, CA).

The possession order under this procedure must be made by a judge, who has no discretion to suspend the order or grant a stay of execution unless the owner acquiesces: McPhail v Persons Unknown [1973] 3 All ER 393, CA (where the court stated that since the owner could resort to immediate self-help—see (b) above—he should not be in a worse position, through having the order suspended, if he went to court instead).

Where a local authority seeks a possession order, it might be possible for the squatters to argue that the council has not authorized the proceedings by resolution, so that they are ultra vires the council (see LB of Southwark v Peters [1972] 70 LGR 41, CA); but the squatters cannot raise as a defence breach by the authority of the duty to provide temporary accommodation under the National Assistance Act 1948, s21 (LB of Southwark v Williams [1971] 2 All ER 175, CA).

It is not unknown for squatters to be granted legal aid to defend possession proceedings, and an adjournment for a legal aid application may be a useful delaying tactic.

(d) Damages and costs   The owner will normally be unable to recover exemplary (i.e. punitive) damages: Cassell & Co Ltd v Broome [1972] 1 All ER 801, HL (and see 'Clerk and Lindsell on Torts', 1969, para 1357: 'what is not permissible is to punish a trespasser by awarding damages as a mark of retribution for his malice or ill manners'). Further, it seems that no damages or mesne profits can be claimed if the owner uses the expedited procedure introduced by the 1970 Orders ('Supreme Court Practice', 1973, Vol I, p. 1482, note 113/1—8/3). Subject to those qualifications, the owner may claim both for physical damage to his property and the reasonable rental value in recompense for the squatters' occupation, either as damages for trespass or as mesne profits as part of his claim for recovery of the land.

The principal difficulty for the owner claiming damages lies in enforcing them against squatters who may be 'men of straw'; perhaps for the same reason, it is rare for squatters to be ordered to pay the owner's costs, even if the squatters are identified (costs are not obtainable against unidentified occupiers).

(e) The supply of electricity, gas and water   As occupiers, squatters may be able to enforce the provision of these services, which may be particularly important if the elderly or very young have been 'squatted' (see Electric Lighting (Clauses) Act 1899, Sch, para 27(1); Gas Act 1972, Sch 4, para 2(1); Water Act 1945, Sch 3, para 30(1); but cf. (1974) LAG BUL. 49).

References

'The Grief Report', a Shelter report on temporary accommodation by R. Bailey and

Joan Ruddock (1972).

'Bed and Breakfast', a Shelter report on temporary accommodation by R. Bailey (1974).

Matthews, G. (1974), 'Knowhere to Go' (sic), The Cyrenians, Canterbury.

Harding Boulton, A. (1972), 'Law and Practice of Social Security', Jordan, Bristol.

Bailey, R. (1973), 'The Squatters', Penguin, Harmondsworth.

'Russell on Crime' (1964), 12th ed, Stevens, London.

Megarry, R.E. and Wade, H.W.R. (1966), 'The Law of Real Property', Stevens, London.

'Clerk and Lindsell on Torts' (1969), 13th ed, Sweet & Maxwell, London.

Chapter 9 **Landlord and Tenant: the Private Sector**

We have come a long way since Lord Brougham defended the mass eviction of tenants in nineteenth-century Ireland on the ground that it was the landlord's 'undoubted, indefeasible and most sacred right' to do as he pleased with his own property (House of Lords, 23 March 1846). During the present century, the old laissez-faire attitude has been rejected in favour of substantial protection for the private tenant under the Rent Acts, which place a compulsory ceiling on rents and restrict the landlord's right to regain possession. The extent of this protection has varied with changes of government: what has remained constant is the complexity of the legislation, which has been subjected to constant judicial criticism (e.g. a 'welter of chaotic verbiage', a 'labyrinth and jungle'). Yet legal aid is still not available for the multitude of Rent Act cases going to rent officers, rent assessment committees and rent tribunals, rather than to the courts (see ch 13(A)(2)). Hence landlords are professionally represented before such bodies far more frequently than tenants.

Although the Rent Acts are Parliament's main protection for private tenants, other legislation can be useful: the Housing and Public Health Acts will be considered later (ch 12), but three other examples can be given here. First, the Accommodation Agencies Act 1953 tries to stop profiteering from the housing shortage by making it an offence to demand or accept payment for (a) registering or agreeing to register details of anyone seeking the tenancy of a house or flat, or (b) supplying or agreeing to supply details to anyone of houses or flats to let: if the Act is broken, and the police do not prosecute, then the local authority can do so (Local Government Act 1972, s222), and the prospective tenant can recover by civil proceedings any sums paid; however, no offence is committed where the payment is only due after the prospective tenant takes up the tenancy: Saunders v Soper [1974] 3 All ER 1025, HL (and see Ruth Holt (1975) LAG BUL. 75). Second, the better-known Race Relations Act 1968 includes housing in the areas of prohibited discrimination (i.e. discrimination based on colour, race or national origins): the race relations board first tries to settle the tenant's complaint between the parties, failing which it can go to a county court and the landlord can be

ordered to pay damages and/or be prohibited from further
discrimination. Third, the Gas Act 1972, Sch 4, para 12, and Electricity
Act 1957, s29, lay down the maximum sums landlords may charge for
metered supplies of gas and electricity (details are obtainable from local
gas and electricity consumer councils, and overpayments may be
deducted from the rent).

This chapter concentrates on the three major sources of legal worries
for underprivileged tenants: rent, responsibility for the condition of the
property, and ending the tenancy. It does not deal with tenancies initially
granted for more than twenty-one years, 'business tenancies', or
agricultural tenancies.

(A)   The Types of Tenancies to which the Rent Acts apply

Although most private tenants of unfurnished or furnished dwellings are
within the Rent Acts, the amount of protection relating to the rent and
the ending of the tenancy depends on the particular technical class into
which the tenancy falls (though this decision is not normally important
when considering responsibility for the condition of the property). The
broad distinction is between 'fully covered tenancies' and 'Part VI
lettings' (not now between 'unfurnished' and 'furnished' lettings). If a
tenancy is 'fully covered' (an expression not used as such in the
legislation), further analysis is then required: in order to discover the rent
ceiling, it must be decided whether it is a 'protected tenancy' or a
'statutory tenancy', and then whether it is a 'regulated tenancy' or a
'controlled tenancy'; but when the ending of a 'fully covered tenancy' is
considered, the only relevant division is normally between a 'protected
tenancy' and a 'statutory tenancy'. There is some overlap, since although
a 'statutory tenancy' only arises when a 'protected tenancy' ends, a
'regulated tenancy' followed by a 'statutory tenancy' means both are
together treated as one 'regulated tenancy', and a 'controlled tenancy'
followed by a 'statutory tenancy' leads to both being together treated as
one 'controlled tenancy' (RA 1968, ss3, 7). Thus the Rent Acts' 'family
tree' is as shown in figure 1.

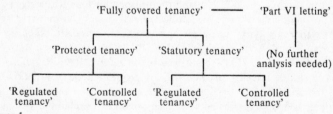

Figure 1

We must define these baffling expressions before the 'meat' of the Rent Acts is considered: but at this stage we can formulate the necessary questions. First:

In all cases: 'Is it a 'fully covered tenancy' or a 'Part VI letting'?'
(If it is neither, the Rent Acts do not apply; if it is a 'Part VI letting', no further analysis is needed; but if it is a 'fully covered tenancy', the following questions are necessary:) Second:

As regards the rent or the ending of a 'fully covered tenancy':
'Is it a 'protected tenancy' or a 'statutory tenancy'?'
(It must be one or the other; having decided which, as regards its ending, no further analysis is normally needed; but as regards its rent, further analysis is required:) Third:

As regards the rent of a 'protected tenancy' or a 'statutory tenancy':
'Is it a 'regulated tenancy' or a 'controlled tenancy'?'
(It must be one or the other.)

(1)   Is it a 'fully covered tenancy' or a 'Part VI letting'?
For there to be either a 'fully covered tenancy' or a 'Part VI letting', the dwelling must be within certain rateable value limits: these are now generous, so that most privately rented property is within the Rent Acts. In essence, the dwelling must have had a rateable value not exceeding £1,500 in Greater London, or £750 elsewhere, either on 1 April 1973, or, if the dwelling was not then shown on the valuation list, on the day it was first listed (RA 1968, ss1, 6, and 71, as amended by the Counter-Inflation Act 1973 and the RA 1974: all subsequent references to the RA 1968 are to that Act as amended). The rateable value can be obtained from the local authority.
(a) 'Fully covered tenancy'   A 'fully covered tenancy' is one, whether unfurnished or furnished, which satisfies the conditions in the RA 1968, s1, and does not fall within the exceptions listed in ss1, 2, 4, and 5.
   Under s1(1) there must be a tenancy of a 'house or part of a house . . . let as a separate dwelling', which satisfies the rateable value limits given above. 'Let' refers to a strict landlord and tenant relationship, where the right to exclusive possession is given, so that mere licensees (e.g. lodgers) having no exclusive possession cannot have 'fully covered tenancies': it does not matter what the parties call the transaction, what is important is the substance of what the occupier is given (A. Arden (1974) LAG BUL. 155); similarly 'service occupiers', who are employees required to occupy property for the better performance of their duties, are mere licensees (compare 'service tenants', who are simply allowed to reside in their employers' property, and may hold 'fully covered tenancies': A. Arden

(1974) LAG BUL. 108). 'Separate dwelling' means that a tenant sharing living accommodation with his landlord (e.g. a kitchen or sitting room, but not a bathroom, lavatory or coal house) cannot have a 'fully covered tenancy', whether or not he shares with others also: he only has a 'Part VI letting' (RA 1968, s101; Goodrich v Paisner [1956] 2 All ER 176, HL); though if the tenant shares such accommodation simply with people other than his landlord, he can still have a 'fully covered tenancy' of his separate (non-shared) accommodation (RA 1968, s102).

Assuming the tenancy satisfies these conditions, it will nevertheless fail to be 'fully covered' if it falls within one of the exceptions listed in the RA 1968, ss1, 2, 4, and 5, the most important of which are as follows.

(i) Where the landlord is a local authority, etc.   If the landlord is a local authority, the Crown, the Housing Corporation, or a housing trust, the tenancy is not 'fully covered' (RA 1968, ss4, 5). Since local authority lettings greatly outnumber private lettings (see ch 1(B)) this exception is important: for council housing, see ch 10.

(ii) Where it is a 'resident landlord tenancy'   This exception is considered in detail below (see (b)(ii)), since such cases come within 'Part VI lettings'. Basically, the exception covers two distinct cases: first, where the landlord has, on or after 14 August 1974, let part of a building, whether unfurnished or furnished, and has resided throughout the tenancy in another part of that building (RA 1968, ss1(1)(d), 5A); and second, where the landlord has before 14 August 1974 let part of a building furnished, and has resided at all times since 14 August 1974 in another part of that building (RA 1974, Sch 3, para 1): thus here it is important to decide what is meant by 'furnished' (see (b)(ii) below). If the landlord chooses to move into the building after 14 August 1974, he cannot affect the position of tenants already there (whether of unfurnished or furnished property): if they were 'fully covered' before he moved in, they remain so.

It is uncertain how many tenancies fail to be 'fully covered' through this 'resident landlord' exception. The D of En estimated in 1974 that only 5 per cent of all private landlords were 'resident', and that 600,000 of a total of 750,000 furnished tenants would be 'fully covered'. Yet the Francis Report contained a 1970 survey showing that 39 per cent of furnished tenants in the stress areas covered lived in the same building as their landlords (Cmnd 4609, p. 290).

(iii) Where the tenant pays for board or attendance   If the dwelling is 'bona fide let at a rent which includes payment in respect of board or attendance', the tenancy is not 'fully covered' (RA 1968, s2(1)(b)). 'Board' appears to mean meals etc of an adequate nature, and not e.g. mere bedtime cocoa. 'Attendance' means a service provided by the landlord which is personal to the tenant, e.g. removal of his rubbish: it would not include the cleaning by the landlord of a hallway common to the tenant's and other property; and for this 'attendance' exception to apply, the amount of rent covering the attendance must form a substantial part of the whole rent (RA 1968, s2(3)): see further A. Arden (1975) LAG BUL. 73.

(iv) Where the rent payable is nil, or less than two-thirds of the rateable value   If no rent is payable, or the rent is less than two-thirds of the rateable value, the tenancy is not 'fully covered' (RA 1968, s2(1)(a)); there are detailed rules for picking the appropriate rateable value (RA 1968, ss2(1) (proviso), 6, and 7(3); (1974) LAG BUL. 193).

(v) Where it is a student tenancy or a holiday tenancy   If the tenancy is granted to a student by a 'specified educational institution', it is not 'fully covered' (RA 1968, s2(1)(bb); SI 1974/1366); neither is a tenancy granted to any person for holiday purposes (RA 1968, s2(1)(bbb)(sic!)). A student tenancy can be a 'Part VI letting' (but a holiday tenancy cannot: RA 1968, s70(5)).

(b) 'Part VI letting'   A 'Part VI letting', i.e. one falling within the RA 1968, Pt VI, is defined in ss70, 71, 101, and 102A.

(i) The main definition   By s70 (the main definition) Part VI applies to 'a contract ... whereby one person grants to another ... in consideration of a rent which includes payment for the use of furniture or for services, the right to occupy as a residence a dwelling', provided exclusive occupation is given and the rateable value limits given above (and see s71) are satisfied.

Since this definition covers contracts, and not just tenancies, it can extend to mere contractual licences (compare 'fully covered tenancies': (a) above): thus e.g. a lodger or 'paying guest' who has exclusive occupation of a furnished 'bed-sit' may have Part VI protection (despite the absence of exclusive possession: Luganda v Service Hotels Ltd [1969] 2 All ER 692, 695, CA). However, s70(3) excludes from Part VI cases where a substantial part of the rent (roughly 20 per cent or more) represents payments for board (see (a)(iii) above); and hotel guests would further be excluded on the ground that they normally have no 'right to occupy as a residence' (but cf. Luganda v Service Hotels Ltd, above). It seems that 'services' in s70(1) is a wider word than 'attendance' in s2(1)(b) (see (a)(iii) above): thus 'services' can include e.g. the provision of hot water by the landlord to the tenant and others in the same block, which would not constitute 'attendance'.

(ii) The relationship between 'Part VI lettings' and 'fully covered tenancies'   If the tenancy is 'fully covered', it normally cannot also be a 'Part VI letting' (s70(3)(c)). We saw that the fact that a tenancy is furnished does not normally prevent it being 'fully covered' ((a) above), so that such a tenancy, despite its furniture, cannot also be a 'Part VI letting'. However, we also noted (in (a) above) that two cases of 'resident landlord tenancies' are not 'fully covered' but are 'Part VI lettings' instead, and these must now be examined.

'Resident landlord tenancies' granted on or after 14 August 1974   Where a landlord has granted a tenancy on or after 14 August 1974 of a dwelling, whether unfurnished or furnished, which forms part only of a building which is not a purpose-built block of flats, and the landlord resided in some other part of that building at the time of the grant and has so resided ever since, then the tenancy is not 'fully covered' (RA 1968, s5A(1)), but is a 'Part VI letting' even if it is unfurnished (RA 1968, s102A). For the meaning of 'resident landlord' see A. Arden (1974) LAG BUL. 302.

A house converted into flats is within s5A(1), but not a purpose-built block, i.e. one which as first constructed contained two or more flats (s5A(6)). Special provisions allow the landlord certain 'void' periods where there is an interruption of his residence (up to six months, on notice to the tenant, if he sells, and up to twelve months if he dies: s5A(2)).

However, s5A is inapplicable if the tenancy is granted to a tenant who was previously a 'fully covered tenant' in that building: the new tenancy is also 'fully covered' (s5A(5)(a)).

Normally, if a landlord renews a 'resident landlord tenancy' it remains a 'Part VI letting', save that if the new tenancy is for a fixed term (see (D)(1)(a) below) and the tenant's former tenancy was within s5A, the new tenancy is nevertheless 'fully covered' (s5A(5)(b)).

'Resident landlord tenancies' granted before 14 August 1974   Where a landlord has granted a tenancy before 14 August 1974 of a furnished dwelling, which forms part only of a building which is not a purpose-built block of flats, and the landlord resided in some other part of that building on 14 August 1974 and has so resided ever since, then the tenancy is not 'fully covered', but is treated as being within s5A above (RA 1974, Sch 3, para 1), and is a 'Part VI letting' (RA 1968, s102A). If the pre-14 August 1974 tenancy was not 'furnished', it is 'fully covered' notwithstanding the landlord's residence in the building: thus it is here necessary to consider what is meant by 'furnished'.

The tenancy will be 'furnished' if the annual value of the furniture (roughly 15 per cent of its valuation at the start of the tenancy) forms a substantial percentage (roughly 20 per cent or more) of the annual rent: so to find this percentage, the sum is: $\dfrac{\text{annual value of furniture}}{\text{annual rent}} \times 100;$

but the House of Lords has refused to approve any specific percentages as 'substantial' (Palser v Grinling [1948] 1 All ER 1, HL), and judges vary considerably ((1973) LAG BUL. 223). However, an important 1974 decision shows that changing social and economic conditions are relevant, there being now a great shortage of houses to rent and a glut of cheap second-hand furniture, so that even a fully furnished house can be 'unfurnished' if the annual value of the furniture to the tenant is slight (Woodward v Docherty [1974] 2 All ER 844, CA: flat let fully furnished at a rent of £10 per week held 'unfurnished' since the furniture was worth only £40 per year to the tenant). Clearly, evidence from a furniture valuer can help the tenant considerably. A county court can decide this unfurnished/furnished question by declaration, even if no other proceedings are on foot (RA 1968, s105).

(iii) Types of 'Part VI lettings'   For the reasons given above, the main sorts of 'Part VI lettings' are: certain 'resident landlord tenancies'; lodgers with exclusive occupation of furnished accommodation, but without board; and tenants, whether unfurnished or furnished, who share living accommodation with their landlords (RA 1968, s101: see (a) above).

(2) Is a 'fully covered tenancy' a 'protected tenancy'? Or is it a 'statutory tenancy'?
If the tenancy is 'fully covered', it is important as regards both its rent and its ending to inquire whether it is a 'protected tenancy' or a 'statutory tenancy': it must be one or the other (see figure 1 above).
(a) 'Protected tenancy'   A 'protected tenancy' is simply a 'fully covered tenancy' which is still contractual, i.e. it has not been extended by the RA 1963, s3 (see (b) below) beyond the term agreed.
(b) 'Statutory tenancy'   Since a 'protected tenancy' is contractual, it can be ended by either landlord or tenant, or automatically (see (D)(1) below). But as we shall see ((D)(3)(a)(i) below), immediately a 'protected tenancy' ends, a 'statutory tenancy' springs up (RA 1968, s3), which may be treated as either 'regulated' or 'controlled' (RA 1968, s7: see (3) below). A tenant under a 'statutory tenancy' is difficult to remove, for as will be seen ((D)(3)(a)(ii) below) he need only depart if the court so orders in certain limited circumstances (RA 1968, s10). While in possession, the 'statutory tenant' has the benefit and burden of all the provisions of the original 'protected tenancy', so far as consistent with the Act (RA 1968, s12(1)).

(3) Is a 'protected' or 'statutory' tenancy a 'regulated tenancy'? Or is it a 'controlled tenancy'?
If the tenancy is either 'protected' or 'statutory', it is important as regards its rent to ask whether it is a 'regulated tenancy' or a 'controlled tenancy': it must be one or the other (see figure 1 above).
(a) 'Regulated tenancy'   Under the Housing Finance Act 1972, a large number of 'protected' or 'statutory' tenancies became regulated, since the 1972 Act laid down a system of phased conversion of 'controlled tenancies' to 'regulated tenancies' between 1973 and 1975; however, this phased conversion process was permanently halted by the Housing Rents

and Subsidies Act 1975, s9 (see (b) below), and the process never applied
to unfit premises, as to which the old law applicable to 'controlled
tenancies' remains (see (b) below). The RA 1968, s7(2) provides that a
'regulated tenancy' is 'a protected or statutory tenancy which is not . . . a
controlled tenancy'. Thus to ensure that a 'protected' or 'statutory'
tenancy is 'regulated' it is necessary to establish that it is not 'controlled'.
(b) 'Controlled tenancy'   A 'protected' or 'statutory' tenancy will
only be 'controlled' if all the following conditions are satisfied:

   (i) The original contractual tenancy started before 6 July 1957.

   (ii) The dwelling was erected, or converted into a separate and
self-contained unit, on or before 29 August 1954.

   (iii) The rateable value of the dwelling on 7 November 1956 did not
exceed £40 in London or £30 elsewhere.

   (iv) The original contractual tenancy was granted for twenty-one years
or less.

   (v) Either the original tenant, or his first successor on his death, is still
alive. (Conditions (i)-(v) are in the RA 1968, Sch 2).

   (vi) No 'qualification certificate' has been issued for the dwelling. By
the HFA 1972, Pt III, where there is a 'controlled tenancy' the landlord
can apply to the local authority for a certificate that the dwelling is
provided with all the standard amenities (e.g. toilet, sink: see ch 11(C)(2))
for the exclusive use of its occupants, is in good repair, and is in all other
respects fit for human habitation (see ch 12(A)(1)). These are called the
'qualifying conditions'. The tenant may object to the authority that they
are not satisfied. If the authority considers that the 'qualifying
conditions' are satisfied, it must issue a 'qualification certificate'. The
tenancy thereupon ceases to be 'controlled' and becomes 'regulated', so
that application may be made to the rent officer for registration of a 'fair
rent' or the parties can agree a 'fair rent' (see (B)(1) below). Any increases
to the 'fair rent' level will normally be phased (see (B)(1)(c)(vi) below).

   (vii) The dwelling has not become decontrolled under the 'general
decontrol' provisions. By the HFA 1972, s35, many 'controlled tenancies'
not already decontrolled under the 'qualification certificate' procedure
(see (vi) above) were converted to 'regulated tenancies' under a phasing
system between 1973 and 1975, the applicable date depending on the
rateable value of the dwelling on 31 March 1972. But these 'general
decontrol' provisions never applied to unfit dwellings (see ch 12(A)(1)) as
to which one or more of certain statutory notices had been served not
later than three months before what would otherwise be the conversion
date (HFA 1972, s36). Moreover, this phased conversion process has now
been permanently halted by the HRSA 1975, s9. If these old 'general
decontrol' provisions operated on a particular tenancy, then as from the
applicable date the 'controlled tenancy' became a 'regulated tenancy' for
which a 'fair rent' could be registered or agreed, the increases being phased

(see (B)(1) below).

(viii) The dwelling is not 'furnished' (RA 1974, s1(3); see (1)(b)(ii) above).

Having dealt with these vital but arid definitions, we can now apply them to the practicalities of rent control and the ending of tenancies under the Rent Acts.

(B) Rent Control

The Rent Acts contain extensive and regrettably complicated provisions restricting the rents landlords may charge. Fully covered tenancies are dealt with differently from Part VI lettings, so that the two systems must be separately considered. Under both systems, rent increases may be subject to temporary freezes imposed by order of the Secretary of State (HRSA 1975, s 11).

(1) Fully Covered Tenancies
(a) Rent limit for tenancies which are both protected and regulated

(i) Where no rent has been registered   If no rent has been registered for a protected (i.e. contractual) and regulated tenancy, then the position is as follows.

Where the tenant was granted a regulated tenancy before 1 January 1973   The RA 1968 originally provided that where no rent was registered, the contractual rent limit should either be the rent payable under any other regulated tenancy of the property granted not more than three years before the present regulated tenancy began, or the rent payable under the present tenancy (as at 8 December 1965 if granted before that date), subject in either case to adjustments in respect of changes in responsibility for repairs, the provision of services, the use of furniture, the amount of rates, or improvements (RA 1968, ss20(3), 21); this rent limit still applies to a pre-1 January 1973 regulated tenancy if the rent under the tenancy, as varied by any agreement before 1 January 1973, exceeded this limit (HFA 1972, s42(2)(b)).

But this limit will cease completely (by HFA 1972, s42), if the parties enter into a 'rent agreement with a tenant having security of tenure' (see below): thus the old rent limit stays only so long as no such agreement is entered into, and the availability of such an agreement to unfreeze the rent is now an alternative to an application to register a fair rent.

Where the tenant was granted a regulated tenancy on or after 1 January 1973   Here the old initial rent limit (in RA 1968, ss20(3), 21: see above) has been completely removed (HFA 1972, s42). Further, the existing rent can now be increased by a 'rent agreement with a tenant having security of tenure' (which term includes the grant of another regulated tenancy to the same tenant, but excludes any increase simply to cover higher rates for the property): HFA 1972, s43. The procedure is not available where a rent has been registered. This rent agreement must be in writing, signed by the parties, and must state that the tenant's security of tenure under the Rent Acts (see (D)(3)(a) below) will not be affected if he refuses to enter into the agreement, and that the agreement will not deprive either party of the right to apply for registration of a fair rent at any time. Special requirements relating to the agreement apply where the tenancy has become regulated under the 'qualification certificate' or 'general decontrol' procedure (see (A)(3)(b) above), and where grant-aided improvements have been approved (HFA 1972, ss44, 45). If any of these rules is not observed, the increase in rent provided for by the agreement is irrecoverable from the tenant (HFA 1972, s46).

Where the premises are not occupied by a tenant   Here, in view of the removal of the old rent limit (by HFA 1972, s42, noted above), the landlord can charge what rent he likes, subject to the tenant's right to registration of a fair rent.

(ii) Where a rent has been registered   Where a rent has been registered for a protected and regulated tenancy, then that is the maximum rent recoverable notwithstanding any agreement to the contrary (RA 1968, s20(2)); though this is subject to the landlord's right to add the rates if paid by him and to the right of both parties jointly to apply for cancellation of the registration (see (c)(vii) below).

Where a protected tenancy is on foot and the registered rent is higher than the agreed rent the landlord cannot automatically raise the agreed rent up to the registered level, since this would be a breach of contract. If the tenancy is for a fixed term, e.g. three years, the landlord is stuck with the agreed rent during the term. But if the tenancy is periodic, e.g. weekly, the landlord may convert the contractual protected tenancy into a statutory tenancy by notice to quit (see (D)(1)(b) below), and may thereafter raise the statutory rent to the registered limit by a notice of increase (RA 1968, s22(2)(b); see (b)(ii) below), though this is subject to special phasing provisions (see (c)(vi) below); moreover the landlord may also achieve the same effect by serving a notice of increase during the contractual period, taking effect not earlier than the earliest date at which a notice to quit could take effect (RA 1968, s26(3)): we shall see that four weeks' written notice to quit is the minimum required to end a periodic tenancy of a dwelling ((D)(1)(b) below).

(b) Rent limit for tenancies which are both statutory and regulated.

(i) Where no rent has been registered   Here the maximum recoverable rent for the statutory period is normally the rent for the last contractual period (RA 1968, s22(1)); but the rent can be raised by a 'rent agreement' (HFA 1972, s43: see (a)(i) above), the effect of which will be to create a new contractual tenancy. The maximum rent for the statutory period may be adjusted to take account of variations in rates, the provision of services, the use of furniture, or improvements (RA 1968, ss23-5).

(ii) Where a rent has been registered   If a rent has been registered for a statutory tenancy, that is the maximum recoverable rent (save that the landlord can add the rates if paid by him), notwithstanding any agreement to the contrary (RA 1968, s22(2)). However, both parties may apply jointly to cancel the registration (see (c)(vii) below). If the registered rent is higher than the rent for the statutory period (see (i) above), then the latter rent may be increased up to the registered rent by the landlord serving a notice of increase taking effect not earlier than the date of registration of the rent, nor more than four weeks before the notice of increase is served (RA 1968, s22(2)(b), (3): though this is subject to special phasing provisions (see (c)(vi) below)). The notice may thus have limited retrospective effect.

(c) The system of registration of rents under regulated tenancies   We have seen that, in determining rent limits, it is important to ascertain whether the rent has been registered. We shall now look at this rent registration system.

(i) Rent officers and rent assessment committees   It is the job of the rent officer to fix a 'fair rent' for a regulated tenancy on application. There are about 320 rent officers in England and Wales, and objections to their decisions are taken to a rent assessment committee (usually consisting of a lawyer, a valuer, and a lay member). An appeal lies from a rent assessment committee to the High Court on a point of law only (Tribunals and Inquiries Act 1971, s13(1)).

(ii) Applications and procedure   An application for registration may be made by the landlord or tenant or both (RA 1968, s44(1)), or by a local authority (RA 1968, s44A). The application must be in the prescribed form (form RR1) and contain a statement of the proposed rent (RA 1968, s44(2)). No fees are payable, and the rent officer cannot make an order for payment of costs. After the rent officer receives the application, the subsequent procedure is, briefly, as follows (RA 1968, Sch 6): the rent officer may by written notice obtain further information from the parties, and will give the non-applying party a chance to make representations to him; then, if the application is a joint one or no representations are made by the non-applying party, and the rent officer considers the proposed rent is fair, he may register that rent without further proceedings and notify the parties accordingly.

But where representations are made or he does not consider the proposed rent to be fair, he serves a notice on the parties informing them of the time and place at which he proposes to consider the fair rent, in consultation with the parties. For this purpose he will also normally inspect the property. After the hearing (see (iii) below) he will determine and register a fair rent or confirm the existing rent and note the confirmation on the register, and notify the parties accordingly. A dissatisfied party may object within twenty-eight days, in which case the rent officer must refer the matter to the rent assessment committee (an out of time objection may also be referred). Both parties may make written or oral representations before the rent assessment committee.

The procedure is the same where it is desired to secure alteration of an existing registered rent, but applications for alteration by landlord or tenant alone cannot be entertained before the expiry of three years (tenant's application) or two years and nine months (landlord's application) from the last registration or confirmation, except on the ground of change of circumstances (RA 1968, s44(3), (3A)).

The Francis Report noted that tenants' applications were running at a low level: landlords were responsible for 70 per cent of all applications, and 90 per cent of these landlords gained increases: but where tenants did apply, 85 per cent of them achieved reductions (Cmnd 4609, p. 16). Thus a tenant considering an application should not be frightened that the rent officer will increase the rent.

(iii) The hearing   The keynote of proceedings before both rent officers and rent assessment committees is informality: although each party may be represented by a 'person authorized by him' (whether or not a lawyer), the rules of evidence are not strictly observed, nor is evidence given under oath; indeed, since legal aid is not at present available for representation at such proceedings (see ch 13(A)(2)), the tendency is for the tenant to be professionally represented in far fewer cases than the landlord (Francis Report, Cmnd 4609, p. 51) (but the legal advice scheme enables some help to be given by a lawyer: see ch 13(A)(1)). The Francis Report did not favour professional representation, one reason being that there is 'little scope for advocacy' since the officers or committees tend to rely very much on their own knowledge of important matters like 'scarcity' (Cmnd 4609, pp. 52-3).

(iv) Assessing a 'fair rent'   The RA 1968, s46 specifies those matters which must be taken into account, and those to be disregarded, in arriving at a fair rent.

Regard must be had to 'all the circumstances', and in particular to 'the age, character, locality and state of repair of the dwelling-house', and 'the quantity, quality and condition' of any furniture provided. Thus e.g. if the landlord has failed to carry out his repairing obligations, the disrepair will be relevant in assessing the fair rent: a surveyor's evidence is valuable here.

Certain other matters are directed to be disregarded. First, the rent officer must disregard the 'personal circumstances' of the parties: thus e.g. the tenant's poverty is not relevant for fair rent purposes (but may be material in considering his eligibility for a rent allowance: see ch 11 (A)). Second, the rent officer must disregard any disrepair of the property, ill-treatment of any furniture provided, or other defect attributable to a failure by the tenant or his predecessor to comply with the terms of the tenancy (i.e. if the tenant fails to obey the terms of the tenancy, the rent shall not be diminished: though, as we saw, disrepair caused by the landlord's default is material). Third, any improvement to the property or its furniture carried out by the tenant or his predecessor other than under the terms of the tenancy must be disregarded (i.e. if the tenant carries out improvements when under no obligation to do so, the rent does not increase). Fourth, the addition of certain amenities to the locality, and any deterioration in or disappearance of amenities, must be disregarded: if the provision or improvement of an amenity in the locality is to be disregarded for these purposes, the provision or improvement must have been made at the cost of a person other than the landlord or a superior landlord (unless it was provided or improved by a public body which is a superior landlord), and if the deterioration in or disappearance of amenities in the locality is to be disregarded, the deterioration or disappearance must not have been due to any act or omission of the landlord or a superior landlord; further, in order to be disregarded the amenities must have been provided or improved, or must have deteriorated or disappeared, after the date of the earlier application for registration (where the rent is already registered), or after 8 March 1971 (where no rent is yet registered).

But the fifth and most difficult matter which must be, in effect, disregarded is 'scarcity value'. If demand for rented property in a particular area exceeds supply, the market rent will obviously be higher than if there was no scarcity. By the RA 1968, s46(2), it must be assumed for 'fair rent' purposes that there is no scarcity; but a set-off under s46(2) can only be made on the basis of shortage over a really substantial area: a scarcity within a small area caused by a particular amenity is too limited for consideration under s46(2): Metropolitan Holdings v Finegold [1975] 1 All ER 389. The Francis Report found that in practice evidence of scarcity is hardly ever presented by the parties, so that rent officers and rent assessment committees rely on their own local knowledge as to e.g. the availability of council housing: they do not now assess scarcity as a percentage of the market rent, but tend to find the fair rent of unfurnished properties by looking at a combination of the registered rents for comparable properties, the market rents of properties for which there is no scarcity, and the various conventional valuation criteria, e.g. fair return on capital value, i.e. capital value with vacant possession: Mason v Skilling [1974] 3 All ER 977, HL; the fair rent thus calculated will be less than the market rent where there is a scarcity element, and the Report concluded that registered rents are on the average about 20 per cent lower than the related market rents (Cmnd 4609, pp. 58-9, 62). If the property is furnished, an additional sum must be added to give the landlord a reasonable return for the furniture.

In arguing for or against a particular rent, the tenant should refer to comparable registered rents in the area: for this purpose he can search the rent officer's register, which is open to free public inspection; such a search may give the tenant valuable ammunition, for the 'comparables' approach seems now to be preferred by rent officers, rent assessment committees, and indeed the courts (Tormes Property Co Ltd v Landau [1970] 3 All ER 653, 655; Mason v Skilling [1974] 3 All ER 977, HL).

(v) Entry on the register   Once determined, the fair rent (or note of confirmation) is entered on the register. The amount must include any sums payable by the tenant to the landlord for the use of furniture or for services (RA 1968, s47(1)). Where the landlord bears the rates, the registered rent must exclude the rates (i.e. it will be the net rent), but the fact that the rates are so borne must be noted on the register, and the rates can be added to the rent limit and so recovered from the tenant (RA 1968, s47(2), (3)). Further, the fair rent may be registered as variable to take account of agreed payments to the landlord varying with the cost of services, maintenance or repairs (RA 1968, s47(4)).

Upon registration, the fair rent normally has retrospective effect back to the date of the application, and that date will be entered in the register (RA 1968, s48). Thus the tenant can recover any rent paid between application and registration in excess of the registered rent (see (e) below).

(vi) Phasing of rents   Where the tenancy has become regulated under the 'qualification certificate' or 'general decontrol' procedure (see (A)(3)(b) above), or where certain grant-aided improvements have been completed prior to first registration, any increase up to the registered rent is to be phased under detailed regulations (HFA 1972, s38, Sch 6).

Where a regulated tenancy is outside these 'phasing of increase' provisions of the 1972 Act, it will normally come within the general 'phasing of increase' provisions in the HRSA 1975, s7, under which the landlord may gradually increase the rent of a regulated tenancy up to the registered figure by notices of increase (see (a)(ii), (b)(ii), above), but only to the extent permitted by Sch 2 of the 1975 Act; this does not however affect rent increases under the RA 1968, s47(4) (variable rents: see (v) above): HRSA 1975, s7(5). Sch 2 of the 1975 Act provides for phasing over a period of two years beginning with the date of registration of the rent, whether before or after the coming into force of the Act (11 March 1975), save that if a rent is registered between 8 March 1974 and 11 March 1975, the two-year period runs from 11 March 1975. During the relevant two-year period, and as regards periods in respect of which rent is due after 11 March 1975 ('rental periods'), a landlord's notice of increase can only have a limited effect: for a rental period beginning during the first of the two years, the permitted increase is an increase up to an amount which is the total of the recoverable rent immediately before registration (the 'previous rent limit'), added to either the sum of 40p per week, or one-third of the registered rent less the previous rent limit, whichever is the greater (Sch 2, para 3(2)); and for a rental period beginning during the second of the two years, the permitted increase is an increase up to an amount which is the total of the previous rent limit, added to either the sum of 80p per week, or two-thirds of the registered rent less the previous rent limit, whichever is the greater (Sch 2, para 3(3)); however, further detailed adjustments are needed where the registered rent includes a payment in respect of services (Sch 2, para 2).

(vii) Cancellation of registration   We have seen that the registered rent is the maximum that can be charged, whether the regulated tenancy is protected or statutory, 'notwithstanding anything in any agreement' (RA 1968, ss20(2), 22(2)), and that a 'rent agreement with a tenant having security of tenure' cannot be entered into where there is a subsisting registration (HFA 1972, s43). But the parties may now jointly apply for cancellation of the registration, thus avoiding the need to apply for a new registration, and substituting their agreed higher rent for the registered rent (RA 1968, s48A). If the following conditions are satisfied, the rent officer must cancel the registration: the application must be made by the parties jointly, and accompanied by a copy of the rent agreement (meaning an agreement increasing the rent under a protected tenancy or granting a new tenancy at a rent exceeding the old one); this rent agreement must not take effect before the expiration of three years from the date of the last registration or confirmation of the rent, and the tenancy must not be capable of ending (except on the tenant's breach of the tenancy) earlier than twelve months after the date of the application.

The tenant is protected in two ways: the rent officer must be satisfied, before he can cancel, that the substituted rent under the agreement does not exceed a fair rent; and a fresh registration can be applied for at any time after cancellation.

(d) Rent limit for controlled tenancies   Those controlled tenancies surviving the decontrol procedures of the HFA 1972 (e.g. because of unfitness: see (A)(3)(b) above) have a rent limit imposed by the RA 1968, s52: the basic limit is a rent of which the annual rate is equal to the aggregate of:

(i) the 1956 gross value of the property (RA 1968, Sch 8), multiplied by the 'appropriate factor' (RA 1968, Sch 9);

(ii) the annual amount of rates borne by the landlord for the rental period including 6 July 1957 (RA 1968, Sch 4);

(iii) the annual amount agreed by the parties or determined by the court as a reasonable charge for any services for the tenant provided by the landlord during the rental period including 6 July 1957 or for any furniture which the tenant was entitled to use during that period.

Adjustments to this rent limit may be made to take account of subsequent variations in the landlord's rates (RA 1968, s54), or in the provision of services or use of furniture (RA 1968, s55); also, increases may be made in respect of subsequent improvements (RA 1968, s56) or repairs (HRSA 1975, s10). If the landlord fails to repair, and the tenant is not responsible for the repairs, the tenant can apply to the local authority for a 'certificate of disrepair' resulting in a reduction of rent (RA 1968, Sch 9).

Protected and statutory tenancies   Having ascertained the rent limit, the landlord cannot automatically raise the existing rent to that level: where the controlled tenancy is statutory, he may raise the rent by serving a notice of increase giving at least three months' notice (RA 1968, s53); but if the tenancy is still protected, i.e. contractual, the landlord can only raise the rent if the tenancy so provides (RA 1968, s60(1)), though if he serves a notice of increase and the protected tenancy could, by a notice to quit served at the same time, be brought to an end before the date specified in the notice of increase, the notice of increase shall operate to convert the protected tenancy into a statutory tenancy as from that date (RA 1968, s60(2)).

Level of controlled rents   Controlled tenants, as may be expected, pay a greatly reduced rent in comparison with regulated tenants: in 1971 the government stated that controlled tenants were 'being subsidised by their landlords' and that the typical rent was 85p a week outside London and £1.50 a week in London ('Fair Deal For Housing', Cmnd 4728, para 6).

(e) Recovery of overpayments   Whether the tenancy is regulated or controlled, the landlord cannot recover more than the relevant limit, and if the tenant has overpaid, the excess can be recovered from the landlord by deduction from future payments of rent or by action provided the excess was paid not more than two years previously (RA 1968, ss33, 62). A regulated tenant can similarly recover any excess rent paid to a landlord who has failed to observe any of the requirements of a 'rent agreement' (HFA 1972, s46: see (1)(a)(i) above).

It is an offence to make an entry in a rent book or similar document indicating that a tenant is in arrears in respect of an irrecoverable sum (RA 1968, ss33, 62), but the landlord does not commit an offence simply by charging more than the relevant limit (though the Francis Report recommended the creation of such an offence, pointing out that 27 per cent of tenants in Greater London with registered rents were paying more than the registered figures: Cmnd 4609, p. 117).

(2)   Part VI Lettings
A rather different system of registration of rents applies to Part VI lettings.

(a) Rent limit   No rent limit is normally imposed until a rent tribunal has had the contract referred to it (see below). But once a rent has been registered after determination by a rent tribunal, that is the maximum recoverable rent, regardless of changes of tenant (RA 1968, s76(1)); however, the landlord can add the rates if paid by him (s76(1A)), and an application can later be made for reconsideration of the registered rent (see (b)(ii) below).

(b) The system of registration of rents for Part VI lettings

   (i) Rent tribunals   The registration of rents for Part VI lettings is exclusively in the hands of rent tribunals, and outside the jurisdiction of rent officers or rent assessment committees. There are roughly forty rent tribunals in England and Wales, and each tribunal normally consists of a chairman (usually a lawyer), a valuer and a lay member. An appeal lies on a point of law to the High Court (Tribunals and Inquiries Act 1971, s13(1)).

   (ii) Applications and procedure   The application for registration may be made by landlord, tenant or local authority (RA 1968, s72(1)): a tenant normally applies on form FR2/3, together with a statement of particulars on form FR5. No fees are payable, and the tribunal cannot make an order for payment of costs. But the tenant may be better off claiming a rent allowance (see ch 11(A)), rather than applying to a rent tribunal, in view of the relative ease with which a disgruntled landlord can end a Part VI letting (see (D)(3)(b) below).

   The subsequent tribunal procedure is as follows: the landlord is informed of the application and requested to give particulars of the property and tenancy on form FR4; the members of the tribunal then inspect the property, usually on the day of the hearing; after the hearing (as to which see (iii) below) the rent decided on will be registered with the local authority (RA 1968, s74).

   Either party, or the local authority, can apply for reconsideration of an already registered rent, but applications for alteration by landlord or tenant alone do not have to be entertained before the expiry of three years from the last registration or reconsideration, except on the ground of change of circumstances (RA 1968, ss73(5), 75).

   (iii) The hearing   The proceedings are informal, and the Francis Report noted that the parties are 'seldom represented, the great bulk of the landlords as well as the tenants being individuals' (Cmnd 4609, p. 144); however, some professional help can be given under the legal advice scheme (see ch 13(A)(1)). The rules of evidence are not strictly followed, nor is evidence given on oath. The tribunal members will elicit the relevant information from the parties and witnesses.

   (iv) Assessing the rent   The Part VI code gives less indication of the matters to be considered in assessing the rent than the fully covered code. The tribunal, after making such inquiry as it thinks fit and hearing representations, may approve the rent, or reduce or increase it to such sum as it thinks reasonable, or dismiss the reference (RA 1968, s73(1)). However, if a rent has already been registered for the property under the 'fully covered' provisions, the tribunal cannot reduce the rent under the Part VI letting below that registered figure (RA 1968, s73).

The usual method of assessment, as noted in the Francis Report (Cmnd 4609, pp. 146-50), is for the tribunal initially to find what would be a reasonable rent if the property were unfurnished, disregarding for this purpose any 'scarcity value' in the market rent: it will accordingly look at fair rents registered for comparable unfurnished properties in the area. Then the tribunal will add to the 'unfurnished' rent a sum to cover the landlord's costs plus a reasonable profit for providing furniture, and all services in fact provided even though not under contractual obligation. It is important for the tenant to search the local authority's register (see (v) below) before the hearing, and find a 'comparable' registered Part VI letting with a lower rent.

A study of rent tribunal cases in London, also referred to by the Francis Report, showed that, of the 100 cases examined, in 63 cases the tribunal reduced the rent, the average reduction being of 15.3 per cent (Cmnd 4609, p. 456).

(v) Entry on the register   After the hearing the tribunal tells the local authority of its decision, and the local authority must then register details of the contract, the property, and the rent (RA 1968, s74 (1),(2)). If the landlord pays the rates, this must be noted on the register, but the rates must be deducted from the registered rent (s74(2A)); however, they can be recovered from the tenant in addition to the registered rent (s76(1A)). The register is open to free public inspection.

Upon registration of a reduced rent, the reduction is effective from the date of registration only (RA 1968, s76(1): cf. regulated tenancies, where the tenant benefits from the retrospective effect of registration: see (1)(c)(v) above).

(c) Recovery of overpayments   As we have seen, the registered rent is the maximum recoverable by the landlord. Any excess paid is recoverable by the tenant (RA 1968, s76(2)). Contrary to the 'fully covered' position (see (1)(e) above), any person requiring or receiving an excessive sum also commits a criminal offence (for which only the local authority can prosecute), and the convicting court can order repayment of the excess to the tenant (RA 1968, s76(3), (4)). Thus a tenant who knows of the registered rent but offers more may himself be guilty of aiding and abetting the landlord's crime. The Francis Report noted evidence of landlords charging rents above the registered figures, but pointed out that there is no obligation on the landlord to inform a new tenant of an existing registration other than by making the prescribed entry in the rent book, and many furnished weekly tenants have no rent book (Cmnd

4609, p. 158).

(3)   Premiums
Any person who requires or receives a premium (i.e. broadly, a capital sum) as a condition of the grant, renewal, continuance or assignment of a protected tenancy (RA 1968, ss85, 86), or a Part VI letting whose rent is registered (s87), commits a criminal offence (subject to certain exceptions), and the person paying the premium may recover it (s90). 'Premiums' include refundable deposits (s92), excessive payments for furniture and fittings (ss88, 89, and 92), certain advance payments of rent in the case of regulated tenancies (s91), and payments to third parties (Elmdene Estates Ltd v White [1960] 1 All ER 306, HL). A requirement that the tenant must pay his landlord's legal costs can amount to a premium.

(4)   Rent Books
The purpose of a rent book is primarily to set out the receipts for rent; it does not normally include the actual contract of letting, which is often made orally.

The landlord is only under a duty to provide a rent book if the rent is payable weekly, and the rent does not include a payment for board the value of which forms a substantial part of the rent (Landlord and Tenant Act 1962, s1). This limited obligation applies whether or not the letting is within the Rent Acts.

The rent book must contain:

(i) the name and address of the landlord;

(ii) if it is a Part VI letting, particulars of the rent and other terms of the contract, and the information required by SI 1972/1827 as amended by SI 1973/1055 (this includes information about the tenant's rights regarding rent and security);

(iii) if it is a fully covered tenancy, the information required by SI 1972/1827 and 1973/1055;

(iv) a summary of the overcrowding provisions in the HA 1957 (s81 of that Act: see ch 12(C)(1)); and

(v) details of the local rent allowance scheme (HFA 1972, s24(11); SI 1972/1827, 1973/1055; for rent allowances, see ch 11(A)).

Failure to comply with these requirements results in the landlord being guilty of a criminal offence (L & TA 1962, s4: local authorities have been urged to prosecute: MHLG Circular 59/1962, para 3); but he may nevertheless recover rent from the tenant (Shaw v Groom [1970] 1 All ER 702, CA).

The Francis Report noted that many weekly tenants had no rent book, and that a landlord who retains custody of a rent book may still technically be 'providing' it within the 1962 Act; the Report pointed out that 'rent books are perhaps the most important and effective vehicle for conveying information to tenants about their rights under the Rent Act', and that a fully paid up rent book is required by some local authorities when allocating council accommodation (see ch10(A)(1)(c)); it was therefore suggested that the 'weekly' limit in the 1962 Act should be extended, and that the book should remain in the tenant's custody (Cmnd 4609, pp. 216-17).

(C)   The Condition of the Property

A fertile source of dispute between landlord and tenant is the problem of responsibility for repairs. The old rule was that landlords were under no duty to make their properties fit for habitation or otherwise to repair them, and they would often impose onerous repairing obligations on their tenants. Such burdens have now largely been lifted from short-term tenants (including statutory tenants: see (A)(2)(b) above), by a hotchpot of implied obligations imposed on landlords by Parliament and the judges. Some tenants have trouble in identifying and contacting their landlords concerning repairs, e.g. where rent is paid through agents: however, every residential tenant can now make a written demand to the landlord's agent for the landlord's name and address, and must also be sent the name and address of anyone taking over the landlord's interest (HA 1974, ss121-2).

(1)   Implied Obligations on the Landlord
(a) Lettings for less than seven years: covenant to repair   If a landlord lets a house (or part of a house) after 24 October 1961, for a term of less than seven years, then the HA 1961, ss32-3, impose on the landlord the following implied covenants:
    (i) to keep in repair the structure and exterior (including drains, gutters and external pipes), and
    (ii) to keep in repair and proper working order the installations for the supply of water, gas and electricity, and for sanitation (including basins, sinks, baths and sanitary conveniences), and for space heating or water heating.
    The obligation to 'keep' in repair obliges the landlord to put property in repair if it is in disrepair at the start of the tenancy (Proudfoot v Hart (1890) 25 QBD 42, CA). The Act provides that the landlord cannot foist these responsibilities on to the tenant, unless a county court so allows with the parties' consent. The landlord may enter and view the state of repair on giving twenty-four hours' written notice (and where it is a protected or statutory tenancy he has a general right to enter and carry out repairs under the RA 1968, ss12(2), 112).
    There are certain limitations on the landlord's liability, however: he is

not responsibile for repairs which the tenant must carry out through having broken his obligation to use the premises in a 'tenant-like manner' (i.e. to take proper care of the property), nor where the property has been damaged by fire, flood or other inevitable accident. Further, in order to be liable the landlord must know that repairs are required: it has been held that a landlord who is unaware of the defect will be free of liability for resulting damage even where, because the defect was hidden, the tenant was quite unable to tell the landlord about it (O'Brien v Robinson [1973] 1 All ER 583, HL); but if the landlord's employee knows of the defect, this will fix the landlord with knowledge (Sheldon v West Bromwich Corp (1973) 25 P & CR 360, CA). Since the landlord has no incentive to inspect, a tenant who is aware of a defect should inform the landlord in writing forthwith.

Where the landlord breaks these implied covenants, the tenant may sue him for damages, and/or repudiate the tenancy.

(b) Lettings at low rents: fitness for human habitation   If a landlord lets a house (or part of a house) at a rent not exceeding £80 p.a. in inner London or £52 p.a. elsewhere at the start of the tenancy (or half these figures if the tenancy commenced before 6 July 1957), then by the HA 1957, s6 there is implied a condition that the house is fit for human habitation at the commencement of the tenancy, and an undertaking that the landlord will keep it so throughout, even though the rent later exceeds the limit. 'Rent' here does not mean rent net of rates or other outgoings, but rather the actual agreed rent paid to the landlord, regardless of whether the landlord pays the rates etc (Rousou v Photi [1940] 2 All ER 528, CA). For the decision as to whether a house is 'fit', see ch 12(A)(1). Section 6 will, however, be excluded if the house is let for three years or more on the terms that the tenant will render it fit for human habitation.

There are similarities between s6 and the HA 1961, ss32-3, (see (a) above), for the parties cannot, save as mentioned above, contract out of the implied condition and undertaking (not even with the court's blessing); the landlord may enter and view the state of repair on giving twenty-four hours' written notice; and the landlord must be aware of the defect which renders the house unfit if he is to be liable (McCarrick v Liverpool Corp [1946] 2 All ER 646, HL). Further, where the landlord breaks the condition the tenant can sue for damages and/or repudiate the tenancy; damages alone can be claimed for breach of the undertaking. But there will only be a breach of s6 if the house is capable of being made fit at reasonable expense (Buswell v Goodwin [1971] 1 All ER 418, CA).

(c) Furnished lettings: fitness for human habitation   Where a landlord lets a furnished house, there is an implied condition that it shall be reasonably fit for human habitation at the start of the tenancy (but the landlord is under no obligation to keep it thus fit). It has been held that an action lies on this condition if e.g. the house is infested with bugs, or if the last occupier suffered from pulmonary tuberculosis, or if the drains are defective. The tenant may sue for damages and/or repudiate the tenancy. This condition evolved from case law, not statute.

(d) Non-derogation from grant   Where the tenant has the right to share common facilities, e.g. a kitchen or a lavatory, the shared area will be excluded from the letting since there is no exclusive possession; thus the above implied obligations are inapplicable. But such a right to share can be an easement (Miller v Emcer Products Ltd [1956] 1 All ER 237, CA), so that if the facilities become unfit through disrepair the tenant may sue for breach of the landlord's general obligation not to derogate from his grant (i.e. not to render the interest granted materially less enjoyable).

(e) General liability in tort: occupier's liability and defective premises   So far we have looked at the implied contractual obligations of the landlord which benefit the tenant alone: but the landlord may also be liable under the general law of tort to third parties on the premises (e.g. the tenant's family or visitors) through the provisions of the Occupiers' Liability Act 1957. Basically, this Act imposes (s2) a 'common duty of care' on the 'occupier' to ensure that people lawfully on the premises will be 'reasonably safe'. Normally, the 'occupier' will be the tenant. But the landlord could be liable as 'occupier' for defective common parts (staircases, hallways, etc) which he keeps in his possession, and he cannot exclude this liability to the tenant's visitors by any provision in the lease (s3): such exclusion would only be effective with regard to his contractual liability as against the tenant.

Moreover, the landlord may be liable to third parties in tort for defective premises even if he is not an 'occupier' within the 1957 Act, s2. For by the Defective Premises Act 1972, s4, where the landlord is under an obligation to the tenant (either expressly or by the HA 1957 or HA 1961: see (a),(b) above) for repair of the premises, or has the right to enter and repair, then the landlord owes to 'all persons who might reasonably be expected to be affected by defects in the state of the premises' a duty to take reasonable care to see that they are 'reasonably safe from personal injury or from damage to their property' caused by such defects, provided he knows or ought to have known of the defect in question. Further, the parties cannot contract out of the 1972 Act.

(2)   Remedies for Breach
(a) Going to court   The obvious remedy by court action is damages (including e.g. damages for personal injuries caused by the disrepair). But the court may also order specific performance by the landlord of his repairing covenants: HA 1974, s125.

(b) Going to the rent officer or rent tribunal   The tenant may secure a reduction in his rent from a rent officer or rent tribunal on account of the disrepair (see (B)(1)(c),(B)(2)(b) above).

(c) Going to the local authority   The tenant can request (and sometimes require) the local authority to force the landlord to repair under the Housing and Public Health Acts (see ch 12). This course is often preferable to court action.

(d) Going it alone   The tenant cannot simply stop paying rent in retaliation for the disrepair. But he has an 'ancient common law right' to pay for the necessary repairs himself and then deduct the cost from future rent (Lee-Parker v Izzet [1971] 3 All ER 1099): before having the work done, he should fully inform the landlord of his proposals and send him the builder's estimate, and to be absolutely safe, a county court declaration should be obtained authorizing this course (coupled with the necessary claim for damages); see further S. Sedley, (1973) LAG BUL. 173, (1974) LAG BUL. 161.

(D)   Ending the Tenancy

A tenancy, like a marriage, is easy to enter into but difficult to end. It will be seen that there are certain general fetters on a landlord who seeks to turn his tenant out, whether or not the premises are within the Rent Acts, but where the Rent Acts apply the restrictions are considerably more onerous. Not surprisingly, frustrated landlords have sometimes tended to resort to extra-legal measures to displace recalcitrant tenants, and the Francis Report recorded disturbing evidence relating to landlords who stamped on bedroom floors to keep tenants awake at night, turned off essential services, removed slates from the roof to let the rain in, and even assaulted tenants with knives and threw petrol bombs into their letter boxes (Cmnd 4609, p. 108).

(1)   Methods of Ending a Contractual Tenancy

We have seen that a protected tenancy remains contractual in nature (see (A)(2)(a) above): thus in order to end it, the landlord must first end the contractual term, before he can seek to establish one of the necessary Rent Act grounds for possession (see (3)(a) below). The Rent Acts simply impose further restrictions on a landlord who has already ended the contractual tenancy at common law, and we must therefore briefly consider the more important ways in which such a contractual tenancy may be ended (the details are outside the scope of this book).

(a) Automatic determination   This will arise where the tenancy is for a fixed term, e.g. three years, rather than periodic, e.g. weekly. A fixed term will end automatically at common law when the term expires, without the need for a notice to quit (unless expressly required by the contract).

(b) Notice to quit   Where there is a periodic tenancy, a precise and unequivocal notice to quit, expiring at the end of a completed period, is necessary to end it (and such a notice is also required if a fixed term tenancy provides for it). Subject to contrary agreement, if the periodic tenancy is yearly, half a year's notice is needed, and in other cases a full period's notice must be given (e.g. one month's notice expiring at the end of a month of the tenancy for a monthly tenancy). Further, by the RA 1957, s16, whether or not the letting is within the Rent Acts, four weeks' notice is the minimum that either party can give to end a residential tenancy, notwithstanding any contrary agreement; the notice must be in writing, and contain prescribed information: HA 1974, s123.

(c) Forfeiture   A landlord may retake possession of the premises on the tenant's breach of covenant or contractual obligation, provided the lease expressly reserves this right (or is drafted as a series of conditions, which is rare). Special rules govern forfeiture for breaches of covenants unrelated to rent (Law of Property Act 1925, s146; Leasehold Property (Repairs) Act 1938).

(d) Surrender   This happens where the tenant gives up his lease to his landlord, thereby extinguishing it in the landlord's interest. It can be done either expressly by document, or by operation of law, e.g. where the tenant gives up the keys to the landlord who accepts them and re-lets the property to someone else.

(2)   Unlawful Eviction and Harassment

Whether or not they are within the Rent Acts, all tenants are given both criminal and civil remedies for unlawful eviction and harassment.

(a) Criminal proceedings   If the landlord forcibly takes possession, he may be prosecuted under the Forcible Entry Acts (see ch 8(B)(1)). More importantly, unlawful eviction and harassment are crimes per se under the RA 1965 (even if the tenancy is outside the Rent Acts).

First, by the RA 1965, s30(1), if any person 'unlawfully deprives' a 'residential occupier' of his occupation or attempts to do so, he is guilty of an offence unless he proves he reasonably believed that the occupation had ceased. The eviction is 'unlawful' where the tenancy is still in existence, or, if it has previously ended, where the landlord evicts without a court order (see (3)(a) below if the tenancy is 'protected' under the Rent Acts, and the RA 1965, s32, if it is not); also, forfeiture (see (1)(c) above) without a court order is unlawful where the property is still occupied (RA 1965, s31). 'Residential occupier' is widely defined (s30(5)), and would cover not only any tenant, but also a lodger (though not an unlawful squatter).

Second, by the RA 1965, s30(2), if any person, with intent to cause a 'residential occupier' to leave or to refrain from exercising any of his rights (e.g. to apply to a rent officer), does acts calculated to interfere with his peace or comfort or that of members of his household, or persistently withdraws or withholds services, that person is guilty of an offence.

The maximum penalty for either of these s30 offences is now a £400 fine and/or six months' imprisonment (magistrates' court), or an unlimited fine and/or two years' imprisonment (Crown Court): s30(3).

The police were directed by the Home Office in 1965 not to prosecute for s30 offences, and they will only intervene to stop a breach of the peace. But local authorities may prosecute (RA 1968, s108), and have been urged to do so swiftly (D of En Circular 15/1973). Thus the tenant should first report the landlord to the legal department (or harassment officer) of the local authority: a letter from the authority may suffice to persuade the landlord to mend his ways. If he is prosecuted by the authority and convicted, the court may order him to pay compensation to the tenant (Powers of Criminal Courts Act 1973, s35), and the certificate of conviction will be useful evidence in a civil court (Civil Evidence Act 1968, s11). If the authority does not act, the tenant may prosecute privately, but this is unwise, since no legal aid is available, the average penalties on conviction are low (see the Francis Report, Cmnd 4609, p. 104), there may be several months' delay before the hearing, and a civil action is much more effective (see below).

(b) Civil proceedings

(i) The possible causes of action   It is best to plead all the available causes of action: these broadly fall into two classes, breach of the terms of the lease, and tort.

Breach of the lease   The tenant may sue for breach of the landlord's express, or more usually implied, covenant or obligation for quiet enjoyment (i.e. freedom from disturbance), or, in the case of shared facilities, for breach of the obligation not to derogate from the grant (see (C)(1)(d) above).

Tort   The most suitable tort will normally be trespass (where the landlord has entered without permission), or breach of the criminal provisions of the RA 1965 (see above: this constitutes the tort of breach of statutory duty: Warder v Cooper [1970] 1 All ER 1112).

(ii) The remedies available

Damages   Various sorts of damages may be recovered. Special damages represent the loss the tenant has already incurred, and must be specifically claimed, since they will not be presumed: they will include the cost of moving, and any higher rent already paid for the new accommodation. General damages represent loss which the law presumes will be suffered, e.g. the future cost of higher rent. Aggravated damages are designed to compensate the tenant for further loss arousing the indignation of the court, e.g. for inconvenience, discomfort and humiliation (£100 in Mafo v Adams [1969] 3 All ER 1404, CA; £300 in Asinobi v Chuke [1971] CLY 6561, CA). Exemplary (or punitive) damages can only be recovered in tort (normally trespass) and are intended to punish a landlord whose conduct was calculated to make him a profit which might well exceed the compensation payable to the tenant as damages (Lavender v Betts [1942] 2 All ER 72; Cassell & Co Ltd v Broome [1972] 1 All ER 801, HL).

Injunction   An injunction (coupled with damages) is the best remedy, since it will restrain the landlord from evicting or harassing the tenant, or order the tenant's reinstatement if already evicted. Breach of the injunction is contempt of court, punishable by imprisonment or fine.

(iii) Procedure   The action may be started in the High Court, or (more usually) a county court (provided the damages claimed do not exceed £1,000). Help from a solicitor or law centre is in practice essential: the procedure is complicated, and although it can all be completed in a single day ((1973) LAG BUL. 230), the adviser must give it full attention; delay may be fatal, for the landlord may re-let following an eviction. Detailed notes for solicitors on the county court injunction procedure, together with draft particulars of claim, are obtainable from LAG. Briefly, the procedure is as follows. The initial instructions should if possible be taken under the legal advice scheme (see ch 13(A)(1)), and immediate application should then be made to the secretary of the local Legal Aid Office for an emergency legal aid certificate (see ch 13(A)(2)) if the tenant is eligible (this application should be delivered by hand and meanwhile the secretary should be telephoned for permission to commence the action). Simple particulars of claim can then be drawn up (an injunction cannot be requested by itself: it must be added to a damages claim), together with affidavits from the tenant and any witnesses.

A county court summons must then be issued. Thereafter, in an urgent case the judge may grant the injunction ex parte (without prior notice to the landlord), on the evidence of the affidavits: but this injunction will normally only last for a week, after which the landlord may object to its continuation until the main hearing. In a less urgent case, application can be made on notice to the landlord for an interim injunction lasting until the main hearing. In every case, the necessary papers must be served on the landlord.

If the landlord ignores the injunction, the tenant may ask the court to commit him to prison (or fine him) for contempt, even if the tenant decides never to return to the property (Jennison v Baker [1972] 1 All ER 997, CA).

(3)   Further Provisions applying to Rent Act Tenancies

Apart from the general provisions regarding the ending of tenancies already considered, if the tenancy is covered by the Rent Acts, additional fetters are imposed on the landlord. These differ depending on whether it is a fully covered tenancy or a Part VI letting.

(a) Fully covered tenancies

(i) The statutory tenancy   When a contractual tenancy has ended in any of the ways noted above (see (1)), then if that contractual tenancy was a protected tenancy under the Rent Acts, and the tenant continues substantially to occupy the property as his residence, a statutory tenancy will immediately arise (RA 1968, s3). The result is that the tenant is given a right to stay in possession unless the court on certain limited grounds orders him to leave (RA 1968, s10: see below), and while in possession he has the benefit and burden of all the provisions of the original contractual tenancy, so far as consistent with the Act (RA 1968, s12(1)).

A tenant is still deemed to be occupying the property for these purposes where he sub-lets part (provided he resides in the remainder); or where he is absent temporarily (provided he leaves his goods or a member of his family on the property); or even where he deserts his wife, leaving her in occupation (Matrimonial Homes Act 1967, s1(5)).

Since a statutory tenancy is not contractual in nature, it cannot normally be transferred by the tenant; but there can be a change of statutory tenant by an agreement to which the landlord is a party (RA 1968, s14), and when a statutory tenant (or even a protected tenant) dies, a statutory tenancy passes by succession to his widow, or if none (or if the tenant was a woman) then to certain members of the tenant's family, followed by a second succession on the first successor's death (RA 1968, Sch 1); and further, where the statutory tenant's marriage ends by decree of divorce or nullity, the court can order that his or her former spouse should take over the statutory tenancy (MHA 1967, s7).

(ii) Ending the statutory tenancy   How can such a statutory tenancy be ended? The statutory tenant can normally end it only if he gives such notice as would have been required under the provisions of the original contractual tenancy, or if no notice was so required, he must give not less than three months' notice (RA 1968, s12(3)); if, after giving such notice, he then yields up possession leaving no spouse in occupation, the statutory tenancy ends. But even if the statutory tenant is anxious to give possession, if he has left a deserted and blameless wife on the property who refuses to depart, the statutory tenancy cannot end unless and until the court so orders on the landlord establishing one of the grounds for possession considered below (Middleton v Baldock [1950] 1 All ER 708, CA); however, if the woman left on the property happens to be only the tenant's mistress, her presence will not be sufficient to preserve the statutory tenancy (Colin Smith Music Ltd v Ridge [1975] 1 All ER 290, CA).

More importantly, the landlord can in general only end the statutory tenancy against the tenant's will if one of certain limited grounds for possession exists, and the court considers it reasonable to make such an order (RA 1968, s10). The matter normally goes to a county court (RA

1968, s105). The more common of these grounds are:

suitable alternative accommodation is available to the tenant: this may be satisfied by an offer of part of the existing property (Mykolyshyn v Noah [1970] 1 WLR 1271, CA) or by a certificate from a housing authority that it will provide suitable accommodation; however, the court can consider not just the physical character of the accommodation offered, but also environmental matters (Redspring Ltd v Francis [1973] 1 All ER 640, CA);

the rent has not been paid or the tenant has broken any other of his obligations;

the tenant or any person for whom he is responsible has been guilty of conduct which is a nuisance or annoyance to adjoining occupiers, or has been convicted of using property for immoral or illegal purposes or of allowing such use;

the tenant or any person for whom he is responsible has caused the condition of the property or its furniture to deteriorate through waste, neglect or default;

the tenant has given notice to quit and in consequence the landlord has contracted to sell or let the property, or has taken any other steps as a result of which he would be seriously prejudiced if he could not gain possession;

the tenant has assigned or sub-let the whole property without the landlord's consent;

the property was let to the tenant in consequence of his being employed by the landlord, he has ceased to be so employed, and the landlord reasonably requires the property for another employee;

the landlord reasonably requires the property for occupation as a residence for himself, his child over eighteen, his parent, or, in the case of a regulated tenancy only, his spouse's parent; but the landlord must not have bought the property after certain specified dates, and the court cannot make the possession order if the tenant shows that greater hardship would be caused by granting the order than by refusing it;

the tenant has been charging a sub-tenant of part of the property an excessive rent.

The first ground is contained in the RA 1968, s10(1), (4), and the others in Sch 3, Pt I. In the case of all nine grounds, the judge has a wide discretion in deciding whether it is reasonable to make an order, and thus may e.g. give the tenant the chance to clear off his rent arrears so as to avoid making a possession order: the Court of Appeal will rarely interfere. The judge is given a further discretion by the RA 1968, s11: even if minded to make a possession order, he may adjourn the proceedings for such period as he thinks fit, and on making the possession order he may stay or suspend execution or postpone the date of possession, again for such period as he thinks fit: he can indeed suspend possession indefinitely: Yates v Morris [1950] 2 All ER 577, CA; he may also impose such conditions regarding rent and otherwise as he thinks fit, and on compliance with such conditions he may discharge or rescind the order.

However, in the case of certain other grounds the judge is given no discretion as to the making of the order: if the landlord establishes one of these special grounds, the order must be made (although the judge has a limited discretion to give the tenant four to six weeks in which to leave: see ch 10(E)(2)(c)).

The more important of these grounds are:

the landlord, who was the owner-occupier of the property before he let it, now requires it back for use as a residence for himself or any member of his family who resided with him when he last lived in the property (RA 1968, Sch 3, Pt II);

the landlord, who acquired the property with a view to retiring to it and then let it, has now retired and requires it as a residence; or has now died and a member of his family who resided with him at his death requires the property as a residence (RA 1968, Sch 3, Pt II);

(but the above two grounds—'owner-occupation' and 'retirement'—only apply where the tenancy is regulated, and the tenant must normally have been given prior written notice that possession might be recovered on the relevant ground, though the court can waive this last requirement);

the property is overcrowded (within the meaning of the HA 1957: see ch 12(C)(1)(a)) in such circumstances as to render the occupier guilty of an offence (RA 1968, s17);

the premises are unfit for human habitation under the HA 1957, ss16, 22 or 27: see ch 12 (A)(4)(b)(i)-(iii); this ground applies even though the premises are unfit through breach of a contractual or statutory duty on the landlord to maintain the property (Buswell v Goodwin [1971] 1 All ER 418, CA).

If the judge makes a possession order, then once the final time limit for the tenant's departure has expired, the landlord must instruct the court bailiff to remove the tenant if he remains: this procedure can take a month.

(b) Part VI lettings   The security for Part VI lettings is very different: the tenant (which term includes some licensees: see (A)(1)(b)(i) above) can apply to a rent tribunal (see (B)(2)(b) above), but it can only prevent a notice to quit from taking effect for a limited time. Thus the security only applies to a periodic tenancy, which the landlord seeks to end by notice to quit: a fixed term tenancy expiring by effluxion of time, e.g. a tenancy for one year, has no protection, nor is any security given (by the Rent Act) if the landlord seeks to forfeit for breach of covenant (see (1)(c) above).

(i) Powers of the rent tribunal   There are two ways in which security may be obtained for a periodic Part VI letting, and certain circumstances in which this security may be excluded or reduced.

Automatic security   If a tenant or a local authority has referred the rent to the rent tribunal, then if the landlord serves a notice to quit after the reference but either before the tribunal's decision or within six months after it, then that notice cannot take effect until the expiration of six months from the tribunal's decision, unless the tribunal decides on a shorter period (RA 1968, s77).

Application for security   If a tenant or a local authority has referred the rent to the rent tribunal during the current tenancy, and a notice to quit has been served, whether before or after the reference, then at any time before the expiry of the period at the end of which the notice takes effect (whether by virtue of the contract or of s77 above), the tenant may apply to the rent tribunal for an extension of that period (RA 1968, s78). Thus if e.g. the landlord delays serving his notice to quit until more than six months from the tribunal's decision on the original reference, the tenant can still apply under s78 for security before the notice expires (Preston Rent Tribunal v Pickavance [1953] 2 All ER 438, HL). But if the notice to quit has expired before the tenant applies, nothing can be done.

Assuming these conditions are satisfied, the notice to quit is suspended until the tribunal's decision, whereupon the tribunal may extend the period of the notice to quit by up to six months (s78(3)): the tenant should offer evidence of his efforts to secure alternative accommodation (e.g. registration with accommodation agencies, acceptance on the council's housing list). Successive applications may be made ad infinitum: in some cases, tenants have by such repeated applications gained up to ten years' security, but it is unusual for more than two extensions to be granted.

On a first application for security under s78, the tenant must also refer the rent to the tribunal if it has not been so referred during the current tenancy, notwithstanding the fact that, as the Francis Report recognized, he may be quite satisfied with the rent, which may have been fixed a few months earlier by the tribunal under a previous tenancy of the same property (Cmnd 4609, p. 162). Thus the question of rent will often merely be a cloak for a security application, consideration of the rent being largely academic.

Exclusion or reduction of security   There are two provisions which limit the availability of either s77 or s78 to the Part VI tenant. The first relates to notices to quit served by former owner-occupiers: by s79, the notice to quit cannot be extended if the landlord, who lived in the property before letting it, requires it back for use as a residence for himself or any member of his family who resided with him when he last lived there; but the tenant must have been given prior written notice that the landlord is the owner-occupier within s79. The second provision relates to the tenant's default: by s80, where a period of security has already been granted under s77 or s78, the landlord may apply to the tribunal for a reduction of that period if the tenant has broken the terms of the tenancy, or has been guilty of causing or permitting misbehaviour on the property, or a deterioration in the condition of the property or its furniture; if the tribunal reduces the period of security under s80, the tenant cannot subsequently apply under s78 for an extension.

(ii) Powers of the court   The landlord must apply to court (normally a county court) for possession once the period of the notice to quit (as extended where appropriate by the rent tribunal) has expired, if the tenant remains. The landlord can also go to court before a period of extension under s77 or s78 (above) has expired, whereupon the judge has the same power to reduce that period under s80 (above) as the tribunal had (s80A).

The tenant has no defence once the period of the notice to quit (as extended or reduced) has expired; but the judge has a limited discretion to give him four to six weeks in which to leave (see ch 10(E)(2)(c)). The landlord normally applies for, and is frequently awarded, costs against the tenant.

Once the final time limit given to the tenant by the judge has expired, then the landlord must instruct the court bailiff to remove the tenant if he remains (see (a)(ii) above).

References

'Report of the Committee on the Rent Acts', Chairman: H.E. Francis QC, Cmnd 4609 (1971).
'Fair Deal For Housing', Cmnd 4728 (1971).

Chapter 10

Landlord and Tenant: the Public Sector

We are here concerned with 'council housing' in the popular sense, i.e. permanent local authority housing, as opposed to emergency accommodation (for which see ch 8(A)(2)).

Most books on English land law are conspicuously silent as to the position of council house tenants, as opposed to private sector tenants: yet the former greatly outnumber the latter (see ch 1(B)), and well over four million households in England and Wales now live in council houses.

We shall see that local authorities are given considerable discretion in providing, allocating and managing council houses, but there are nevertheless certain limitations and obligations.

As regards the provision of council houses, several specific and unrelated responsibilities exist (Housing Act 1957, ss42, 76, and 91; HA 1969, s70; Land Compensation Act 1973, s39); but these haphazard provisions have been criticized by the Central Housing Advisory Committee as inadequate for the purpose of ensuring that authorities are better informed of the local housing situation: the Committee recommended that authorities should have 'a wide general duty to survey the overall housing situation in their areas' ('Council Housing Purposes, Procedures and Priorities', 1969, para 35; this report is subsequently referred to as the Cullingworth Report).

With regard to the allocation and management of council houses, the HA 1957, s111(1), lays down that the 'general management, regulation and control' of council houses is vested in and may be exercised by the local authority. Despite the apparent width of this discretion, certain restrictions are imposed, which are considered below.

(A) Choosing Tenants for Council Housing

The Cullingworth Report noted that every year local authorities allocate about 350,000 houses, about 145,000 to existing council tenants transferring to different houses and over 200,000 to households living in the private sector or without separate accommodation (para 54). Since it is becoming increasingly difficult for applicants refused council housing to secure accommodation in the private sector, the allocation policies are of vital concern.

Council houses are allocated to two main classes of people: those on the authority's housing list, and those displaced by public action. We shall deal with these two classes in turn, and then with the related problem of transfers and exchanges of council houses. While the Cullingworth Report is widely referred to in the following discussion, it is not law: it can however provide useful ammunition when approaching a local authority.

(1) Housing Lists
The commonest way of securing a council house is to reach the top of the housing waiting list. The applicant must therefore first get himself on the list, and then satisfy the necessary criteria for priority once there.

(a) Restrictions on admission to the housing list   Some authorities will not allow an applicant even admission to the housing list unless he satisfies certain requirements, relating e.g. to residence or employment in the area for a minimum period, or to the level of his income. The Cullingworth Report recommended that there should be no residential qualification for admission to a housing list, and that it should be 'fundamental that no one should be precluded from applying for, or being considered for, a council tenancy on any ground whatsoever', since only if all applications are admitted is it possible to assess needs (para 169). The Report suggested that this principle should be enshrined as a statutory obligation (in London minimum residential qualifications for acceptance on a housing list have already been abolished by the London Government Act 1963, s22(3)).

Quite apart from any such admission requirements, some private tenants in multi-occupied houses may be frightened to apply in case this alerts the authority to offences being committed in relation to multiple occupation or overcrowding, resulting in trouble for the tenants and their landlords (see ch 12(C)): this fear is justified, for the Cullingworth Report recorded that some housing tenancy committees 'sneak' by referring cases to the health department where applicants are living in overcrowded or unsuitable accommodation and the committees have decided not to re-house them (para 386).

(b) Selection schemes   Once an applicant is on the housing list, what chance does he have of getting a council house? Obviously, there is no duty to provide a council house for every family in need of it, and indeed, authorities are given a wide discretion in the selection of tenants (by HA 1957, s111 (1)). Nevertheless, a 'reasonable preference' must be given to 'persons who are occupying insanitary or overcrowded houses, have large families or are living under unsatisfactory housing conditions' (HA 1957, s113(2)). Moreover, in practice each authority works to its own favourite selection scheme. The Cullingworth Report examined several such schemes, but confined itself to formulating general principles only, since 'their detailed application in any particular area must be determined in the light of the local housing situation' (para 125). The Report recommended as follows: authorities should not take up a 'moralistic' attitude towards applicants who are e.g. unmarried mothers, cohabitees, or 'dirty' families (para 96); applicants whose health is such that they should have priority should be considered outside the normal selection procedures: urgent cases should be eligible for immediate rehousing, and others should be given an appropriate 'weighting' in the selection scheme for the degree of ill-health (para 111); the imposition of residential qualifications for rehousing (as distinct from acceptance on the list—see (a) above) was occasionally justifiable in areas of extreme housing pressure (para 154); and most importantly, more weight should be given to 'social need', assessed by taking into account both the housing conditions of the individual household (e.g. amenities, security of tenure) and the ability of that household to cope with those conditions (i.e. the 'medical' and 'social' factors of rehousing need): thus the highest priority should go to households unable to cope with their bad conditions (paras 117-18). The Report concluded its general comments on selection schemes by stating that cases of severe ill-health, social need, eviction and homelessness should all be dealt with as priorities outside the main selection schemes (para 136).

Turning to individual schemes, the Cullingworth Report commented briefly on the four main types, i.e. 'date order' schemes, 'points' schemes, 'merit' schemes and 'combined' schemes. 'Date order' schemes (where allocation is in order of date of application) were only approved in areas where there is no real housing problem and then only so long as individual hardship cases and key workers are dealt with separately (para 128). 'Points' schemes (where allocation depends on amassing sufficient 'points' for e.g. sharing, lack of facilities, room deficiency, etc.) were said to be 'excellent in concept but exceedingly difficult to devise in detail with fairness', and in practice they can be similar in effect to date order schemes if a large number of points is allocated for length of waiting time or if the range of housing need is narrow (paras 130-1); points for length of residence (as distinct from length of housing need) were said to be undesirable except for purposes of differentiating between cases of equal housing need (para 170). 'Merit' schemes (where each application is treated on its merits), although allowing judgment on factors difficult to 'point', were said to be 'unworkable' for larger authorities and incapable of publication (paras 133-4). 'Combined' schemes involve a combination of the above schemes, e.g. a 'merit' scheme for priority cases such as severe ill-health, homelessness and eviction, a 'points' scheme for ordinary families, and a 'date order' scheme for single people (para 135): the

Report noted that all authorities deal with cases of 'exceptional hardship' outside their normal schemes, but that the definition of 'exceptional' varied (para 135).

As an overlay to its general and particular comments on selection schemes, the Cullingworth Report emphasized that they should always be published and readily available (para 137); advisers should thus secure copies of their local schemes.

(c) Problem cases: the homeless, evicted tenants, and tenants with rent arrears   We are here concerned with the claim to permanent council housing of those who are homeless, have been evicted or have rent arrears (for their claim to temporary accommodation, see ch 8(A)). Although homelessness is often caused by eviction which in turn is caused by rent arrears, this is not necessarily so, and thus it is proposed to separate these three problems. We have already seen ((b) above) that the Cullingworth Report recommended that cases of homelessness and eviction should be dealt with as priorities outside the main selection schemes.

The homeless   There is a natural reluctance to allow a family to claim immediate entitlement to permanent council housing merely because it is homeless (for whatever reason), since this is regarded as unfair to those who have been on the housing list for some time. The Cullingworth Report showed great differences of practice between authorities, but the most usual action taken was to provide temporary accommodation only, although some authorities rehoused permanently people who had been in temporary accommodation for a period (para 336). As regards deliberate attempts at queue-jumping, D of En Circular 18/1974 stated that authorities are 'bound to take a serious view' of those who 'give up their accommodation and plead homelessness in a deliberate attempt to induce their Council to give them an unmerited priority for housing', but 'in the last resort if homelessness becomes a real prospect, even if it does seem to have been self-inflicted, Councils should give the degree of help necessary to secure that people are not left without shelter' (para 33): such help will no doubt continue to be mainly in the form of temporary, rather than permanent, accommodation.

Evicted tenants   If the eviction has been caused by the tenant's fault, there is once again great reluctance to give permanent council housing: 'if eviction for rent arrears merely leads to rehousing by the council . . . then why should anyone trouble to pay the rent? . . . if eviction ceases to have unpleasant consequences . . . the principal restraint upon irresponsible behaviour is removed' (T. Hearn, a London housing manager, in a letter to 'The Times', 18 February 1974).

Tenants with rent arrears   The availability of rent allowances (see ch 11(A)) should reduce this problem, but many authorities do insist on a 'clear' rent book before considering a private sector tenant eligible for a council house. The Cullingworth Report recommended that 'rent arrears should not automatically preclude a family from obtaining a council house', since such families are 'the most vulnerable', for whom authorities should take increased responsibility (para 350).

(d) Coloured people   Local authorities who allocate housing are bound by the Race Relations Act 1968, and so must not discriminate on grounds of colour, race or national origins (see LB of Ealing v Race Relations Board [1972] 1 All ER 105, HL). The Cullingworth Report, in a detailed survey of this delicate issue (paras 352-428), concluded that coloured people were handicapped by general policies and practices—e.g., being largely newcomers, they will sometimes fall foul of residential requirements; the Report rejected the suggestion that the disadvantages of coloured people should be offset by specially favourable treatment over council housing, but recommended a policy of dispersal so as to avoid concentrations of them.

(2)   Persons displaced by Public Action
Persons displaced by public action merit separate treatment as regards the allocation of council housing, and indeed many authorities deal with such cases quite apart from their general selection schemes (though some award these cases a large number of 'points', thus technically bringing them within 'points' schemes: see the Cullingworth Report, para 135).

By the Land Compensation Act 1973, s39(1), where a person is displaced from residential accommodation due to certain types of public action, and 'suitable alternative residential accommodation on reasonable terms is not otherwise available' to him, then the local authority has a duty to secure that he will be provided with such accommodation. In examining s39, it is necessary to consider what types of public action it covers, what type of accommodation must be provided, which 'persons' are protected, and the 'operative date' for eligibility.

The public action covered   Section 39(1) covers acquisition by an authority possessing compulsory purchase powers, improvement or redevelopment on land previously acquired by such an authority, the service of an improvement notice under the HA 1974, Pt VIII (see ch 12(A)(6)), and the making or acceptance of a housing order or undertaking ('housing orders' include demolition and closing orders under the HA 1957, Pt II: s29 of the 1973 Act; see ch 12(A)(4)(b)(ii),(iii)).

The type of accommodation to be provided   It has been held that a 'fully covered' Rent Act tenant (see ch 9(A)(1)) who is displaced cannot force the authority by mandamus to provide immediate and permanent council housing giving him security of tenure equivalent to that under the Rent Acts: the duty to give suitable alternative accommodation on reasonable terms is satisfied by the initial provision of temporary accommodation, followed by the offer of a council house, when available, on the usual conditions (see (B) below): R v Bristol Corp, ex p Hendy

[1974] 1 All ER 1047, CA; Savoury v Secretary of State for Wales, 'The Times', 10 December 1974. Thus the displaced person cannot jump the housing list queue. It is also open to the authority to argue that suitable alternative accomodation is in fact 'otherwise available' so that the authority need not provide it.

The persons protected   Section 39(1) does not expressly solve the problem of whether sub-tenants, 'Part VI' tenants and lodgers are entitled to be rehoused, but it would appear that they are now so entitled: this can be inferred from s39(3), which states that s39 does not apply to trespassers, or persons allowed into short-life property pending its demolition or improvement; and Circular 18/1974 stated that s39 covers 'all those displaced—whether families (with or without children) or lodgers or single residents' (App, para 7).

The 'operative date' for eligibility   If the displacement is caused by acquisition under a compulsory purchase order, or improvement or redevelopment on land previously so acquired, then to qualify for rehousing applicants must have been resident when the order was first published prior to its submission for confirmation (or if no confirmation was needed, when the draft order was prepared). If the displacement is caused by the service of an improvement notice or the making or acceptance of a housing order or undertaking, then applicants must have been resident when the notice was served, the order was made, or the undertaking was accepted (s39(6)).

(3)   Transfers and Exchanges

A sensible policy on transfer and exchange can benefit either the authority (by permitting a more equitable distribution, with e.g. the larger families taking over the larger houses), or the tenants (e.g. by relieving overcrowding or allowing them to move nearer to their work), or both.

Although the terms 'transfer' and 'exchange' have no precise legal meaning, a 'transfer' has been defined as occurring when a council tenant moves to a vacant council dwelling, while an 'exchange' occurs where tenancies are interchanged between tenants (whether in the private or public sector) with no vacant accommodation being employed (see 'Transfers, Exchanges and Rents', a Central Housing Advisory Committee Report, 1953). Thus transfers, unlike exchanges, absorb vacant dwellings which might have been used for other housing purposes. Apart from considering transfers and exchanges strictly so called, we shall look also at the related problem of transmission on death or marital breakdown.

(a) Transfers   Transfers, as noted above, may be in the council's interest or the tenant's interest. As regards 'council's interest' cases, e.g. where there is under-occupation, the authority will often, on grounds of humanity, be reluctant to force a family to move from a house it has come to regard as its home. In 'tenant's interest' cases the authority has to balance the tenant's needs against the competing claims of slum clearance cases and other priority cases on the housing list: whether the person at the top of the transfer list wins over the person at the top of the housing list will often depend on the application by the authority of its 'points' scheme to both lists.

(b) Exchanges   Exchanges are normally allowed by the authority, since they do not affect the pool of vacant accommodation needed for urgent cases, but often the authority will introduce other dwellings, vacant or occupied, thus widening the proposed exchange to benefit the authority also. Tenants proposing exchanges often seek counterparts by advertising in the press, or at newsagents' shops, etc.

Exchanges between different authorities can be useful where tenants change jobs to other areas. Mutual exchange bureaux maintained by authorities can ease this process, but the idea of a national bureau, acting as a clearing house for exchanges throughout the country, has attracted 'considerable scepticism' from authorities (Cullingworth Report, para 184). However, in the London area the Greater London Council is required by the London Government Act 1963, s22(5), to maintain an exchange bureau for its area, and can charge for use of this service, notwithstanding the Accommodation Agencies Act 1953 (see the beginning of ch 9).

(c) Removal expenses and help with house purchase costs   By the HFA 1972, s93, authorities may pay the removal expenses of any council tenant who moves, whether to another council house or not. Further, if the tenant is purchasing the house he is moving to, the authority may pay any expenses involved (other than the price): but this will not apply to the purchase of a council house owned by that authority unless the house has never been let (s93(2)).

(d) The transmission of tenancies on death or marital breakdown

Death   The succession provisions of the Rent Act 1968 (see ch 9(D)(3)(a)(i)) do not apply to council tenants (RA 1968, s5). If the original tenants were husband and wife holding on a joint tenancy, on the death of one spouse the other will normally take the tenancy automatically, and if the husband was sole tenant, in practice the widow will usually be allowed to succeed him.

Where both parents have died leaving adult children in a council house the tenancy of which was held by one or more of the parents, it is more common for a transfer to the children to be made where they have lived in the house for a considerable time than where they have only recently joined the parental household (Cullingworth Report, para 208).

Marital breakdown   The Matrimonial Homes Act 1967, s7 (allowing the court in cases of divorce or nullity to transfer the interest of a protected or statutory tenant under the Rent Acts to his or her former spouse: see ch 9(D)(3)(a)(i)) does not apply to council house tenants (RA

1968, s5), although the Finer Report recommended the removal of this restriction on s7 (Cmnd 5629, para 6.86). Further, it has been doubted whether the general power of the court to order a transfer of property on terminating a marriage (Matrimonial Causes Act 1973, s24(1)(a)) can apply to council tenancies: Brent v Brent [1974] 2 All ER 1211, 1215; however, it now appears that this power could apply to a council tenancy in an appropriate case: see Thompson v Thompson, LSG, 12 March 1975, p. 290, CA, and Hale v Hale, 'The Times', 25 February 1975, CA.

In cases of divorce, nullity or judicial separation decrees, the policy of authorities in practice appears to be 'the tenancy follows the children', i.e. the spouse who gains custody of the children will get a transfer of the tenancy (see the Cullingworth Report, para 207). In the case of other matrimonial orders (normally made by the magistrates' courts), if the order includes a non-cohabitation clause, the practice once again is for 'the tenancy to follow the children', but it would clearly be wrong for a magistrates' court to insert such a clause merely with a view to the transfer of the tenancy. In the absence of such a court order relieving the parties from the duty of cohabiting the authority will not normally involve itself in the dispute (see e.g. Bradley v Bradley [1973] 3 All ER 750, 752, CA), but the spouse remaining on the property has the normal right to stay there and pay the rent on behalf of the tenant-spouse under the Matrimonial Homes Act 1967, s1 (which applies to council houses: Tarr v Tarr [1972] 2 All ER 295, HL), until evicted by the authority.

These 'rules of thumb' operated by authorities on marital breakdown were criticized in the Finer Report (Cmnd 5629, paras 6.81-6.84).

The Cullingworth Report suggested that, as regards death and marital breakdown situations, 'the position of council tenants should be neither more nor less favourable than that of private tenants' (para 209), but this seems to overlook the basic lack of security of council tenants (see (E) below).

(B)   The Form and Content of the Tenancy Agreement

The normal council house tenancy is on a weekly periodic basis: it follows that the authority must generally supply a rent book (Landlord and Tenant Act 1962, s1: see ch 9(B)(4)), but that it is not legally necessary for the tenancy to be in writing (Law of Property Act 1925, s54(2)), and in practice 'the vast majority of local authority houses are . . . let on oral agreements which the tenant is deemed to have accepted subject to certain conditions which are set out in a leaflet, or on the back of the rent book' (Macey and Baker, 1973, p. 267). These 'conditions' will cover the matters of rent, condition of the premises, and ending the tenancy (all discussed below). They will also prohibit the tenant from assigning, sub-letting or otherwise parting with the possession of the premises or part thereof except with the council's written consent, this term being obligatory under the HA 1957, s113(5): it has been suggested that this may not prevent the taking of lodgers without consent since this is not 'parting with possession' (Davies, 1974, p. 147: and see Lam Kee Ying Sdn Bhd v Lam Shes Tong [1974] 3 All ER 137, PC), but in any event councils have been urged actually to encourage their tenants to take lodgers (Cullingworth Report, para 200; Circular 18/1974, App, para 9(vi)). Further, the conditions will normally provide that the council shall have reasonable access for purposes of inspection (see also HA 1957, s111(2), providing for inspection 'at all times'), and repair. Finally, the conditions will often impose rather more pernickety restrictions, e.g. on keeping pets and erecting television aerials.

(C)   Rents of Council Houses

The subject of council house rents has recently been a newsworthy political football (remember Clay Cross!). Before 1972, authorities had a wide discretion to 'make such reasonable charges for the tenancy or occupation of the houses as they may determine' (HA 1957, s111(1)), and there were tremendous regional variations: 'for 3-bedroom houses of the Parker Morris standard, built between 1965 and 1970, rents charged by differing authorities varied from less than £1.50 per week to nearly £7' (Macey and Baker, 1973, p. 414). In 1972 the Conservative government, following its proposals in 'Fair Deal For Housing' (Cmnd 4728), passed its Housing Finance Act: this Act (in Pts V and VI) sought to rationalize council house rents by imposing the concept of fair rents already applied in the private sector for regulated tenancies by the RA 1968 (see ch 9(B)(1)(c)(iv)), directing that authorities should be able to make a profit from council houses, and introducing bodies known as 'rent scrutiny boards' (though called by some 'latter-day Star Chambers') to supervise the fair rent fixing process (HFA 1972, ss49-51). The tenant was given very little chance to participate in this system. However, in February 1975 the Labour government enacted the Housing Rents and Subsidies Act 1975, which basically restores the pre-1972 position on council house rents.

(1) 'Reasonable' Rents
Each authority now once again has a wide discretion to charge 'reasonable' rents (HA 1957, s111(1): see above; HRSA 1975, s1(1)); but this is without prejudice to the duty to operate a rent rebate scheme under the HFA 1972 (see ch 11), and it is provided by s113(1A) of the HA 1957 that an authority 'shall from time to time review rents and make such

changes, either of rents generally or of particular rents, as circumstances may require', which 'appears to impose a duty on the authority and not merely [a power]': Smith v Cardiff Corp [1955] 1 All ER 113, 117. Further, the extent to which a profit can be made from council housing is strictly limited: an authority can make provision for a working balance in its Housing Revenue Account 'which is no larger than is reasonably necessary having regard to all the circumstances', but otherwise it 'shall not make provision for a surplus in that account' (HRSA 1975, s1(3)).

The pre-1972 case law on 'reasonable' rents is thus largely resurrected. The following principles are established.

First, every authority must balance the interests of its tenants and the interests of the 'general body of ratepayers' (Belcher v Reading Corp [1949] 2 All ER 969, 983), and the charges have to be reasonable in fact, not just in the opinion of the authority (Smith's case, above, at p. 121).

Second, the authority may operate a 'differential rent scheme', i.e. it may charge individual tenants different rents for similar accommodation based on each tenant's means, so that some may pay more than the 'economic' (or 'cost') rent, i.e. the rent at which a house must be let to cover the cost of erection, maintenance and management (Summerfield v Hampstead BC [1957] 1 All ER 221, Leeds Corp v Jenkinson [1935] 1 KB 168, CA); such a scheme survives the repeal by the HFA 1972 of the power in the HA 1957, s113(3) to grant rebates (see Luby v Newcastle-under-Lyme Corp [1964] 3 All ER 169, 172, CA; cf. Evans v Collins [1964] 1 All ER 808, 810); but the authority should have regard to the terms of its (mandatory) rent rebate scheme under the HFA 1972 (see HRSA 1975, s1(1)), and there is no obligation to operate a differential rent scheme (Luby's case and Evans's case, above): in its absence a poor tenant must rely on rent and rate rebates (see ch 11).

Third, the authority can make a blanket calculation of the total rents to be charged by reference to the 'economic' rent (see above), and it can assess its rents by reference to the needs and capacities of tenants in broad groups rather than of individual tenants (Evans's case, above).

Fourth, the view that tenants who have occupied council houses for a long time should be immune from rent increases 'has no justification at all' (Belcher's case, above, at p. 981).

(2)   Challenging 'Reasonable' Rents

The rents may be challenged as unreasonably low by a ratepayer (Evans's case, above), but are more often challenged by tenants for being unreasonably high. Before launching an action, the tenant should remember three things: first, the onus of proof lies firmly with him (Smith's case, above, at p. 121); second, at the end of the day he could receive a notice to quit for his pains (see(E)(2) below); and third, the cases 'cumulatively do emphasize . . . that very wide discretion which local

authorities have under s111 ..., and also the reluctance which courts
have shown to interfere in matters which are very often matters of social
policy and not really matters of law at all' (Evans's case, above, at p. 812):
hence the following judicial remarks: '. . . the object of the Act is not to
provide subsidized houses for people who can afford to pay economic
rents' (the Leeds case, above, at p. 181), and '. . . he has been living for
years at the expense of his neighbours . . . [he] is not entitled to insist on
being favoured above his neighbours who live outside the charmed circle'
(Summerfield's case, above, at pp. 223, 226).

If, undeterred at the prospect of the judges attempting to do what the
HFA 1972 failed permanently to achieve, the tenant wishes to take his
local authority to court, the usual procedure is to seek a declaration that
the rent scheme is ultra vires (i.e. beyond the powers of) the authority
because of unreasonableness, and therefore void, coupled where
appropriate with an injunction to prevent implementation of the scheme
(see e.g. Belcher's case and Smith's case, above).

A group of council tenants is not a class able to bring a representative
action (Smith v Cardiff Corp [1953] 2 All ER 1373, CA; cf. John v Rees
[1969] 2 All ER 274); thus each tenant should proceed as an individual.

(3)   Procedure for Increasing Rents

There is a general power for the Secretary of State to make orders
providing for the restriction or prevention of rent increases in the public
sector, or for the restriction of rents on new lettings (HRSA 1975, s11).

Quite apart from any such temporary freezes on rent increases, the rule
at common law is that, subject to contrary stipulation in the tenancy
agreement, a landlord cannot increase the rent under a periodic tenancy
unless that tenancy is first ended by notice to quit or the tenant
consents. However, in order to save the council tenant from distress at
receiving a notice to quit when all the authority really wants is a rent
increase, the authority now has power to increase the rent of a periodic
tenancy without a notice to quit, by a notice which gives the tenant four
weeks' warning of the increase and tells him of his right to terminate the
tenancy if he so wishes: Prices and Incomes Act 1968, s12 (this must now
be read subject to any statutory rent freeze). Alternatively, the authority
often provides in its tenancy conditions that the rent is 'liable to be
increased or decreased on notice being given': a reasonable notice of
increase served under such a condition is valid even though it may fail to
comply with the Prices and Incomes Act 1968, s12, and even though the
increase is dependent on the whim of the authority, since the new rent
will be sufficiently certain at the time it falls to be paid: GLC v Connolly
[1970] 1 All ER 870, CA (once again, this is subject to any statutory rent
freeze).

(D)   The Condition of the Property

(1)   Landlord's Obligations

Not unpredictably, no reference is usually made in the tenancy conditions to the council's repairing obligations. Thus the normal implied statutory and common law obligations (see ch 9(C)(1)) will apply in appropriate cases (see e.g. Sheldon v West Bromwich Corp (1973) 25 P & CR 360, CA; Summers v Salford Corp [1943] 1 All ER 68, HL).

In addition, it will often happen that a council landlord, unlike his private sector counterpart, will have originally built or arranged for the building of the house in question: if so, the tenant (whether original or subsequent) may sue the council in tort for defects in the property arising through negligent building (although this liability may be excluded by the tenancy agreement): Dutton v Bognor Regis United Building Co Ltd [1972] 1 All ER 462, CA; further, if the provision of the dwelling took place after 1 January 1974, the tenant may sue for breach of the separate statutory duty to build dwellings properly and so that they are fit for habitation, contained in the Defective Premises Act 1972, s1(1),(4), (this liability cannot be excluded by agreement: s6(3)). The council may similarly be liable in tort to the tenant for works of construction, repair, maintenance, demolition, etc. carried out negligently on or in relation to the property after erection: see Dutton's case (above) and the Defective Premises Act 1972, s3.

In view of the widespread belief that councils are under no repairing obligations (see e.g. (1973) LAG BUL. 48), it might be wise to require all council rent books to state the council's (otherwise implied) duties.

Apart from an action against the council on these implied obligations, a tenant whose property is in disrepair may choose instead to pursue the remedies offered by the housing and public health codes relating to defective premises: but as we shall see (ch 12) proceedings under these codes normally emanate from the local authorities themselves; nevertheless, there are procedures enabling a private individual to initiate action under the HA 1957, s157 and the Public Health Act 1936, s99, which could be useful to a council tenant whose landlord proves reluctant to serve the relevant notice on itself (see ch 12(A)(2), (B)(2)(b)).

(2)   Tenant's Obligations

The tenant is normally required by the tenancy conditions to keep the house clean, the garden cultivated, and to repay to the council the cost of cleansing due to his having permitted the property to become dirty or verminous, or of repairing due to his having caused damage to the structure, fixtures or fittings.

If the tenant is obliged by the conditions to effect internal decorative repairs, then this must be read subject to the Law of Property Act 1925, s147, which allows him to apply to the court in certain circumstances for relief from liability if the landlord has been unreasonable in insisting on performance of this obligation (whether by way of forfeiture or damages).

(E)   Ending the Tenancy

We have seen that a private sector landlord is subject to severe restrictions in the legal process of eviction (imposed principally by the RA 1968: see ch 9(D)(3)), but he is under no obligation to consider the wisdom of the actual decision to seek possession. By contrast, in the public sector a local authority is subject to very little legal restraint once it has decided to set in motion the legal process of eviction, but it is obliged by ministerial Circulars carefully to consider whether seeking possession is the wisest course.

It is thus proposed to consider first the matters an authority is directed to bear in mind in deciding whether to evict and, second, the eviction processes open to it.

(1)   Preliminaries to the Decision to Evict

Prior to 1972, ministerial Circulars were not illuminating as to the considerations authorities had to bear in mind in deciding whether to evict (see MHLG Circulars 58/1966, para 6; 62/1967, para 7); but in 1972 more specific advice was given regarding the most common cause of eviction, rent arrears, in D of En Circular 83/1972: this referred to the new summary county court rent action introduced in 1972, coupled with an attachment of earnings order under the Attachment of Earnings Act 1971 where the tenant has regular employment, as offering 'a better solution to this problem than recourse to eviction' (para 8).

The most comprehensive guidance yet on this issue appeared in the Appendix to Circular 18/1974, under the heading 'Evictions and Rent Arrears': this emphasized that rent arrears should not be treated 'simply as a financial problem attracting as routine penalties the issue of an eviction notice with the possible execution of any subsequent possession order', since this would be to 'create homelessness with which the local authority itself will have to deal' (see ch 8(A)(2)); instead, the Circular set out a range of eight possible measures, in ascending order of seriousness, ranging from special arrangements for rent collection where the tenant is in difficulties and checking his entitlement to rent and rate rebates (see ch 11(A),(B)), through financial support by social services authorities and direct payment of the rent element in SB from the social security office to the housing authority (see ch 4(I)), until the final possibility of an eviction notice followed by proceedings for possession is reached: but this final remedy must be used 'only if the authority is satisfied, or can arrange, that other accommodation is available'. The 1974 Circular is particularly important in the light of the argument already advanced (see ch 8(A)(2)(b)) that in the exercise of their powers under the HA 1957 housing authorities are under an implied obligation to have regard to Circulars (the relevant statutory power here being found in s111(1) of the HA 1957, which provides that the 'general management, regulation and control' of council houses may be exercised by local authorities). The Finer Report regretted that the 1974 Circular did not 'go farther and give firm guidance to local authorities that eviction simply for rent arrears is no longer tolerable' (Cmnd 5629, para 6.65).

Thus the decision to evict, especially in cases of rent arrears, should only be taken after careful consideration, and indeed the Cullingworth Report found that much 'leniency' is shown to council tenants in arrears, eviction being resorted to 'only in extreme cases' (para 345). But in areas where the housing situation is desperate, authorities will often be influenced by 'the knowledge that there are far more deserving families already living in Part III accommodation or even sleeping "under the arches", (Macey and Baker, 1973, p. 333).

(2) Eviction Processes

We have seen that the most important ways in which private sector contractual tenancies may end (subject to Rent Act protection thereafter) are through automatic determination, notice to quit, forfeiture and surrender (ch 9(D)(1)).

As regards public sector tenancies, surrender can obviously occur just as much as in the private sector. Automatic determination will however rarely occur, since as we have noted most public sector tenancies are periodic (and on a weekly basis). Forfeiture on breach of the terms of the tenancy can occur if the tenancy agreement reserves the right to forfeit or if the tenant's obligations are worded as a series of conditions, and in practice one of these methods is invariably used: nevertheless, where the tenant has broken his obligations the authority will rarely in practice bother to forfeit in view of the comparative ease with which it may end the tenancy by notice to quit. Thus notice to quit followed by a county court possession order is the normal way of ending the tenancy against the tenant's will whether he happens to be at fault or not (since, as will be seen, Rent Act protection is excluded); this process must therefore be examined in detail.

(a) Form and service of notice to quit   The tenancy agreement normally contains a term that it may be ended by four weeks' notice from either party: this is in fact the minimum period allowed by law (RA 1957, s16: see ch 9(D)(1)(b)). The notice may be signed on behalf of the authority by the 'proper officer of the authority' (this would include the housing manager and not just the clerk of the council or his lawful deputy), and any document purporting to bear his signature (including facsimile signature) is deemed to have been duly authorized by the authority: Local Government Act 1972, s234.

The methods of service of the notice are set out in the LGA 1972, s233, and include service by post: but it seems that if the ordinary post is used rather than the registered or recorded delivery services, it is open for the tenant to show he never received the notice: see Sharpley v Manby [1942] 1 KB 217, CA. If the authority cannot ascertain the tenant's new address after reasonable inquiry, it can affix the notice conspicuously to some part of the property (LGA 1972, s233(7)).

(b) Exclusion of fetters in the Rent Acts   Having duly determined the tenancy by notice to quit, the authority will not normally be hampered in court by having to prove a Rent Act ground for possession (see ch9(D)(3)(a)). This is because the RA 1968, s5, provides that where the landlord is a local authority the tenancy is neither protected nor statutory (see ch9(A)(1)(a)). But in order for this exemption to apply, the authority must show that it requires possession for the purpose of exercising its powers 'under any enactment relating to housing', by the HA 1957, s158(1): see St Pancras BC v Frey [1963] 2 All ER 124. It has been held that s158(1) is not restricted to cases where e.g. possession of compulsorily purchased property is required by the authority, and that it extends to the requiring of possession for reletting following the expiration of a notice to quit, since the power to terminate the tenancy by notice for reletting is within the power of 'general management, regulation and control' of council houses vested in authorities by the HA 1957, s111(1), which is an 'enactment relating to housing': Shelley v LCC [1948] 2 All ER 898, HL, as explained in St Pancras BC v Frey (above).

The apparent width of s158(1) is qualified by the insistence of the courts that the authority must give some evidence that it requires possession for housing purposes, rather than merely e.g. for the 'purpose of erecting a school, or widening a road, or for some other purpose which was not included in the Housing Act': R v Snell, ex p St Marylebone BC [1942] 1 All ER 612, at 614-15. The bare service of a notice to quit is thus not by itself evidence that it was given for the purpose of the authority exercising its housing powers, in the absence of further evidence of the purpose for which possession is required (St Pancras BC v Frey, above). But it would be enough for the authority to give evidence that it required the property for re-letting to someone else on the housing list (R v Snell, above; Harpin v St Albans Corp (1969) 67 LGR 479), or (perhaps) evidence that the tenancy is 'not in all respects satisfactory' without any statement of the purpose for which possesssion is required (Jenkins v Paddington BC [1954] JPL 510).

(c) The court   Until recently, an authority could swiftly recover possession in the magistrates' court under the Small Tenements Recovery Act 1838; but this procedure is no longer available after 1 October 1972, so that the authority must now use either the High Court or (more normally) the county courts: in either case, the judge may fix the date for giving possession and suspend the execution of the possession order in his discretion (see, as to the county courts, the 'County Court Rules', Order 24, r11, and Order 25, r72) and 'the usual order is from four to six weeks' (McPhail v Persons Unknown [1973] 3 All ER 393, at 398-9, CA); the time allowed must however be reasonable (see e.g. Jones v Savery [1951] 1 All ER 820, CA: three months reduced on appeal to one month; cf. GLC v Connolly [1970] 1 All ER 870, CA: order deferred for two months; contrast the position under the RA 1968, where as we saw the judge can suspend possession indefinitely: ch 9(D)(3)(a)(ii)).

The judge will normally make an order for payment of the authority's costs by the tenant.

(d) Defences   In view of what has been said above regarding the absence of Rent Act protection, it is no defence for the tenant to allege unreasonableness on the authority's part, hardship, or his unblemished tenancy record (see Shelley v LCC, above). The possible defences appear to be: (i) that in launching possession proceedings the authority has failed to take account of Circulars; (ii) that the authority does not require the property for housing purposes; (iii) that if the notice to quit was sent by ordinary post, it was never in fact received by the tenant; and (iv) that the issue of the notice to quit, though technically in order, was for the purpose of trying to recover an unlawful rent increase and is therefore ultra vires the authority (GLC v Connolly [1970] 1 All ER 870, 875, CA). The details of these points are dealt with above (and see D. Yates and J. Linden (1973) LAG BUL. 198).

(F)   General Comparison of the Council House Tenant with the Private Tenant

We have seen that the council house tenant is generally at a disadvantage when compared to his private sector counterpart. With regard to rents, the HFA 1972 sought to achieve parity but gave the council tenant much less opportunity to be heard in the assessment process than the private tenant. In the matter of repairs, although many of the implied obligations on the landlord are common to both sectors, the council tenant has to face the reluctance of the authority to serve notices on itself under the housing and public health legislation relating to defective premises.

But it is in the context of security of tenure that the council tenant is most vulnerable. Yet the extent of his insecurity seems in doubt. Thus Circular 58/1966 stated that: 'Not many families are rendered homeless as a result of eviction from council property' (para 6), and the Cullingworth Report, as we saw, found that eviction was resorted to 'only in extreme cases' (para 345); but Circular 18/1974 reported that: 'The quarterly returns made by social services authorities ... show that, outside London, most applicants for temporary accommodation ... claim that their homelessness is due to eviction by local authorities for rent arrears' (App, para 2). If the true answer to this security problem is that the council tenant has protection in practice, but not in law, so long as he behaves himself (see Sills v Watkins [1955] 3 All ER 319, 320, CA; R v Bristol Corp, ex p Hendy [1974] 1 All ER 1047, 1049, CA), then to avoid causing him distress through any apparent uncertainty, the law should be married to the practice and 'security of tenure similar to the Rent Acts protection [should] be extended to tenancies in the public sector' (Finer Report, Cmnd 5629, para 6.90).

References

'Council Housing Purposes, Procedures and Priorities', Ninth Report of the Housing Management Sub-Committee of CHAC, HMSO (1969).

'Transfers Exchanges and Rents', Fourth Report of the Housing Management Sub-Committee of CHAC, HMSO (1953).

'Report of the Committee on One-Parent Families', Chairman: the Hon. Sir Morris Finer, Cmnd 5629 (1974).

Macey, J.P., and Baker, C.V. (1973), 'Housing Management', The Estates Gazette, London.

Davies, K. (1974), 'West's Law of Housing', The Estate Gazette, London.

'Fair Deal For Housing', Cmnd 4728 (1971).

Chapter II **Financial Benefits**

We are here concerned with the provisions enabling local authorities to provide financial relief for those in housing difficulties, primarily from the viewpoint of the tenant, rather than that of the local authority or the landlord.

(A) Rent Rebates and Rent Allowances

We shall here examine the model schemes introduced by the Housing Finance Act 1972, Pt II and D of En Circular 74/1972 for local authorities to help public and private sector tenants with payment of their rent (but only in outline, since as will be seen authorities can devise their own schemes and otherwise vary the model schemes: thus advisers should always examine the particular scheme operated by the client's local authority).

The basic calculations are the same for all tenants.

(1) The Persons Eligible
(a) General eligibility   Rent rebates must be given to council tenants, and rent allowances to private sector tenants, provided in each case they satisfy the financial conditions outlined below (HFA 1972, ss18, 19). Entitlement in the private sector extends to 'fully covered' tenants, 'Part VI' occupiers, and lodgers, etc. even if they pay for board (s19(4); see ch 9 (A)).
(b) Special cases
   (i) Supplementary benefit claimants   Public or private sector tenants on SB are eligible for rent rebates or allowances, but this does not affect the claimants themselves (unless 'wage-stopped': ch 4(F)(2)) since their SB will be calculated with regard to their full rent, and the full rent must be paid (even by council tenants) to their landlords: the local authorities then pay the rebates or allowances direct to the DHSS (D of En Circular 154/1973).
   It may be better for an SB claimant to come off SB completely and

to claim the rent rebate or allowance (and a rate rebate: see (B) below) instead: see (1974) LAG BUL. 84, and D of En Circular 148/1974.

(ii) Separated 'spouses'   Where the original tenant has left the property but his spouse (or former cohabitee) remains in occupation, then if the person in occupation pays the rent, he or she may be treated as the tenant for rebate or allowance purposes (HFA 1972, Sch 4, para 1(3)).

(iii) Substitution of higher income resident   If someone residing with the tenant has a higher income than the tenant, the authority may treat that other person as the tenant for the purpose of the calculations detailed below (Sch 3, para 5), but this power should only be used 'very sparingly' (Circular 74/1972, para 21).

(2)   Calculating the Amount Payable
The rebate or allowance is basically the difference between the tenant's weekly rent and a special 'minimum weekly rent' which he must meet himself, and which depends upon the relationship between his weekly income and his weekly 'needs allowance'. But we must first define the necessary factors in this calculation.
(a)The necessary factors

(i) Income   The weekly income of the applicant and his 'spouse' (which includes cohabitee) must be ascertained. Weekly earnings are normally calculated by taking the average gross amount (i.e. before deductions) over the last five weeks if the person is paid weekly, or two months, if paid monthly (HFA 1972, Sch 4, para 3). Income will include e.g. family allowances, FIS (see ch 5), and maintenance payments. Uninvested cash exceeding £800 is treated as producing a notional weekly income of 0.1 per cent of the excess over £800 (Sch 3, para 9(4)). But the following items (inter alia) are disregarded: rent received from a sub-tenant (excluding any sums attributable to furniture or services), payments received from dependent children or non-dependants (e.g. lodgers), £2.50 of a wife's earnings, attendance allowances, SB, and the first £2 of certain other benefits and pensions (Sch 3, para 9(2)).

(ii) Rent   The rent which is eligible to be met by a rebate or allowance is calculated on a weekly basis and is normally the 'occupational element' of the full rent, less the 'occupational element' of any rent payable by a sub-tenant: the 'occupational element' is found by deducting rates, and charges for furniture and certain services (HFA 1972, s25). But if an applicant for an allowance (not a rebate) is paying an excessive rent, the authority may take a lower figure before calculating the occupational element (Sch 3, para 17; Sch 4, para 14).

(iii) Needs allowance   The tenant's weekly needs allowance, regarded as essential for basic living standards, depends on his circumstances and is as follows (Sch 3, para 8):

Single person with no dependent children	£19.35
Single parent with a dependent child or children	£26.75
'Married' couple (which includes cohabitees)	£26.75
Add, for each dependent child of a single parent or 'married' couple	£4.05

These sums are increased in cases of handicap. A child is 'dependent' if it is either under sixteen or in full-time education.

(b) The final calculation   This is dealt with by Sch 3, paras 10-14. The tenant will normally have to pay a 'minimum weekly rent', and only the balance of the eligible weekly rent (see above) will be met by the rebate or allowance, less any reduction for 'non-dependants', and subject to minimum and maximum figures. The details are as follows.

(i) The 'minimum weekly rent'   This depends on the relationship between the tenant's weekly income and his weekly needs allowance (both calculated as above).

First, where the tenant's income equals his needs allowance, then the 'minimum weekly rent' is £1 or 40 per cent of the eligible rent (see above), whichever is the greater: we shall call this figure '£X'.

Second, where the tenant's income is less than his needs allowance, the 'minimum weekly rent' is £X less 25 per cent of the difference between the needs allowance and the income: if the result of this percentage equals or exceeds £X, the 'minimum weekly rent' is zero.

Third, where the tenant's income exceeds his needs allowance, the 'minimum weekly rent' is £X plus 17 per cent of the difference between the income and the needs allowance: thus high income tenants pay the whole rent.

(ii) The basic rebate or allowance   The basic rebate or allowance will be found by deducting the 'minimum weekly rent' from the eligible weekly rent.

(iii) Reductions for non-dependants   The basic rebate or allowance must be reduced under para 12 if certain non-dependants reside with the tenant, since they are regarded as notional contributors to the rent; the weekly reduction may be up to £1.50 per non-dependant.

(iv) Minimum and maximum rebates or allowances   The final rebate or allowance figure, after the 'non-dependants' reduction where applicable, is ignored if it is less than 20p, and if it exceeds £8.00 in Greater London or £6.50 elsewhere the excess is not payable.

(3) Local Variations to the Schemes
Local authorities may depart from the model rebate and allowance schemes in the HFA 1972 outlined above, in two ways: first, they may grant a higher rebate or allowance if the applicant's 'personal or

domestic circumstances are exceptional', and second, they may make their schemes up to 10 per cent more generous (but not less generous) than the model schemes (HFA 1972, ss21-2).

(4)   Making Applications
Application forms are normally obtainable from, and returnable to, the authority's housing or treasurer's department: the relevant pay slips (see (2)(a)(i) above) should be enclosed, with proof of the amount of rent payable.

(5)   Payment of the Rebate or Allowance
The authority in practice pays a rebate by deducting it from the tenant's rent (unless he is on SB: see (1)(b)(i) above).

An allowance must be paid with regard to the 'reasonable needs and convenience of the tenant' (Sch 4, para 12 (3)(b): but see (1)(b)(i) above if he is on SB). Circular 74/1972 (as amended by Circular 148/1974, App) directs allowance payments at the same intervals as the rent is paid, save that payment at shorter intervals can be made by agreement, and payment of the allowance fortnightly is permissible if the rent is payable weekly (App F); it suggests payment through the Post Office or into the tenant's bank or savings account (para 49). Where the tenant fails to pay his rent regularly, the authority may pay the allowance directly to his landlord (HFA 1972, Sch 4, para12 (2)).

The rebate or allowance period ends after twelve months for pensioners, or seven months for non-pensioners, and any changes of circumstances within that period must be notified to the authority; further applications must be made not earlier than one month before, nor later than one month after, the end of the prior period (Sch 4, paras 4, 5 and 10).

(6)   Appeals
Although the tenant may make representations to the authority within one month of its decision (Sch 4, para 15), there is no appeal as such. But the tenant could try writing (via the D of En) to the Advisory Committee on Rent Rebates and Rent Allowances set up under the HFA 1972, s23.

(B)   Rate Rebates

The new statutory rate rebate scheme, introduced by the Local Government Act 1974, ss11-14, SI 1974/411, and D of En Circular 41/1974, is very similar to the rent rebate and allowance schemes previously considered, and can be looked at under the same framework.

(1)   The Persons Eligible
(a)   Normal 'residential occupiers'   All residential ratepayers satisfying the financial conditions outlined below must be given rebates, whether they are owner-occupiers, or public or private sector tenants (and if tenants, regardless of whether the rates are paid by the tenants directly, or as part of their rent), provided in all cases the rateable value of the property does not exceed £1,500 in Greater London or £750 elsewhere (LGA 1974, ss11, 13; SI 1974/412, reg 3).
(b) Special cases
   (i) Supplementary benefit claimants   Normally, SB claimants have their full rates included in the assessment of their requirements by the SBC (see ch 4(B)(3)): thus they cannot claim rebates unless 'wage-stopped' (SI 1974/411, reg 27; see ch 4(F)(2)), or unless their SB is less than the total rate rebate and rent rebate or allowance which they would have received had they not been on SB (SI 1974/1552, reg 3; Circular 148/1974).
   (ii) 'Poverty' cases   An authority may reduce or remit the payment of rates on 'poverty' grounds (General Rate Act 1967, s53): in such a case, the claimant will only get a rebate as to any balance of rates (LGA 1974, s14(3)).
   (iii) Substitution of higher income resident   There is a similar power to that under the rent schemes (see (A)(1)(b)(iii) above) for the authority to pick another resident with a higher income for the purpose of computing the rebate (SI 1974/411, reg 5), which is to be used 'sparingly' (D of En Circular 85/1974).

(2)   Calculating the Amount Payable
The rebate is calculated in basically the same way as under the rent schemes (see (A)(2) above), with rates taking the place of rent.
(a) The necessary factors
   (i) Income   The weekly income of the occupier and his 'spouse' (which includes cohabitee) is calculated in the same way as under the rent schemes, save that rent from a tenant or sub-tenant is included (SI 1974/411, regs 8, 18; cf. (A)(2)(a)(i) above).
   (ii) Rates   The full general (not water) rates charged on the occupier are normally brought into account, treated on a weekly basis (SI 1974/411, reg 9).
   (iii) Needs allowance   This is the same as in the rent schemes (SI 1974/411, reg 7; see (A)(2)(a)(iii) above).
(b) The final calculation   The final calculation is similar to that under the rent schemes: thus the occupier will normally have to pay the 'minimum weekly rates', and only the balance of the weekly rates will be met by the rebate, less any 'non-dependants' reduction, and subject to minimum and maximum figures, as follows (SI 1974/411, regs

10-14).

(i) The 'minimum weekly rates'   First, where the occupier's income equals his needs allowance, then the 'minimum weekly rates' are 33p or 40 per cent of the rates, whichever is the greater: we shall call this figure '£X'.

Second, where the occupier's income is less than his needs allowance, the 'minimum weekly rates' are £X less 8 per cent of the difference between the needs allowance and the income: if the result of this percentage equals or exceeds £X, the 'minimum weekly rates' are zero.

Third, where the occupier's income exceeds his needs allowance, the 'minimum weekly rates' are £X plus 6 per cent of the difference between the income and the needs allowance: thus high income occupiers pay full rates.

(ii) The basic rebate   To find the basic rebate, deduct the 'minimum weekly rates' from the full rates.

(iii) Reductions for non-dependants   There are similar reductions to be made from the basic rebate in the case of non-dependants to those under the rent schemes (see (A)(2)(b)(iii) above), but the amounts are smaller (reg 12).

(iv) Minimum and maximum rebates   The final rebate figure, after any 'non-dependants' reduction, is ignored if less than 5p, and any excess over £3.00 in Greater London or £2.50 elsewhere is not payable.

(3)   Local Variations to the Scheme
The scheme outlined above is the statutory scheme, and authorities may make their own schemes up to 10 per cent more (but in no way less) generous: LGA 1974, ss12, 14(2). So advisers must obtain the relevant scheme.

(4)   Making Applications
Application forms are normally obtainable from and returnable to the authority's treasurer's department, and the relevant pay slips (see 2(a)(i) above) should be included.

(5)   Payment of the Rebate
The rebate normally takes effect in practice by way of a deduction from the rates, and may be granted at the same intervals as the rates are paid (SI 1974/411, reg 16). The maximum rebate period, the necessity for notifying changes of circumstances. and the procedure for further applications, are all as for the rent schemes (SI 1974/411, regs 19, 20 and 25; see (A)(5) above).

(6)   Appeals
There is no appeal as such, merely a right to make representations to

the authority within one month of its decision (SI 1974/411, reg 28); but pressure on local councillors may succeed.

(C)   Grants for Improvement, Repair and Conversion

Local authority grants for improving, repairing and converting properties are not the prerogative of the underprivileged: before the Housing Act 1974 there was evidence of considerable abuse of grants by developers, causing large rent increases and evictions (Pearson and Henney, 1972), and the really poor will still often be unable to get grants by virtue of the general rules considered below, e.g. a periodic or short-term tenant (see ch 9(D)(1)(a),(b)) cannot apply and must ask his landlord to do so, a decayed property may not satisfy the requirement of fifteen or thirty years' probable life after completion of the work, and a potential applicant (owner-occupier or landlord) may be deterred by the contribution required of him towards the cost. Hence grants often go to young, middle-class people taking over working-class property (Buxton, 1973, p.167).

Nevertheless, grants can help impecunious owner-occupiers, and periodic or short-term tenants whose landlords agree to apply. If the landlord of such a tenant refuses to apply, the tenant can ask the authority to compel the landlord to provide the standard amenities (see ch 12(A)(6)); but whether the landlord does improvement work voluntarily or compulsorily, the tenant must remember that his rent can be increased as a result (see ch 9(A)(3)(b), (B)(1)(c), (B)(2)(b)). The converse situation, where a landlord wishes to use a grant to improve or convert property against his tenant's will, is considered below (see (6)).

(1)   General Outline of the Grants Scheme
There are four types of grant ('intermediate', 'repairs', 'improvement' and 'special': see below); but every application must normally satisfy certain common conditions:

(a) the property must not normally have been built after 2 October 1961 (HA 1974, s56(3));

(b) the applicant must normally have the freehold of the property, or a lease with five or more years to run (s57(3): this excludes periodic and short-term tenants);

(c) the applicant must not normally have begun the work (s57(5));

(d) unless applying for a 'special' grant, the applicant must certify his intention to reside in the property for the next four years, or to let it for the next five years (s60). Conditions (b), (c) and (d) do not apply to an application for an 'intermediate' grant where the authority is compelling the provision of standard amenities (s67(2); see ch 12(A)(6)).

If the authority refuses a grant, it must give written reasons (s80).

If the grant is approved, the authority must calculate the 'eligible expense', which varies according to the type of grant (see below), and the applicant will only receive at the most the 'appropriate percentage' of that expense, depending on where the property is situated, as follows (s59):

(a) 75 per cent (or 90 per cent in hardship cases) in a 'housing action area';

(b) 60 per cent in a 'general improvement area';

(c) 50 per cent in other cases.

An authority may declare a district a 'housing action area' under the HA 1974, Pt IV, where it is subject to housing stress (typically, a city centre or older industrial district); while it may declare a district a 'general improvement area' under the HA 1969, Pt II and the HA 1974, Pt V if it is a residential district of basically sound older houses, free of stress conditions and capable of voluntary improvement by houseowners with the aid of grants and in response to environmental improvements.

The authority can award less than the appropriate percentage of the eligible expense, save for 'intermediate' grants, but must give written reasons for so doing (s80).

To curb abuse, conditions are now imposed on all except 'special' grants relating to the future owner-occupation or availability for letting of the dwelling and lasting for up to seven years (ss73-5), on breach of which the authority can demand repayment of the grant with interest (s76).

Having considered the general provisions of the scheme, we can now turn to the individual types of grant.

(2)   The Intermediate Grant

This is designed for improvement by the provision of missing 'standard amenities', i.e. a fixed bath or shower with hot and cold water supply (normally in a bathroom), a wash-hand basin with hot and cold water supply, a sink with hot and cold water supply, and a WC (normally within the building): s58, Sch 6.

(a) Conditions for grant   The authority must approve an intermediate grant (s67(1)), provided certain conditions are fulfilled, the most important being that the dwelling must attain the 'full' or 'reduced' standard on completion of the work (s66). To attain the 'full' standard the dwelling must:

(i) be provided with all the standard amenities for the exclusive use of its occupants;

(ii) be in good repair;

(iii) satisfy certain thermal insulation requirements;

(iv) be fit for habitation under the HA 1957 (see ch 12(A)(1));

(v) have a likely future life of fifteen years as a dwelling.

The 'reduced' standard applies where the authority exercises its powers to modify any of conditions (i)-(v) (which it must do if it is compelling the provision of standard amenities and the full standard will not be attained: s67(2); see ch 12(A)(6)).

(b) Amount of grant   The authority must determine separately the proper expense of work involving solely the provision of standard amenities, and of related work of repair or replacement: the amount of the grant must then be the appropriate percentage (see (1) above) of the whole 'eligible expense': the eligible expense is the aggregate of (i) not more than the total of the amounts specified in Sch 6, Pt I for each of the standard amenities to be provided, and (ii) not more than £800 for related work of repair or replacement (s68).

(3)   The Repairs Grant

This is designed for work of repair or replacement in a housing action area or general improvement area (see (1) above) not being work associated with the improvement or provision of the dwelling (s56(2)). It is discretionary, and the authority must consider whether the applicant could finance the work himself without a grant and without undue hardship (s71 (1), (2)).

(a) Conditions for grant   Before it can approve the grant, the authority must be satisfied that the dwelling is within a housing action area or general improvement area, and will be in good repair on completion of the work (s71(3), (5)).

(b) Amount of grant   The authority must determine the proper expense of the work, and the amount of the grant cannot then exceed the appropriate percentage (see (1) above) of the 'eligible expense': the eligible expense here is the proper expense of the work up to a limit of £800 (s72).

(4)   The Improvement Grant

This is designed for the general improvement of a dwelling (beyond merely the supplying of standard amenities), or for the provision of a dwelling by converting a building (s56(2)); it is discretionary (s61(1)).

(a) Conditions for grant   The authority can only approve the grant if the dwelling will attain the 'required standard' on completion of the work (s61(3)), i.e.:

   (i) be provided with all the standard amenities (see (2) above) for the exclusive use of its occupants;

   (ii) be in good repair;

   (iii) be able to satisfy specified structural and amenity requirements (see MHLG Circular 64/1969, App B, para 7);

   (iv) be likely to provide satisfactory housing accommodation for thirty years.

The authority may modify conditions (i)-(iv) (s61(4), (5)). Where the applicant certifies his intention to reside in the dwelling (see (1) above), it must not exceed the prescribed rateable value limit (s62): this is £300 for property in Greater London and £175 for property elsewhere (SI 1974/1931).

(b) Amount of grant   The authority must determine the proper expense of the work, not more than 50 per cent of which can be for works of repair and replacement (s63). The amount of the grant cannot then exceed the appropriate percentage (see (1) above) of the 'eligible expense': the eligible expense here is the proper expense of the work up to a limit of £3,200 in normal cases, or £3,700 for the provision of a dwelling by converting a building of three or more storeys (s64; SI 1974/2004).

(5)   The Special Grant
This is designed for the improvement of a house in multiple occupation (see ch 12(C)(2)(a)) by the provision of standard amenities (see (2) above; s56(2)), and is entirely discretionary (s69(1)).

Amount of grant   The authority must decide the proper expense of the work, and the amount of the grant cannot then exceed the appropriate percentage (see (1) above) of the 'eligible expense': the eligible expense here is the proper expense of the work up to the limit of the total of the amounts specified in Sch 6, Pt I for each of the standard amenities to be provided, but further amounts can be added for the provision of more than one amenity of the same description (s70).

(6)   The Tenant's Position Regarding Unwanted Improvements or Conversions
Until now we have assumed that, if the property is tenanted, the tenant is anxious for the grant-aided work to be carried out. What is the position if he objects to such work, e.g. on the ground that it will cause him undue disturbance, or an increase in rent (see ch 9(B))?

We saw earlier that exclusive possession is essential to a tenancy (see ch 9(A)(1)(a)): thus the normal rule is that the landlord (and his surveyor, builder, etc) commits a trespass if he enters without the tenant's consent, unless the landlord is doing repairs which are his responsibility (see ch 9(C)(1)), or is permitted to enter by the lease or some statutory authority (e.g. the HA 1957, s161 where he is complying with a local authority's notice under Pt II of that Act regarding an unfit house: see ch 12(A)(3)-(5)). Where the landlord merely wishes to improve the property, and the lease is silent on the point, he can only override the tenant's objections by applying to a county court under the HFA 1972, s33: but the only work the court can authorize the landlord to carry out is that required to bring the dwelling up to the 'qualifying conditions' (s33(1)), which are that it must be provided with all the standard amenities (see (2) above) for the exclusive use of its occupants, be in good repair, and be in all other respects fit for habitation (see ch 12(A)(1)): s27(1), (4). Thus any work in excess of that required to satisfy the 'qualifying conditions' cannot be authorized; and there are additional hurdles which the landlord must surmount to succeed under s33: first, the tenancy must be statutory (whether regulated or controlled) and not contractual (s33(1): see ch 9(A)(2),(3)); second, the authority must have approved the landlord's application for a grant for the work, or have certified that the dwelling will satisfy the qualifying conditions on completion of the work (s33(2)); third, the court may impose conditions regarding the time at which the work is to be done and the accommodation for the tenant and his household whilst it is in progress (s33(3)); and lastly, in deciding whether or not to make the order, or to impose conditions, the court has a wide discretion, but it must consider all the circumstances, including any disadvantage to the tenant, the temporary accommodation available to him, and his age and health (though not his financial circumstances, which are only relevant for a rent allowance: see (A) above): s33(4).

If the court makes a s33 order, the tenant's rent is liable to increase following the work (see ch 9(B)), and if he moves out temporarily while the work is done he should safeguard his statutory tenancy by leaving some evidence of it on the property, e.g. a notice pinned to the wall (Dawn Oliver (1973) LAG BUL. 168, 169; see Roland House Gardens Ltd v Cravitz, 'The Times', 11 December 1974, CA, and Gofor Investments Ltd v Roberts, LSG, 19 February 1975, p 191, CA).

References

Pearson, P. and Henney, A. (1972), 'Home Improvement—People or Profit?', Shelter, London.
Buxton, R. (1973), 'Local Government', Penguin, Harmondsworth.

Chapter 12   **The Housing and Public Health Legislation**

This chapter deals with the powers and duties of local authorities regarding the condition of existing houses (primarily those in private ownership); their responsibilities for the provision of new council housing were mentioned earlier (see ch 8(A)(2)(b), and the beginning of ch 10).

Despite wide-ranging legislation, the problem of rotten housing remains: in 1968 the government calculated that 1.8 million dwellings (i.e. more than 10 per cent of the country's housing) were unfit for habitation and that as regards the remaining 'fit' dwellings around 2.3 million lacked one or more of an indoor lavatory, a fixed bath, a wash basin and a hot and cold water system ('Old Houses Into New Homes', Cmnd 3602, para 4); and although the government in 1973 forecast a considerable improvement by the end of that year, it pointed out that: 'Much remains to be done. Almost one household in six still lives in a house that is unfit or lacks at least one of the basic amenities . . . . In some places conditions are getting worse, not better' ('Better Homes—The Next Priorities', Cmnd 5339, paras 2, 3).

Part of the problem has been tackled by authorities through the financial incentive of improvement grants (see ch 11(C)). But this chapter concentrates on the physical rather than financial levers available to authorities for dealing with defective houses, i.e. those statutory provisions designed to secure their repair, modernization and improvement, and for dealing with the related problems of overcrowding and multiple occupation.

We shall look at this legislation largely from the viewpoint of the tenant of an unsatisfactory house who wants the help of his local authority in pressurizing his landlord over the condition of the property, rather than the help of the courts to remedy the landlord's breach of his express or implied repairing obligations (see ch 9(C)). Thus we shall exclude from consideration the clearance area procedure for removing groups of unfit houses, and the details of compulsory purchase. The local authority's general liabilities regarding the condition of public sector housing have been dealt with earlier (see ch 10(D)), but where the particular provisions with which we are here concerned can be of use to the council house tenant, his position will be considered alongside that of the private sector tenant.

It will be seen that it may be a two-edged sword for a tenant to enlist the authority's help against his landlord, since he may run the risk of eviction or increased rent.

(A)   Defective Houses—The Housing Legislation

This account deals with the remedying of defects in individual unfit houses under the housing legislation, and the separate but overlapping provisions under this legislation regarding the compulsory modernization and improvement of properties. The alternative procedures under the public health legislation, and the special rules relating to defects in multi-occupied houses, are dealt with later.

(1)   Deciding whether a House is Unfit

Before an authority can be persuaded by a tenant to act against his landlord regarding a defective house it must normally be satisfied that it is 'unfit for human habitation': this term is defined by the Housing Act 1957, s4, which states that a house is deemed unfit for human habitation for the purposes of the Act if and only if it is so defective in one or more of the following matters as not to be reasonably suitable for occupation: repairs, stability, freedom from damp, internal arrangement, natural lighting, ventilation, water supply, drainage and WCs, and facilities for the preparation and cooking of food and for the disposal of waste water (this is often called the 'nine-point standard'). 'House' includes its yard, garden, etc (HA 1957, s189(1)), and any part of a building used as a dwelling (HA 1957, s18(1)).

These matters, as explained in Circulars (MHLG 55/1954, 69/1967, and 68/1969), are the only criteria to be considered in deciding on unfitness for the purposes of the 1957 Act (see the wording of s4: 'if and only if'), so that one must beware of applying cases decided on the common law implied condition of fitness for habitation on the letting of a furnished property (see ch 9(C)(1)(c)): thus infestation by bugs, though still within this common law condition, would appear to be outside s4, which 'defies rational explanation' (Davies, 1974, p. 44). Further limitations on s4 are that neither the absence of an electricity or gas supply, nor the fact that the only toilet is outside, could come within the section. Thus this 'nine-point standard' needs review.

However, there is no requirement that the specified matters must cause danger to health, and the question of unfitness is one of fact to be determined by the standard of 'the ordinary reasonable man': Hall v Manchester Corp [1915] 84 LJ Ch 732, HL. Cases held to be within s4

include: a defective window sash (Summers v Salford Corp [1943] 1 All
ER 68, HL), a defective step (McCarrick v Liverpool Corp [1946] 2 All
ER 646, HL), and a defective ceiling (O'Brien v Robinson [1973] 1 All
ER 583, HL). The test 'must not be measured by the magnitude of the
repairs required. A burst or leaking pipe, a displaced slate or tile, a stopped
drain, a rotten stair tread may each . . . until repair make a house unfit to
live in, though each . . . may be quickly and cheaply repaired' (Summers's
case at p. 70). Further, most back-to-back houses erected after 1909 and
certain underground rooms are deemed by the HA 1957 to be unfit for
habitation (ss5, 18).

It has been held that the tenant of an unfit house cannot withhold part
of his rent in retaliation (Stevenson Ltd v Mock [1954] JPL 275); but
where the unfitness is caused by disrepair, the tenant can deduct the cost
of repairs from future rent in certain circumstances (see ch 9(C)(2)(d)).

If a defective house does not come within s4, all is not lost. The
authority may use its separate powers under the housing legislation
relating to fit houses in disrepair (see (5) below), the provision of standard
amenities (see (6) below), or houses in multiple occupation (see (C)(2)
below); or its powers under the public health legislation (see (B) below);
and the tenant may take his landlord to court for breach of his express or
implied repairing obligations (see ch 9(C)(2)(a)).

(2)   Initiating Action
An authority is under a duty to take action (the nature of which is
detailed below) where it is 'satisfied' that a house is unfit for human
habitation (HA 1957, ss9, 16). The normal procedure in practice is for the
public health inspector to examine the property and then for the medical
officer to report to the housing committee, which will take further action
if 'satisfied' on unfitness. Thus the tenant should write initially to the
local chief public health inspector, enclosing if possible a surveyor's
report on the property (which could be paid for under the legal assistance
scheme: see ch 13(A)(1)), asking for an inspection of the property, and
setting out the tenant's name, the address of the property, his complaints,
the name and address of the landlord or his agent, and the times when the
property may be inspected: a draft letter is contained in 'How To Fight
For Better Housing Conditions', obtainable from Community Action. If
it is necessary to telephone the inspector to press for attention, this
should be done before 10 a.m., after which time inspectors go on their
rounds. If nothing happens within a reasonable time, the next step is to
write to the Town Clerk (or equivalent officer) demanding action and
threatening to make a formal complaint (see below): again, a draft is
contained in the above booklet.

What if nothing is achieved after pursuing these courses, either because
the complaint is never relayed to the housing committee or the committee

refuses to be 'satisfied' of unfitness in the face of clear evidence? In the former situation, the tenant should complain to a local justice of the peace or parish or community council (for a draft form, see the above booklet), since these bodies have power to complain to the medical officer of health in writing that any house is unfit, whereupon he must inspect the house forthwith and report on it to the local authority giving his opinion as to unfitness (HA 1957, s157(2): see case reported in (1973) LAG BUL. 117). This procedure could be used by a council house tenant. If, however, the problem is that the housing committee refuses to be 'satisfied' despite cogent evidence of unfitness, mandamus (see ch 1(C)) would lie to force the authority to act: see Hall v Manchester Corp [1915] 84 LJ Ch 732, HL; McPhail v LB of Islington [1970] 1 All ER 1004, 1007, CA; and Secretary of State for Employment v ASLEF (No 2) [1972] 2 All ER 949, CA.

A tenant should remember, before initiating action, that by the HA 1957, s33(2), nothing in Part II of the Act (which includes the unfitness procedures detailed below) affects the landlord's right to sue his tenant for breach of the latter's repairing obligations: nevertheless, as we saw, in cases of short leases the repairing obligations will often rest with the landlord (ch 9(C)(1)(a)-(c)).

(3) Action where the Unfit House is capable of Repair at Reasonable Expense

(a) Reasonable expense   Where an authority is 'satisfied' on unfitness (see above), it must then decide whether the house is capable of being rendered fit at reasonable expense, and in deciding this 'regard shall be had to the estimated cost of the works necessary to render it so fit and the value which it is estimated that the house will have when the works are completed' (HA 1957, ss9(1), 39(1)). Bearing in mind the decontrol provisions of the Housing Finance Act 1972 (see ch 9(A)(3)(b)) and the increased capital values of houses, it should now be easier to decide that the expense is reasonable, despite the greater cost of labour and materials; but the expense will not normally be regarded in practice as reasonable unless the authority considers that after the work is completed the house will remain fit for at least five years (this is by analogy with the HA 1957, s69, which states that an owner proposing works of improvement or structural alteration can obtain a statement from the authority as to the likely fitness of the house for at least five years from completion of the work).

The authority need not consider detailed estimates, since it will be presumed that the house is capable of repair unless the authority is satisfied to the contrary (see wording of s9, and Bacon v Grimsby Corp [1949] 2 All ER 875, CA: this case also held that 'value' in s39(1) means freehold value).

(b) Repair notice   Once the authority is 'satisfied' as to unfitness and that the house is capable of being made fit at reasonable expense, it must serve a 'repair notice' on the 'person having control of the house' requiring him to execute the works specified in the notice within a specified reasonable time, and stating that those works will make the house fit for habitation (HA 1957, s9(1)). The 'person having control of the house' is defined as the person receiving the rack (i.e. full) rent or who would so receive it if the house was let (HA 1957, s39(2)), and is hereafter referred to as 'the landlord'. A repair notice cannot specify the adding of amenities unrelated to the question of fitness for habitation: Adams v Tuer (1923) 130 LT 218.

In practice, the authority will try informal pressure on the landlord before serving the notice.

(c) Effects on tenant   Where the work specified in the repair notice is carried out, whether by the landlord or by the authority (see below), then although this will not affect the tenant's security, it can affect his rent, whether he has a 'fully covered tenancy' or a 'Part VI letting', depending on the extent of the work done (see ch 9(A)(3)(b)—qualification certificate for controlled tenancies, and ch 9(B)(1)(c), (2)(b)—powers of rent officers and rent tribunals to vary rents).

A repair notice does not affect the private rights of the tenant against his landlord for want of repair or consequent damage (HA 1957, s10(9); see ch 9(C)).

(d) Failure of landlord to comply   If the landlord does not comply with the repair notice within the time specified, he incurs no penalty, but the authority may do the work itself (HA 1957, s10(1)), recovering the expenses from the landlord (s10(3)), or by instalments from the tenant ('occupier') who may deduct the sums from his rent (s10(5)). The authority cannot be forced to do the work.

If the landlord (or the tenant) obstructs the authority in carrying out the necessary work he is liable to a £20 fine (HA 1957, ss10(2), 161).

(e) Appeal by landlord   The landlord may appeal against the repair notice to the county court, which has wide powers (HA 1957, s11). If the court decides that the house cannot be made fit at reasonable expense, the authority may purchase the house by agreement, or compulsorily (HA 1957, s12): in the latter case the authority must forthwith do all the work specified in the repair notice (s12), and may allow the tenant to remain in occupation (Sch 1, para 3); if the authority chooses not to purchase the house under s12, it must take one of the four general courses of action detailed below, and the tenant will be in danger of losing his home.

(4)   *Action where the Unfit House is beyond Repair at Reasonable Expense*

If the house contains serious defects, the tenant should be aware of the risks of reporting the matter to the authority, since if it is satisfied that the property is beyond repair at reasonable expense, it must take one of the four serious steps discussed below, which could result in the tenant's lawful eviction.

(a) 'Time and place' notice   If the authority is 'satisfied' as to unfitness and that the house is not capable of being made fit at reasonable expense (see above), it must serve on the landlord notice of the time and place at which it will discuss the condition of the house (HA 1957, s16). The tenant has no right to receive a copy of the notice, nor to be present at the hearing.

(b) Courses open to the authority following the hearing   If after hearing the landlord the authority remains satisfied that the house is unfit and beyond repair at reasonable expense, it must take one of the four following courses of action.

(i) Undertaking from landlord

Power to accept undertakings   The authority may accept the landlord's undertaking either to carry out work making the house fit or not to use it for habitation until it has been made fit (HA 1957, s16(4)).

Effects on tenant   As regards acceptance of the former undertaking (concerning work), the authority need not consider the cost of the work, thus benefiting the tenant if expensive work is agreed upon (subject to its effect on the rent: see (3)(c) above). But in the case of the latter undertaking (concerning non-user), acceptance by the authority means that the tenant ceases to have Rent Act protection and the landlord can recover possession (HA 1957, s16(5)); further, it is an offence knowingly to use the property in breach of the undertaking (s16(6)). These grave dangers to the tenant are partly mitigated by the fact that the authority has a limited duty to rehouse him, if displaced, under the Land Compensation Act 1973, though this is not an easy passport to a council house (see ch 10(A)(2)); the displaced tenant may also be entitled to financial benefits from the authority by way of a home loss payment, disturbance payment, and new home acquisition payment under the LCA 1973, ss29-33, 37-8, and 43 (the details of these are beyond the scope of this book: see Dawn Oliver (1974) LAG BUL. 104, 106).

Failure of undertakings   If no undertaking is accepted by the authority, or if one is accepted and later broken, then the authority must, by the HA 1957, s17, take one of the remaining three courses of action referred to below.

(ii) Demolition order   This requires vacation of the house within not less than twenty-eight days and its demolition within the following six weeks or any longer time the authority allows (HA 1957, s21).

Effects on tenant   The tenant may find his landlord indecently anxious for a demolition order, since he will be left with a perhaps valuable site, without the embarrassment of a Rent Act protected tenant.

The authority must serve a notice on the tenant stating the effect of the order and giving him at least twenty-eight days in which to leave: if he fails to do so he ceases to have Rent Act protection and the authority or the landlord may apply to the county court for vacant possession to be given within two to four weeks as the court decides (HA 1957, s22).

The tenant cannot expect any compensation for loss of his interest unless his tenancy was granted initially for more than one year, thus excluding most periodic tenants, and all statutory tenants under the Rent Act (HA 1969, Sch 5). However, he may be entitled to local authority housing, a home loss payment, a disturbance payment, and a new home acquisition payment (see (i) above).

Failure of landlord to comply   If the landlord disobeys the order, he incurs no penalty unless he permits any person to enter after the date of the order; but the authority must enter and demolish the property and can recover the expenses from the landlord (HA 1957, s23).

(iii) Closing order   This is a special order prohibiting the use of the house (or part of it) for any purpose not approved by the authority (HA 1957, s27). It is normally available only in two situations: first, if the authority considers it inexpedient to make a demolition order having regard to the effect of demolition on any other property, it may make a closing order instead (HA 1957, s17(1), proviso); and second, if any part of a dwelling (e.g. an attic) is unfit and beyond repair at reasonable expense, the authority must make a closing order and not a demolition order as respects that part (HA 1957, s18(1): this also covers any underground room, whether or not used as a dwelling, which may be deemed unfit under s18(2)).

Effects on tenant   If the tenant knows about the closing order and nevertheless uses the premises, he may be fined (HA 1957, s27(1)). Also, it has been held that where a closing order is made against part of a house the tenant cannot withhold part of his rent in retaliation: Stevenson Ltd v Mock [1954] JPL 275 (see (1) above). Further, the landlord may recover possession from the tenant, who loses any Rent Act protection (HA 1957, s27(5)), even if the condition of the property is due to breach of the landlord's own duty to repair: Buswell v Goodwin [1971] 1 All ER 418, CA (see ch 9(C)(1)(b)). The tenant's position regarding compensation, rehousing, home loss payment, disturbance payment, and new home acquisition payment is as in demolition order cases (see (ii) above).

Failure of landlord to comply   If the landlord permits the house to be used in contravention of the order, he too may be fined (HA 1957, s27(1)).

(iv) Purchase for temporary housing   If the house is capable of providing accommodation adequate for the time being, the authority may purchase it instead of making a demolition or closing order (HA 1957, s17(2), (3); Circular 55/1954, App II, para 23). The power cannot be used in respect of part of a house (HA 1957, s18(1)). The authority may purchase by agreement or compulsorily, and may carry out the necessary 'patching' work for rendering it capable of providing adequate accommodation for the time being, pending demolition (HA 1957, s29).

Effects on tenant   On completion of the purchase, the tenant will become tenant of the authority, and the HA 1957, s6 (see ch 9(C)(1)(b)) ceases to apply (HA 1957, s29(4)). The authority may allow the tenant to remain in occupation (HA 1957, Sch 1, para 3), but he will lose any Rent Act protection, since the authority can get possession on showing it needs the house for housing purposes (HA 1957, s158(1)-see ch 10(E)(2)(b)).

(c) Appeals   Any 'person aggrieved' by a demolition or closing order, or by the authority's decision to purchase for temporary housing, may appeal to the county court, which has wide powers (HA 1957, s20(1)); but a tenant whose unexpired term does not exceed three years cannot appeal (s20(2)), which thus excludes most periodic tenants, and all statutory tenants under the Rent Act.

(5)   Action where a House is not Unfit but needs Repairs

We have until now been dealing with the authority's powers and duties regarding unfit property. But by the HA 1957, s9(1A), the authority may serve a repair notice (see (3)(b) above) on the landlord where it is satisfied that a house is in such a state of disrepair that, although not unfit, substantial repairs are needed to bring it up to a reasonable standard, having regard to its age, character and locality; however, s9(1A) is inapplicable to 'works of internal decorative repair', and is 'clearly not a provision to be invoked lightly' (MHLG Circular 64/1969, para 16). It would cover e.g. rewiring, and external decorative repairs. Unlike the normal repair notice, there is no 'reasonable expense' qualification.

The procedure for initiating action, the effects on the tenant, and the position where the landlord fails to comply, are all as for the normal repair notice (see (2), (3) above).

(6)   Securing the Provision of Standard Amenities

It may be that a house is fit for habitation (see (1) above), in sound repair (see (5) above), and not a 'statutory nuisance' (see (B)(2) below); yet it may lack one or more of the 'standard amenities' (see ch 11(C)(2)). In such a case the authority can compel the 'person having control' (hereafter called 'the landlord') to provide the missing 'standard amenities' for the dwelling under the HA 1974, Pt VIII: 'dwelling' means a building or part of a building used as a separate dwelling (HA 1974, s129(1)); however, this procedure is inapplicable where all the 'standard amenities' are present, but are not sufficient (in these cases the public health or multi-occupation provisions may however be relevant: see (B), (C)(2), below).

(a) Initiating action   The authority can take action against the landlord in one of two ways: if the dwelling is in a housing action area or general improvement area (see ch 11(C)(1)) the authority can act of its own accord (HA 1974, s85), but if the dwelling is outside such an area, the authority can only act on the written request of the occupying tenant (s89). In either case, therefore, the tenant (whether contractual or statutory: s104(1); see ch 9(A)(2)) should write to the authority requesting it to compel the landlord to provide the standard amenities. But the authority can only act under s85 or s89 if it is satisfied that the dwelling:

(i) is without one or more of the standard amenities, whether or not it is also in a state of disrepair; and:

(ii) is capable at reasonable expense of improvement to the 'full' or 'reduced' standard (see ch 11(C)(2)(a)); and:

(iii) was provided (by erection or conversion) before 3 October 1961.

If the authority is satisfied on these points, then under both s85 and s89 it has a discretion to act (not a duty); but if s89 applies, the authority must notify the requesting tenant if it decides not to act, giving him written reasons (s89(4)): however, there seems to be nothing the tenant can do on receiving such notification.

(b) Provisional notices and improvement notices   If the authority decides to act under s85 or s89, it first serves a 'provisional notice' on the landlord, and a copy on the tenant, specifying the necessary work and giving them an opportunity to discuss the matter with the authority (s85(2),(4);s89(4)). After the authority has considered all representations made to it (including representations concerning housing arrangements for the tenant: see (c)(iii) below), then the next step may depend on whether it is a s85 or a s89 case (see (a) above).

If it is a s85 case, the authority can accept the landlord's undertaking to do the necessary work within nine months, provided the housing arrangements for the tenant (see (c)(iii) below) are satisfactory and the tenant consents to the work: the authority must then serve notice of acceptance of the undertaking on the landlord, with a copy to the tenant, and cannot thereafter serve an 'improvement notice' (see below) unless the landlord breaks the undertaking: s87.

But if it is a s89 case, or a s85 case where no undertaking has been accepted or the undertaking has been broken, then the authority may follow the provisional notice with service of an 'improvement notice', provided the housing arrangements for the tenant (see (c)(iii) below) are satisfactory (ss88-9); the tenant must be sent a copy of the notice. The improvement notice in a s85 case where no undertaking has been accepted can only be served within nine months from service of the provisional notice or, in a s85 case where an undertaking has been accepted but broken, within six months from the expiry of the time limit specified for the work in the undertaking (s88(3)); while in a s89 case, the improvement notice can only be served within twelve months from the date of the tenant's original request (s89(5)).

The improvement notice must specify the necessary work and its estimated cost, and require the landlord to carry it out within (normally) one year and six weeks from the date of service of the notice (ss90(1), 92(1)), subject to rights of appeal to the county court (s91). 'Improvement' includes alteration, enlargement, and repair (so far as necessary to attain the 'full' or 'reduced' standard: see ch 11(C)(2)(a)): s104(1); thus the notice can require considerable work to be done to provide the amenities, e.g. building a bathroom extension to the dwelling (Harrington v Croydon Corp [1967] 3 All ER 929, CA).

(c) Effects on tenant

(i) Rent   On completing the work, the landlord can apply for an increase in rent (see (3)(c) above).

(ii) Contribution to the cost   One of the grounds for appeal to the county court by the landlord against an improvement notice is that some other person having an estate or interest in the dwelling will derive a benefit from the work and should pay the whole or part of its cost (s91(2)(f)), and the court may then order such payment by that other person (s91(6)); this apparent danger to the tenant is mitigated by the opinion of the court in Harrington's case (above) that no contribution could be obtained, under similar wording in the HA 1964, Pt II, from a statutory tenant, nor probably from a short-term contractual tenant (see ch 9(A)(2)).

(iii) Security of tenure   We saw that before accepting a landlord's undertaking or serving an improvement notice the authority must be satisfied as to the housing arrangements for the tenant. 'Housing arrangements' are arrangements agreed in writing between the tenant, and the landlord, the authority or both, and which make provision for the housing of the tenant and his household while the work is being carried out, and/or after its completion (s86). The tenant may appeal to the county court against an improvement notice on the ground that these arrangements are unsatisfactory (s91(3)).

A tenant may fear that, if he requests the authority to act under s89, his landlord will try to evict him soon afterwards in order to stop action by the authority (especially since the authority must notify the landlord of the tenant's request: s89(2)): however, the authority may still serve a provisional notice and an improvement notice even though the tenant leaves the dwelling after making the request (s89(7)), so that unlawful eviction will not enable the landlord to block the notice (and will render him criminally and civilly liable: see ch 9(D)(2)).

(iv) Rehousing   If the housing arrangements for the tenant break down, and he is permanently displaced by the carrying out of work under the improvement notice or landlord's undertaking, then the authority must rehouse him if suitable alternative accommodation is not otherwise available (LCA 1973, s39: see ch 10(A)(2)). He may also be entitled to a home loss payment, a disturbance payment, and a new home acquisition payment from the authority (see (4)(b)(i) above).

(d) Failure of landlord to comply   If the landlord disobeys an improvement notice he does not commit an offence, but the authority may carry out the work itself at his expense, giving the tenant at least twenty-one days' prior notice (ss93-4). The authority can also do the work at the landlord's expense by agreement with him (s97(2)).

(B)   Defective Houses—The Public Health Legislation

(1)   Comparison with the Housing Legislation

The public health legislation (consisting mainly of the PHA 1936 as amended) is very wide ranging: it embraces such diverse matters as sewage, building regulations, air pollution, mortuaries and refuse collection. We are here concerned however only with the provisions concerning defective houses, and mainly from the point of view of the tenant seeking to force his landlord to repair the property, so that the terms 'landlord' and 'tenant' are used throughout in place of the general expressions 'owner' and 'occupier' which are employed in the legislation (see PHA 1936, s343).

It will be seen that there is considerable overlap here with the housing legislation, but there are the following distinctions. First, the public health provisions contain much less sophisticated powers than the housing provisions, since the former relate mainly to specific defects which are hazards to health, while the latter are concerned with improving housing standards generally: thus if a house contains defects sufficiently serious to make it unfit for habitation the housing provisions may be the more suitable, but if the defects are less serious the public health provisions may be used. Second, a statutory nuisance under the public health legislation (see below) can be abated by a lesser standard of work than is required to make a house fit for habitation under the housing legislation, so that the latter legislation (e.g. HA 1957, s9: 'repair notices': see (A)(3) above) is often used if a lasting job is needed, and the former reserved for short-life properties (i.e. those having a probable life of five years or less—see (A)(3)(a) above—or in clearance areas). Third, the public health statutory nuisance procedure normally involves court proceedings, while the procedures under the HA 1957 do not. Fourth, the procedure under the public health legislation may often be simpler and swifter (despite the frequent need for court proceedings) than under the housing legislation, for the public health inspector often has power to instigate public health procedures on his own initiative and need not consider the cost of the work done, while under the HA 1957 authorization frequently has to be obtained through a committee, and the authority must normally decide whether the house is capable of repair at reasonable cost; however, even the public health procedure can take more than three months to complete. Fifth, fines can be imposed for breaches of public health notices, but not normally for notices served under the housing provisions, where often the only sanction is for the authority to do the required work and recover the cost from the owner. Lastly, while there is a procedure for complaint to the Secretary of State on the authority's failure to act under the public health legislation, there is no such procedure to deal with inaction under the housing legislation.

With these points in mind, we can turn to the details of the legislation.

(2) Statutory Nuisances

(a) Definition   The most common ground for action by an authority in this field is where it is satisfied that a 'statutory nuisance' exists. A 'statutory nuisance' is defined as including 'any premises in such a state as to be prejudicial to health or a nuisance' (PHA 1936, s92(1)(a)). 'Prejudicial to health' means 'injurious, or likely to cause injury, to health' (s343(1)), but 'nuisance' is not defined: it is clear from s92(1)(a) that a statutory nuisance can arise from a nuisance which is not prejudicial to health, i.e. the word 'or' is disjunctive, so that in Betts v Penge UDC [1942] 2 All ER 61 it was held that a landlord whose actions caused the property to be in such a state as to interfere with the personal comfort of the tenant had caused a statutory nuisance even though the property was not necessarily injurious to health (here the landlord, without seeking possession, removed the front door and the window sashes in reprisal for the tenant's non-payment of rent and failure to obey a notice to quit: see now the RA 1965: ch 9(D)(2)); compare Springett v Harold [1954] 1 All ER 568, where stained and peeling internal walls and ceilings did not suffice since the property was not thereby rendered injurious to health or unfit for habitation. Thus discomfort or inconvenience alone will not always qualify, and it has been argued that ' "personal comfort" must . . . have some relevance to public health or sanitation in the broadest possible sense', i.e. it must have some possible relation to public health or sanitation, and not every common law nuisance would be caught by the section (see 'Encyclopedia of Public Health Law and Practice', pp. 1148 et seq., and cases there cited: see also Coventry CC v Cartwright, 'The Times', 30 January 1975); even given this limitation, it seems that each of the defects or situations listed in the HA 1957, s4 (see (A)(1) above) or the HA 1961, s32 (see ch 9(C)(1)(a)) can also be statutory nuisances, but each case depends on its own facts.

We have seen that the HA 1957, s9 ('repair notices': (A)(3) above) can only be used if the house is capable of being rendered fit at reasonable expense: it was consequently suggested in Salisbury Corp v Roles (1948) 92 SJ 618 that where s9 cannot be used because this condition is not satisfied, then it is improper for the authority to proceed under the PHA 1936 instead; but there is no such restriction in the 1936 Act itself, and in Nottingham Corp v Newton [1974] 2 All ER 760 it was emphasized that the duty to act under the 1936 Act remains in such a case, though the court has 'considerable tolerance' as to the exact terms of its order (see (d) below; see also Salford CC v McNally [1975] 1 All ER 597).

Section 92(1)(a) would cover a house suffering from e.g. dampness, crumbling ceilings, broken sashcords, dangerous wiring, etc, and even if a single item of disrepair is not sufficient, a combination of such items can in aggregate make the house a statutory nuisance.

(b) Initiating proceedings: normal cases   The authority is normally under a duty to act under the PHA 1936, s93, by serving an 'abatement notice' (see below) where it is satisfied of the existence of a statutory nuisance; but it has a choice as to whether to proceed instead under the HA 1957 (see (A) above): Nottingham Corp v Newton [1974] 2 All ER 760.

Where the tenant considers that the property constitutes a 'statutory nuisance', as defined above, due to conditions which are the landlord's responsibility (see ch 9(C)(1)), then the tenant should write to the local chief public health inspector, as outlined at (A)(2) above. If nothing happens within a reasonable time, the next stage is to write to the Town Clerk (or equivalent officer) asking for action (again, a draft letter can be obtained from the source mentioned at (A)(2) above).

Assuming that the authority can be persuaded to act, it will serve an 'abatement notice' under s93 on the landlord as 'the person by whose act, default or sufferance the nuisance arises or continues', or, in the case of a structural defect, as 'owner' (see PHA 1936, ss93, 343); this notice requires him to abate the nuisance and to execute such works and take such steps as may be necessary for that purpose: if it requires work to be carried out, it must specify that work (see Millard v Wastall [1898] 1 QB 342, 343), and a reasonable time for compliance should be given (Bristol Corp v Sinnott [1918] 1 Ch 62, CA). If the abatement notice is not complied with, or, though complied with, if the nuisance is likely to recur, then the authority must normally make a complaint to the magistrates' court asking for a summons against the landlord so that he may be ordered to abate the nuisance, and the court must normally issue the summons (s94(1)); at the hearing the court has the duties and powers referred to at (d) below. However, if the person causing the nuisance cannot be found and it is clear that it is not the fault of the landlord or the tenant (e.g. where damage has been caused by trespassers), the authority may do the necessary work itself to abate the nuisance (s93) and recover the cost from the landlord (s96).

So far we have assumed that the authority has been persuaded, initially or eventually, to act. But what if the authority refuses to be satisfied of the existence of the statutory nuisance and so does nothing? There are three possible lines of attack. First and most effectively, the tenant may make a private complaint of the existence of the statutory nuisance to the magistrates' court under the PHA 1936, s99, asking for a summons against the landlord so that he may be ordered to abate the nuisance (a specimen complaint form is obtainable from Shelter); if the summons is issued, then at the hearing the magistrates can proceed just as if the complaint had initially been made by the authority (see (d) below), and further, the court may direct the authority itself, whether or not it is the landlord, to abate the nuisance (as in Nottingham Corp v Newton [1974] 2 All ER 760), in which case the authority can recover its expenses from the landlord under s96; s99 is particularly useful where it is alleged that the authority itself caused the statutory nuisance, so that it may be used by a council tenant: see R v Epping (Waltham Abbey) JJ, ex p Burlinson [1948] 1 KB 79, and Salford CC v McNally [1975] 1 All ER 597. Second, mandamus would lie against an authority refusing to be satisfied that a statutory nuisance exists, to force it to act under s93, since the court is prepared to go behind the authority's opinion (see (A)(2) above). Third, complaint may be made under the PHA 1936, s322 to the Secretary of State for the Environment alleging failure by the authority to discharge its functions: he may then investigate the matter and ensure that an abatement notice is issued. The effectiveness of the first remedy renders the remaining two academic.

(c) Initiating proceedings: special cases   We have seen that the authority must normally act under the PHA 1936, s93 where a statutory nuisance exists. It may however be that the authority considers either that this procedure would be too slow in an 'emergency' case, or that while no statutory nuisance exists at present, one has previously occurred and is likely to recur. These two situations have been catered for by subsequent legislation, as follows.

'Emergency' cases   If premises are 'in such a state . . . as to be prejudicial to health or a nuisance', and unreasonable delay would result from following the normal statutory nuisance procedure, then by the PHA 1961, s26 the authority may serve on the landlord a notice setting out the defects and stating that the authority intends to remedy them: after nine days from service of the notice the authority may do the necessary work without the need for any court order and recover the cost from the landlord; this procedure can be used even though the authority could have acted under the HA 1957, s9 ('repair notices': see (A)(3) above).

The authority cannot be forced to use s26, and unfortunately this useful section is often ignored by authorities.

Prohibition notices   We have seen that authorities can only serve an abatement notice under the PHA 1936, s93 where the statutory nuisance actually exists. If however the authority is satisfied that a statutory nuisance has occurred on the premises in the past (even if it has now ceased) and is likely to recur, it may serve a 'prohibition notice' on the landlord under the Public Health (Recurring Nuisances) Act 1969, s1, prohibiting a recurrence of the nuisance and requiring him to do any work necessary to ensure this. A prohibition notice and an abatement notice may be served in the same document, where the nuisance exists at the time of service.

Failure to comply with a prohibition notice means that the authority may apply to the magistrates' court under the 1969 Act, s2, which then has the normal powers under the PHA 1936, s94 (see (d) below), i.e. a prohibition notice is treated as the equivalent of an abatement notice.

The authority cannot be forced to proceed under the 1969 Act, and the 1936 Act, s99 (see (b) above) does not apply (1969 Act, s3(1)).

(d) The powers of the court

Magistrates' court proceedings   We have seen that if an abatement notice is not complied with, or the nuisance is likely to recur, the authority must normally apply to the magistrates' court for a summons against the landlord, under the PHA 1936, s94(1). If the authority proves its case at the hearing, there are the following consequences (which apply not only to a case brought by an authority following breach of an abatement notice or a prohibition notice, but also to a private individual's complaint under s99):

(i) the court must make a 'nuisance order' requiring the defendant to comply with all or some of the abatement notice, or otherwise to abate the nuisance within a specified time, and/or prohibiting a recurrence of the nuisance; further, the court can require the execution of any specified and necessary work (s94(2)); but the court has a discretion whether to require the landlord to do all or part of the work referred to in the abatement notice, and a discretion as to the time for completion of the work (Nottingham Corp v Newton [1974] 2 All ER 760, where it was held that the magistrates must bear in mind the imminence of demolition under a compulsory purchase order, so that they could order the nuisance to be abated by a time after the scheduled demolition date, thereby avoiding the abortive spending of money, provided the house was demolished on time: see also Salford CC v McNally [1975] 1 All ER 597);

(ii) the court may impose a fine of £20 (s94(2));

(iii) the court may order the closure of the building if the nuisance makes it unfit for habitation (s94(2)): in such a case the tenant could be evicted (s289), the authority would be under no duty to rehouse him

under the LCA 1973 (see ch 10(A)(2)), and he would not be entitled
to the financial benefits of the 1973 Act (see (A)(4)(b)(i) above); he
should thus be alive to this danger when he instigates the nuisance
procedure;

(iv) the court must order the defendant to pay the authority's
reasonable legal expenses if the nuisance existed or was likely to recur at
the date of the making of the complaint, regardless of the position at the
hearing itself (1936 Act, s94(3); 1969 Act, s3(2)).

Effects on tenant   Where the required work is carried out, whether
by the landlord or the authority (see below), this may affect the tenant's
rent (see (A)(3)(c) above); and if closure of the building is ordered, the
tenant is liable to eviction (see above).

Failure of landlord to comply   If the nuisance continues after
conviction, a further fine of £50 plus £5 per day may be imposed (s95(1));
should the authority not report the landlord's breach of the order to the
court, the tenant may do so. Further, the authority may do the necessary
work itself (s95(2)), recovering the cost from the landlord (s96) in
(normally) the magistrates' court (s293), or by instalments from the
tenant, who may deduct the sums from his rent (s291). But the authority
cannot be forced to do the work.

(3)   Dangerous Buildings and Structures

Normal cases   Where there is a dangerous building or structure, the
authority may choose to treat it as a statutory nuisance and use the above
procedure. Alternatively, it may proceed under the PHA 1936, s58, which
provides that if a building or structure is in a dangerous condition the
authority may apply to the magistrates' court, which may order the
landlord to do the necessary work to remove the danger, or, if he elects, to
demolish the building or structure, or the dangerous part of it (s58(1)):
the tenant is thus at risk of losing his tenancy if the landlord elects for
demolition. Further, there is no need for the court to specify in the order
the work to be done (R v Bolton Recorder, ex p McVittie [1940] 1 KB
290, CA: compare the statutory nuisance procedure at (2)(d) above), so
that the landlord may get away with a temporary 'patching' job. The
tenant may therefore be better off if the nuisance procedure is adopted.

If the landlord fails to comply with the magistrates' order, he is liable to
a £10 fine and the authority may do the necessary work itself, recovering
the cost from the landlord (s58(2)).

Special cases   Where the authority considers that immediate action
should be taken to rectify a dangerous building or structure, then by the
PHA 1961, s25, it may take that action itself, but it must give notice to
the landlord and tenant if practicable; it may then recover the cost from
the landlord. The authority's surveyor can exercise these emergency
powers in s25 without prior authorization.

(4)   Drains, Sewers and Water Closets

Where a drain, private sewer, soil pipe, rainwater pipe or WC is defective, the authority may choose to employ the statutory nuisance procedure. But it also has special duties and powers related to these items.

Where further drains, sewers and water closets are required   If a building has insufficient drainage, private sewers, soil pipes, rainwater pipes or WCs, or such items are in such a state as to be prejudicial to health or a nuisance, the authority must require the landlord by notice to make such further provision as is necessary (PHA 1936, ss39, 44; PHA 1961, s21); the notice must state the nature of, and time limit for, the work to be done, and if the landlord defaults he is liable to a £5 fine and a further fine of £2 per day for default after conviction (PHA 1936, s290); also, on default the authority can do the work itself and recover the cost from the landlord (PHA 1936, s290) (compare the wider powers in the HA 1961, s15 allowing an authority to require a landlord to provide further amenities in multi-occupied houses: see (C)(2)(c)(i) below).

Authorities often prefer to use these specific public health provisions rather than the general statutory nuisance procedure, since the former are quicker, default action being available to the authority under s290 immediately the time specified in the notice has passed, without the need to go to court (compare s95(2), at (2)(d) above).

Where the existing drains, sewers and water closets need repair   If an existing defective drain, private sewer, soil pipe, rainwater pipe or WC is capable of repair, the authority must require the landlord or the tenant by notice to do the necessary work (PHA 1936, ss39, 45). The above provisions in the PHA 1936, s290, relating to the content of the notice and default will apply. Additionally, by the PHA 1961, s18, if a drain or private sewer is not sufficiently maintained and kept in good repair, but can be repaired for not more than £50 (or £100 in Greater London), then the authority may, after giving seven days' notice to the landlord, have the work done and recover the cost from him.

There are two further provisions relating to blocked or insanitary facilities. First, in the case of blocked drains, private sewers, WCs and soil pipes, the authority may give notice in writing requiring the landlord or tenant to remedy the defect within forty-eight hours, failing which the authority can do the work itself and recover the cost from the person on whom the notice was served (PHA 1961, s17). Second, if a WC is used by two or more families, anyone injuring, fouling or obstructing it is liable to a 50p fine, and if those using it cause it or the approach to it to be insanitary through lack of proper cleaning, they are liable to a 50p fine and a further fine of 25p per day for default after conviction: PHA 1936, s52 (this provision is useful against fellow tenants of unsavoury habits, and also against landlords in appropriate cases).

The last relevant provision is mainly for use against builders and 'do-it-yourself' landlords: by the PHA 1961, s20, a person constructing or repairing a WC, drain or soil pipe carelessly and in such a way that it is prejudicial to health or a nuisance is liable to a £20 fine.

Private prosecutions   Prosecutions for any of these offences concerning drains, sewers and WCs can be brought by the tenant as the 'party aggrieved' under the PHA 1936, s298, if the authority declines to act.

(C)   Overcrowding and Multiple Occupation

The 1969 Report of the Central Housing Advisory Committee on 'Council Housing Purposes, Procedures and Priorities' noted a marked decline in overcrowding since the 1930s (p. 7), and commented that: 'There are now far more rooms than persons in the country . . . . If rooms and persons could be exchanged at will there would be no quantitative housing shortage. This, however, is sheer statistical juggling which ignores the fact that people form households . . .' (p. 63). Thus 'overcrowding' is still a problem, together with the related problem of 'multiple occupation', i.e. where houses are occupied by several different households, even though they may not be overcrowded. These twin problems are dealt with separately by the legislation, and the definitions are important: they are considered in detail below, but basically 'overcrowding' can only apply to a separate self-contained dwelling (which may itself be part of a house), whereas 'multiple occupation' applies to a whole house originally intended for one family which is occupied by persons who do not form a single household.

In practice, authorities enforcing this legislation often have to cope with homelessness brought about by evictions, both legal and illegal.

(1)   Overcrowding
(a) Definition   Only a 'dwelling-house' can be overcrowded (HA 1957, s77(1)). A 'dwelling-house' is 'any premises used as a separate dwelling by members of the working classes or of a type suitable for such use' (HA 1957, s87): 'premises used as a separate dwelling' would include any part of a building so used (MOH Memorandum B on the Prevention and Abatement of Overcrowding, October 1935, para 14), and for there to be a 'separate dwelling' the occupiers must not share living accommodation with anyone else (see ch 9(A)(1)(a)); 'members of the working classes' means 'people in the lower income range' (Guinness Trust (London Fund) v Green [1955] 2 All ER 871, CA).

Assuming the property in question is a 'dwelling-house', it will be overcrowded under the HA 1957, s77(1) if the number of persons sleeping in the house either: (i) is such that any two persons being ten years old or more, of opposite sexes and 'not . . . living together as husband and wife' (which term includes 'common law marriages'), must sleep together in the same room, or: (ii) exceeds the 'permitted number' of persons to rooms laid down in Sch 6 to the 1957 Act; but a child under one year old is ignored, and a child between one year and ten years only counts as half a person (s77(2)).

(b) The duties imposed on local authorities   If it appears to an authority that occasion has arisen for a report on overcrowding, or the Secretary of State so directs, the authority must make an inspection and report to the Secretary of State on the number of new houses needed and how they are to be provided (HA 1957, s76); also, the authority is under a duty to prosecute for overcrowding offences (HA 1957, s85(1): see (c) below).

(c) Overcrowding offences   In view of the danger to health and morals, both the landlord and the tenant may, subject to certain defences, be liable to prosecution where there is overcrowding.

Position of the tenant   If the tenant 'causes or permits' overcrowding he is liable to a £5 fine with an additional £2 a day for continuance after conviction (HA 1957, s78(1)), and loses his security of tenure (see (d) below). However, the tenant may have certain defences.

First, if the only people now sleeping there are the same persons who lived there at 'the appointed day' (normally in 1937 or 1938), or their children if any, then the tenant is not guilty of an offence unless suitable alternative accommodation is offered either to him and he refuses it, or to some person living in the house who is not part of the tenant's family (e.g. a lodger) and the tenant fails to require that person's removal (HA 1957, s78(2)).

Second, if a house only becomes overcrowded because a child attains the age of one or ten (see s77(2), at (a) above), then the tenant is not guilty of an offence from the date that he applies to the local authority for suitable alternative accommodation, unless such accommodation is offered to him and he refuses it, or unless it becomes reasonably practicable to remove from the house any person who is not part of the tenant's family and the tenant fails to require that person's removal (HA 1957, s78(3)): in such cases of overcrowding due to 'natural growth' the tenant should thus apply to the authority for alternative accommodation forthwith.

Third, if the only reason a house is overcrowded is because a member of the tenant's family who does not live there is sleeping there temporarily, no offence is committed by the tenant (HA 1957, s78(4)).

Fourth, a local authority can in exceptional circumstances authorize the tenant by licence to overcrowd for up to one year, in which case he is not guilty of an offence (HA 1957, s80).

Authorities have been urged to bring the second and fourth defences to the tenant's attention when they know that a landlord is taking action to recover possession of an overcrowded house (see (d) below), and to ensure 'speedy action' where a tenant in consequence applies for a s80 licence (MOH Circular 17/1949, para 4).

(d) Effect on the tenant's security of tenure

Action by the landlord   If a dwelling-house is overcrowded within the meaning of the HA 1957 'in such circumstances as to render the occupier guilty of an offence', then by the Rent Act 1968, s17, the Rent Acts do not prevent the landlord gaining possession from the tenant. This section has no application to a tenant who succeeds in one of the defences to a prosecution for overcrowding (see (c) above), nor to 'Part VI' tenants even if overcrowded, since they only have limited security anyway (see ch 9(D)(3)(b)). If a 'fully covered' tenant (see ch 9(A)(1)) shares living accommodation such as a kitchen with another tenant he cannot be guilty of overcrowding (see definition at (a) above), and retains full protection despite the sharing (RA 1968, s102—see ch 9(A)(1)(a)), so that the landlord cannot get possession; while if the tenant shares living accommodation with his landlord he is equally not guilty of overcrowding, although he is treated as a 'Part VI' tenant (RA 1968, s101—see ch 9(A)(1)(a)), and will thus have only the limited security open to such a tenant (see ch 9(D)(3)(b)).

It has been held that where overcrowding arises because a child of the tenant reaches one year (see (a) above), and the landlord commences proceedings for possession, the landlord cannot invoke the RA 1968, s 17, if the tenant then applies to the authority for accommodation under the HA 1957, s78(3) (see (c) above) before the hearing, since he is no longer guilty of an offence (Zbytniewski v Broughton [1956] 3 All ER 348, CA): however, it also appears from this case that the landlord need not show that the tenant has actually been convicted, provided he can show the offence is still being committed at the time of the possession hearing.

Action by the authority   The local authority may serve written notice on a tenant guilty of overcrowding requiring him to abate it within fourteen days, and if within the following three months the house is still overcrowded, the authority may apply to the county court which must order vacant possession to be given to the landlord within twenty-eight days; the authority can then recover its expenses from the landlord (HA 1957, s85).

(e) Rehousing   There are references to the provision of new housing in the HA 1957, ss76 (see (b) above) and 91 (see ch 8(A)(2)(b)), but these are general sections not conferring any right on the individual overcrowded occupier to be rehoused. Since the authority's duty to rehouse under the LCA 1973, s39 (see ch 10(A)(2)) extends to those displaced under demolition, closing and compulsory purchase orders, but not to those displaced by possession orders granted because of overcrowding, the authority should be persuaded to pursue the unfitness procedures where appropriate (see (A) above) to overcrowded houses, or alternatively compulsory purchase. Failing such action, those evicted must rely on emergency accommodation (see ch 8).

(2) Multiple Occupation

(a) Definition   Whereas the overcrowding provisions concentrate on individual 'separate dwellings', which may include parts of houses, the multiple occupation provisions are mainly concerned with whole houses originally intended for single families but now occupied by more than one household, whether or not the houses are now divided into 'separate dwellings' (see Okereke v LB of Brent [1966] 1 All ER 150, CA). While the same house may well be both overcrowded in its 'separate dwellings' and in multiple occupation, the two concepts are distinct: a house in multiple occupation will not necessarily be overcrowded in its 'separate dwellings'.

A house in multiple occupation is statutorily defined as one 'which is occupied by persons who do not form a single household' (HA 1969, s58). Thus a single sub-letting causes multi-occupation, as does the occupation of a house by the same family but in two or more households, and the taking of lodgers (although in certain circumstances lodgers treated as 'part of the family' might form part of that single household: MHLG Circular 67/1969, para 6).

Unlike cases of overcrowding, authorities are under no duty to act where there is multi-occupation: they merely have the following powers.
(b) Powers to limit the number of occupiers
Under the 1957 Housing Act   By the HA 1957, s90, if the local authority considers that excessive numbers of people are being accommodated in a house in multi-occupation, having regard to the available rooms, then it may serve on the landlord, the tenant, or both, a notice stating the maximum permitted number of persons who can sleep in any room (the authority may fix its own limits), and stating the penalty for 'causing or knowingly permitting' this number to be exceeded after twenty-one days from the service of the notice. The penalty is £100 on a first offence (HA 1961, s20). This offence must not be confused with that of overcrowding a 'separate dwelling' (see (1)(c) above), and has no bearing on the tenant's security of tenure (see (d) below). After service of the notice, an offence will only be committed where the permitted number is exceeded through multi-occupation, and not where it is exceeded merely through occupation by a single household: see Wolkind v Ali [1975] 1 All ER 193, 197.

This provision is rarely used in practice, since it brands victims of the housing shortage as criminals without providing alternative accommodation for them.

Under the 1961 Housing Act   By the HA 1961, s19, if a house is defective in certain amenities and services, having regard to the number of people or households living or likely to live there, then the authority may make a direction fixing the maximum number of people or households who may occupy the house (including here, by s19(3), part of the house) in its existing condition. Although s19 is normally used for houses which are already multi-occupied, it can also be used where multi-occupation is anticipated but has not yet occurred: Allen v Khan [1967] 3 All ER 1082. The relevant amenities and services are set out in the HA 1961, s15(1), which is considered in detail at (c)(i) below.

The direction makes it the duty of the 'occupier' (which can include the landlord as well as the tenant: HA 1964, s67(5)), not to permit the number of individuals or households occupying the house to exceed the limit fixed in the direction, or, if the limit is already exceeded at the time of the direction, not to permit any further increase (HA 1961, s19(2)). Thus, unlike the operation of the HA 1957, s90, a s19 direction does not affect the people already in occupation when it is made, but merely prohibits any further increase (see Allen v Khan [1967] 3 All ER 1082): it is therefore a better section from the occupier's viewpoint. A further difference is that while s90 allows the authority to fix the maximum number of occupants having regard to the available rooms, s19 allows it to fix the maximum number having regard to the available amenities and services.

Breach of a s19 direction is an offence carrying a £100 fine on a first conviction (s19(11)). The section does not affect the tenant's security of tenure (see (d) below).

Further, by the HA 1961, s22, as extended by the HA 1969, s64, authorities may make schemes for the registration of houses in multi-occupation and certain other buildings: the schemes may limit the numbers of occupiers and create offences, but are mainly of importance to landlords rather than tenants.

(c) Powers to secure repair, modernization and improvement

(i) Compulsory execution of works   Where a house in multi-occupation is defective with respect to certain amenities and services, having regard to the number of individuals or households living there, then the authority may serve on the landlord or his manager a notice requiring him to do specified work to make the house suitable for such occupation (HA 1961, s15(1)). The amenities and services covered are: natural and artificial lighting; ventilation; water supply; personal washing facilities; drainage and WCs; facilities for the storage, preparation and cooking of food and for the disposal of waste water; and installations for space heating or for the use of space heating appliances. This list differs from that in the HA 1957, s4, defining unfitness for habitation (see (A)(1) above).

Notices under s15 are designed to be used, where appropriate, with s19 directions (see (b) above), since lack of room for the necessary amenities is often a problem: thus the numbers occupying the house may be limited either before or after the specified works have been carried out (MHLG Circular 16/1962, para 29). Further, a s15 notice may specify works to make the house suitable for occupation by a stated smaller number of individuals or households than at present live there, coupled with a s19 direction fixing that smaller number as the limit for occupation (HA 1964, s67).

As regards the work that a s15 notice may cover, it has been held that the provision of a hot water supply to the whole of a multi-occupied house can be required, but this question of washing facilities is in each case one of 'fact and degree' (McPhail v LB of Islington [1970] 1 All ER 1004, CA). Further, although a s15 notice can of course require the provision of additional drainage and WCs, we have seen that authorities have alternative powers to require these under the public health legislation, whether or not a house is multi-occupied (see (B)(4) above).

The notice must allow at least twenty-one days for the work to be carried out (s15(3)), and the tenants must be informed (s15(4)).

Effects on tenant   Although the tenant's security of tenure is not normally affected by a s15 notice (see (d) below), the authority may withdraw the notice if the number of occupiers has later been reduced to a level making the work unnecessary (s15(2)): thus there is a risk of illegal eviction and harassment (see ch 9(D)(2)). Further, completion of the work may result in a rent increase (see (A)(3)(c) above).

Failure of landlord to comply   If the work is not carried out, the authority may do it and recover the cost from the landlord (HA 1961, s18), who may be fined if he 'wilfully fails to comply' with the notice (HA 1964, s65; HA 1969, s61).

Tenement buildings and flats   By the HA 1961, s21, the provisions of s15 are extended beyond houses in multi-occupation to include buildings which are not houses but either (a) comprise separate dwellings, two or more of which have shared WCs and personal washing facilities (i.e. tenement buildings), even though there may be no multi-occupation in the individual dwellings, or (b) comprise separate dwellings, two or more of which are in multi-occupation (i.e. blocks of flats): the former category is included because the need to share facilities may mean that conditions are as bad as in a house originally designed for a single family but now in multi-occupation, and the latter in order that improvements in the common parts of the building, as well as in the multi-occupied flats, may be secured (Circular 16/1962, paras 51-2).

(ii) Application of management code   If the authority considers that a house in multi-occupation is in an unsatisfactory state through failure to maintain proper management standards, it may by order direct the manager of the house (i.e. the person collecting the rents or other payments from the tenants or lodgers) to observe the proper standards of management contained in the 'management code' (HA 1961, ss12, 13). This code, which is set out in SI 1962/668, requires the manager to ensure the repair, maintenance, cleansing and good order of: the water supply and drainage; the kitchens, bathrooms, WCs, sinks and wash-basins in common use; and the stairs, passages, outbuildings, yards and gardens in common use; and to make satisfactory arrangements for the disposal of rubbish; further, the manager is responsible for the installations for the supply of gas, electricity, lighting and heating serving the common parts of the building, the windows and other ventilation throughout the building, the means of escape from fire, and the general safety of the occupants; several other duties are also imposed on the manager. The occupants must co-operate with him so that he can carry out his duties.

Failure to comply   If any person knowingly contravenes the code he may be fined (HA 1961, s13(4)). If it is the manager who breaks the code, the authority may in addition serve a notice on him under s14, requiring him to do specified work to make good his neglect of the proper management standards, allowing at least twenty-one days for the work to be carried out, and notifying the tenants. If the work is not carried out, the authority may do it and recover the cost from the manager (HA 1961, s18), and he may be fined on wilful failure to comply with the s14 notice (HA 1964, s65; HA 1969, s61). The manager can apply to the magistrates' court for an order that any occupier who caused the contravention of the code resulting in the s14 notice should pay the cost of the work (HA 1961, s14(5)). As an alternative to a s14 notice, the authority may make a control order (see (iv) below).

Tenement buildings and flats   The management code provisions extend beyond multi-occupied houses to include certain tenement buildings and blocks of flats, by the HA 1961, s21 (see (i) above).

(iii) Compulsory fire precautions   If the authority considers that a house in multi-occupation has inadequate means of escape from fire, it may serve on the landlord a notice requiring him to provide specified means of escape, allowing him at least twenty-one days to do the work, and notifying the tenants (HA 1961, s16). If the work is not carried out, then the authority may do it, recovering the cost from the landlord (HA 1961, s18), who may also be fined (HA 1964, s65; HA 1969, s61).

Additionally, if the necessary means of escape cannot be provided at reasonable expense for the whole house, but could be so provided if part of the house were not used for habitation, then by the HA 1969, s60, the authority may make a closing order (see (A)(4)(b)(iii) above) on that part, as to which the tenant will lose his security of tenure.

(iv) Control orders   Control orders are drastic orders allowing the authority to act as manager of a multi-occupied house having exceptionally bad living conditions, and are dealt with by the HA 1964, ss73-90. The orders are intended to cover some of the worst cases of squalor in multi-occupied houses where action under the provisions of the HA 1961 (see above) has been inhibited by the residents' fear of eviction if they complain to the authority: thus control orders are designed to be made without prior notice to the landlord (MHLG Circular 51/1964, para 5). However, authorities have been urged only to make the orders on 'hard evidence' of living conditions 'so bad as to necessitate . . . intervention by the local authority as against the more orthodox means of control under the Public Health and Housing Acts' (Circular 51/1964, para 4, and App I, para 12), and authorities tend to avoid taking on the administrative burden of control orders. This is a pity, since they give very comprehensive protection to residents.

A control order can only be made where: first, action has been or could be taken under one of ss12, 14, 15 or 19 of the HA 1961 (i.e. application of the management code, notice to execute works, or direction fixing the maximum number of occupants: see (b), (c)(i), (c)(ii) above), and second, it appears to the authority that the living conditions are such that it is necessary to make the control order to protect the safety, welfare or health of those living in the house (HA 1964, s73).

Once the order is in force, the authority must take all steps immediately necessary to protect the safety, welfare or health of the occupants (HA 1964, s73(2)); further, it has, for five years, the right to act as manager of the house and to grant certain short leases or licences (HA 1964, ss74 and 86); any necessary furniture, fittings and conveniences may be supplied by the authority (HA 1964, s90). However, the house is not to be regarded as a 'council house' within the HA 1957, Pt V (see ch 10): HA 1964, s74(5).

The authority must exercise its powers under the control order so as to maintain proper standards of management in the house and take such action as would have been needed to obey any management code order, notice to execute works, or direction fixing the maximum number of occupants which it would have served if it had not made a control order (HA 1964, s77).

Further, the authority must within eight weeks from the date of the control order prepare a scheme for executing works which it would otherwise have required of the landlord to satisfy the HA 1961, or any other housing or public health legislation (HA 1964, s79).

Effects on occupiers   By the HA 1964, s75, the occupiers (i.e. tenants, licensees, etc) are not affected by the order: the authority is simply substituted for the landlord or owner, and the tenants do not become 'council house' tenants, since they retain their security under the Rent Acts (see (d) below). However, the provisions of the management code imposing duties on the occupiers (see (ii) above) apply equally to occupiers under a control order (HA 1964, s75(4)).

Compulsory purchase   'There may be occasions when compulsory purchase, rather than action under the Act of 1961 or the making of a control order, provides the most effective. . . way of dealing with a situation where bad conditions are coupled with threats of eviction' (Circular 51/1964, para 6); and the making of a control order is without prejudice to the use of the compulsory purchase powers under the HA 1957, Pt V (HA 1964, s74(5); HA 1969, s63), so that an authority can follow a control order by the compulsory purchase (or purchase by agreement) of the property, i.e. it can use the control order merely as a temporary measure, terminating on the compulsory purchase.

(d) Effect on the tenant's security of tenure

Action by the landlord   Normally, action taken by the authority regarding multi-occupation will not affect the tenant's security against his landlord if there is no overcrowding contrary to the HA 1957 (i.e. the RA 1968, s17 is inapplicable: compare the 'overcrowding' provisions at (1)(d) above).

However, if the authority makes a closing order on part of a building because of fire precautions (see (c) (iii) above), then the landlord can recover possession of that part from the tenant, who loses any Rent Act protection over it (HA 1957, s27(5): see (A) (4)(b)(iii) above; HA 1969, s60(6)).

We have seen that the general compulsory purchase powers may be used by the authority in cases of multi-occupation: if a landlord seeks possession from tenants of a multi-occupied house after a compulsory purchase order has been made under the HA 1957, Pt V, but before the authority has become entitled to possession, then the county court may (by the HA 1964, s72) suspend the execution of the possession order for up to three years from the date of the hearing (or until the Secretary of State refuses to confirm the compulsory purchase order or it is quashed by a court), whether or not the tenancy was 'fully covered' (see ch 9(A)): see also D of En Circular 2/1975.

Action by the authority   In normal cases, the tenant is secure as against the authority also. But where the authority acquires the multi-occupied property by compulsory purchase, it will of course be entitled to possession on completion of the procedure, and the protection of the HA 1964, s72 (see above) will not apply against the authority (s72(4)(a)). Further, by the HA 1957, s158(1), nothing in the Rent Acts can stop the authority obtaining possession of any house for the purpose of enabling the authority to exercise its powers 'under any enactment relating to housing' (see ch 10(E)(2)(b)): thus if the authority wishes to do work on the landlord's failure to comply with a notice under the HA 1961, ss14, 15 or 16 (see (c)(i)-(iii) above), it could gain possession where necessary for the carrying out of the work, and the tenant could not claim

Rent Act protection against the authority.

(e) Rehousing   The authority must, under the LCA 1973, rehouse the occupiers (and provide compensation: see (A)(4)(b)(i) above) if either the multi-occupied property is compulsorily purchased, or the part in which the occupiers reside is closed as a fire precaution (see (c)(iii), (iv) above; ch 10(A)(2)). Otherwise, there is no enforceable obligation on the authority to rehouse residents in multi-occupation, though there is a general duty to consider and satisfy the need for further housing in its district (HA 1957, s91: see ch 8(A)(2)(b)), and to review multi-occupation in its district in order to determine what action to take (HA 1969, s70).

References

'Old Houses Into New Homes', Cmnd 3602 (1968).

'Better Homes—The Next Priorities', Cmnd 5339 (1973).

Davies, K. (1974), 'West's Law of Housing', The Estates Gazette, London.

'How To Fight For Better Housing Conditions', Community Action (1973).

'Encyclopedia of Public Health Law and Practice' (1968), Sweet & Maxwell, London.

'Council Housing Purposes, Procedures and Priorities', Ninth Report of the Housing Management Sub-Committee of CHAC, HMSO (1969).

Part III   Legal Services

Chapter 13 **Legal Services**

Previous chapters have described legal provisions of particular relevance to the underprivileged. The effectiveness of such provisions depends ultimately on adequate access for the underprivileged to legal services, courts and tribunals. This is currently an area of concern within the legal profession and elsewhere and recent years have seen both extensions of statutory legal services and the rapid growth of voluntary services. This does not mean that access to the law is equal for all; the statutory services are limited in clientele and scope, the voluntary services by lack of resources, and both are certainly overworked and underfinanced.

(A) Statutory Services

The Legal Aid Act 1974 provides that over a wide range of lawyers' services a client may, on passing a means-test, pay less than, or none of, the full bill. The areas of law involved are largely those traditionally viewed as the province of the legal profession. Legislation to create new legal agencies has been passed but not brought into operation (LAA 1974, s16). The Act distinguishes three schemes—legal advice and assistance, civil legal aid and criminal legal aid.

(1) Legal Advice and Assistance

This scheme (known variously as 'New Legal Aid', 'the £25 Scheme' and the 'Green Form Scheme' and administered by the Law Society) reduces or removes subject to a means-test the need to pay for advice, oral or written, from a solicitor on the legal advice and assistance panel (and a barrister's opinion if necessary) on 'the application of English Law to any particular circumstances', and any possible courses of action to deal with them; and any assistance by a solicitor (or barrister if necessary) in taking such action (LAA 1974, s2(1)). The scheme therefore extends to advice and assistance (e.g. writing letters, completing forms, negotiation) on any of the matters covered by this book and much more besides ((1973) LAG BUL. 84). But the scheme extends only marginally to proceedings; it does not cover proceedings for which civil or criminal legal aid has been granted (see (2),(3) below), nor the institution or conduct of any proceedings before a court or tribunal. The only proceedings or related matters covered are:

(a) magistrates' or county court proceedings in which a solicitor acts for a party at the court's request or at the solicitor's suggestion with the court's approval (LAA 1974, s2(4)); this allows a person in difficulties to be represented in the style of the 'dock brief' and for duty solicitor schemes to use the scheme as a source of funds (see (B)(4) below);

(b) proceedings in which a solicitor acts as a 'McKenzie man' (see (B)(5) below);

(c) assistance prior to a hearing given to a litigant in person (e.g. drafting a submission to a rent officer or SBAT);

(d) negotiating the settlement of civil proceedings.

The means-test is administered by the solicitor providing advice or assistance. Without the consent of a local Legal Aid Committee Secretary, he may not render services of more than £25 in value (LAA 1974, s3); this amounts to about three hours' work for the average solicitor. To benefit from the scheme a client must satisfy two conditions: first, his 'disposable income' must not exceed £29 per week or he must be a SB or FIS recipient; and second, his 'disposable capital' must not exceed £250 (LAA 1974, s1; SI 1975/856, reg 2, SI 1973/349, reg 4).

'Disposable income' is computed by first calculating the sum of net income (i.e. take-home pay), FA and other income of the client and his or her spouse; and deducting from this £6.05 in respect of a spouse and the appropriate SB scale-rate requirements in respect of other dependants (see table 4).

'Disposable capital' is all capital after disregarding furniture, clothes, the first £6,000 of the value of a house (after deducting any mortgage) and half the excess over that figure, and deducting sums in respect of dependants—£125 for the first, £80 for the second, £40 for each further person.

Except for SB and FIS recipients within the capital limit and those with a disposable income of £15 or less, clients must pay contributions related to disposable income up to maxima shown in table 6 (LAA 1974, s4; SI 1975/634, reg 2). The balance of the cost of the advice or assistance given is met first out of any costs paid to or property recovered or preserved for the client (excluding maintenance and several forms of social security payments), on which the solicitor's charges form a first charge; and second, out of the legal aid fund (LAA 1974, s5(3),(4)). Even where there are costs or property subject to the charge it is unlikely to be enforced; it seems some solicitors do not even collect the client's contribution ((1974) LAG BUL. 234,235).

(2) Civil Legal Aid
This scheme covers representation in civil proceedings by a solicitor on the legal aid panel (or a barrister if necessary) and all work preliminary or incidental to the proceedings (LAA 1974, s7(4)). It extends to most civil proceedings in magistrates' courts, county courts and higher courts but not to any tribunals covered by this book (LAA 1974, Sch 1). The scheme is administered by the Law Society through area and local committees composed of barristers and solicitors (LAA 1974, s15). An application can be made in person by any prospective litigant but it is advisable to consult a solicitor (initially under the advice and assistance scheme) who can then help complete the application. This is sent to the local committee office for a decision by the committee which must be satisfied on two counts.

(a) Reasonableness   Aid may not be granted if an applicant cannot show reasonable grounds for taking or defending proceedings; and may moreover be refused if it 'appears unreasonable he should receive it in the particular circumstances of the case' (LAA 1974, s7(5)).

(b) Means   Applicants must satisfy a means-test administered on behalf of the Law Society by the SBC which calculates 'disposable income' and 'disposable capital'.

'Disposable income' is the applicant's net weekly earnings plus any FA, FIS or other income (including a spouse's earnings) less:

(i) £5.15 in respect of a spouse;

(ii) the appropriate SB scale rate requirements for other dependants (see table 4);

(iii) weekly rates and rent (or mortgage, insurance and repair costs of an owner-occupier) less any proceeds from sub-letting (the rent or equivalent must be considered reasonable by the SBC which offers no guidance on this 'rent-stop');

(iv) reasonable employment expenses (e.g. fares to work);

(v) £2 of II disablement benefit or workmen's compensation (see ch 3 (A)(3),(C));

(vi) a further £2 in all cases.

'Disposable capital' is all the capital of the applicant and his or her spouse after disregarding:

(i) furniture, clothes and tools of a trade;

(ii) the first £6,000 of the value of a house (after deducting outstanding mortgage commitments) and half the excess of the value so calculated over £6,000;

(iii) the amount which could be borrowed on the security of a life assurance or endowment policy, less £125;

(iv) the amount of any debts likely to be repaid in the next twelve months;

(v) sums for dependants as for the advice and assistance scheme (see (1) above);

(vi) if disposable income is less than £600 per annum, the difference between it and £600.

The income and capital of an applicant's spouse is not included if they are separated or are opposing parties. Resources in dispute in the proceedings are also excluded (LAA 1974, s11; SI 1960/1471).

Aid is not granted if disposable income is over £1,580 per annum; nor, unless the costs of a case are likely to be high, if disposable capital is greater than £1,200, regardless of income (LAA 1974, s6(1); SI 1975/855).

The SBC normally interviews applicants at local DHSS offices. There is no appeal against refusal on financial grounds, but the SBC is prepared to explain or reconsider decisions if approached via the local committee office (SB Handbook, para 259). An appeal can be made against refusal on grounds of unreasonableness to an area committee and an oral hearing and representation are permitted (SI 1971/62, reg 10).

If a decision to grant aid is taken, the applicant is offered a legal aid certificate on terms which he must accept or decline within twenty-eight days. These terms may relate to the proceedings, such as the limiting of aid initially to the cost of obtaining counsel's opinion; or may require the payment of contributions by the applicant (SI 1971/62, reg 6).

No contribution is required of applicants receiving SB; or of those with disposable incomes of £500 per annum or less and disposable capital of £250 or less. Above these limits and below the eligibility limits (see above), contributions are demanded, subject to a maximum contribution from income of one-third of the difference between £500 and disposable income, and from capital of the difference between £250 and disposable capital. Income contributions are usually paid in twelve monthly instalments, capital contributions in a lump sum on accepting a certificate. Contributions may be raised if costs prove higher than expected but may not exceed the maxima; if costs prove less than anticipated, the balance is returned. Contributions may also be varied on changes in circumstances which must be notified to the Law Society.

An aided litigant who loses his case may be ordered to pay his opponent's costs but such orders are infrequent, the courts being empowered to order payment of costs out of the legal aid fund (LAA 1974, ss13, 14). The successful aided litigant may find not only costs but also damages awarded to him or property adjudged his in the proceedings reduced by the operation of a statutory charge for the amount of the difference between his contributions, if any, and the cost to the legal aid fund; awards of maintenance are exempt from the charge (LAA 1974, ss 8, 9).

In urgent cases an emergency legal aid certificate can be granted (SI 1971/62, reg 11), for example to restore an unlawfully evicted tenant to his home (see ch 9 (D)(2)(b)(iii)). A separate application form must be completed as well as the standard application. It is advisable for an applicant's solicitor to telephone the local committee secretary in advance of the application.

(3)   Criminal Legal Aid

The granting of legal aid in criminal cases is the responsibility of the criminal courts, and not of the Law Society. Criminal legal aid is available in all the criminal courts and for appeals (LAA 1974, s28); it may be given even if the accused pleads guilty, to cover a plea in mitigation or argument on sentence. Representation can be by solicitor or barrister, but in a magistrates' court will normally be by solicitor only, who may be chosen by the accused (LAA 1974, s30(1),(2); SI 1968/1231, para 8). Apart from the scheme here considered, court representation can be obtained under the advice and assistance scheme in exceptional cases (see (1)(a) above), or from a 'duty solicitor' (see (B)(4) below).

Application is normally made to the Clerk of the Court prior to the hearing, but may be made to the court itself at the hearing; before a legal aid order can be made the applicant must complete a detailed statement of means (obtainable from court offices, police stations, and CABx), and if the Clerk then refuses to make the order, he must refer the application to the court (LAA 1974, s29(4); SI 1968/1231, regs 1,2). The Clerk or court can only make the order if satisfied on two counts (doubts being resolved in favour of the accused: s29(6)).

(a) Order desirable in the interests of justice   It must appear 'desirable . . . in the interests of justice' to make the order (LAA 1974, s29(1)). The Widgery Report suggested certain guidelines in applying this test, e.g. whether the charge is a grave one, and whether the accused can follow the proceedings and state his own case (Cmnd 2934, para 180). The test is automatically satisfied where the charge is murder (LAA 1974, s29(1)(a)).

(b) Means   An order cannot be made unless it appears that the applicant's means 'are such that he requires assistance in meeting the costs' (LAA 1974, s29(2)). This is dealt with by SIs 1968/1265, 1970/1994, and 1975/64. In deciding whether the applicant should be given legal aid or required to make a contribution to the costs (see below), the Clerk or court must assess the resources of the applicant and his or her spouse.

The income of the applicant (and spouse) is based on the previous twelve months' net earnings, less 'reasonable sums' for:

(i) annual rates and rent (or, for owner-occupiers, mortgage and insurance costs and a sum for repairs), less any proceeds from sub-letting;

(ii) employment expenses;

(iii) maintenance of a spouse or former spouse, children, and other dependent relatives;

(iv) other matters for which the person 'must, or reasonably may, provide'.

The capital of the applicant (and spouse) is based on the amount or value of every capital resource, disregarding:

(i) furniture, clothes and tools of a trade;

(ii) the first £6,000 of the value of a house less any mortgage, and half the excess of the value so calculated over £6,000;

(iii) any NI death grant or maternity grant (see ch 2(B)(7)(a),(12)).

No maximum figures are prescribed for entitlement to an order (cf.(2)(b) above); but if the 'interests of justice' requirement is satisfied, then an order cannot be refused under the 'means' requirement if the applicant (or spouse) receives SB, or has resources immediately available not exceeding £50 (or £80 if married): SI 1968/1265, reg 3(4); SI 1975/64, reg 2.

The court may (and must if the applicant so requires) request the SBC to assess the applicant's means (LAA 1974, s33).

There is no appeal as such against refusal to grant criminal legal aid, but a conviction may be quashed on appeal if a miscarriage of justice resulted from the lack of representation (e.g. R v O'Brien [1967] Crim LR 367, CA; and see H. Levenson (1974) LAG BUL.245).

If a legal aid order is made, the accused can be ordered to make a contribution towards the costs, or even to pay the full costs, either in a lump sum or by instalments (LAA 1974, s32). No maximum figures are prescribed (cf.(2)(b) above); but no contribution can be ordered if the applicant receives SB, or if his assessed income over the last twelve months was £440 or less and his capital is £50 or less (£720 and £80 respectively if he is married) (SI 1968/1265, reg 4(2); SI 1975/64, reg 3). A Clerk or court can refuse to make a legal aid order unless the applicant first makes a payment in advance on account of any contribution, provided a contribution order is likely to be made and he can afford an immediate payment (LAA 1974, s29(3); SI 1968/1231, regs 1,2). There may be a reference to the SBC in connection with a contribution order, as for legal aid orders (LAA 1974, s33; see above).

(B)   Voluntary Services

The statutory schemes merely make financial adjustments to traditional lawyers' services for the benefit of poorer clients. Recent concern about legal services has focused on the inability of the statutory schemes to make an impact on the legal problems of those in deprived areas or to provide adequate legal services in connection with areas of law such as those covered in this book. The advice and assistance scheme has since 1973 allowed lawyers to assist in such areas of law but, despite considerable publicity, does not appear to have achieved this yet ((1974) LAG BUL. 234). Prompted in part by developments in the United States, the last five years have witnessed a rapid growth of voluntary legal services; the range of agencies offering legal help now varies enormously with the type of problem and the area of the country. This section indicates briefly the types of these agencies; details are contained in the Appendix.

(1)   Legal Advice Centres
A typical legal advice centre offers advice on one or more evenings a week and is staffed voluntarily by local lawyers. Most centres offer free advice, a few make a nominal charge. Clients who need more than advice are usually referred to solicitors or non-legal agencies. A survey in 1972 discovered over sixty such centres in operation and others have started since (Legal Action Group, 1972). The Legal Action Group publishes a directory of legal advice centres.

(2)   Neighbourhood Law Centres
There are currently nine neighbourhood law centres in London and three in the provinces. With some variations they offer a full range of legal services from advice to advocacy and some also undertake work on behalf of local groups and 'preventive' work. Some centres only accept clients from a defined catchment area and refer to solicitors non-urgent cases covered by the statutory schemes. Although the centres use the statutory schemes where appropriate they also undertake work outside those schemes such as tribunal representation; thus there is usually no cost to the client. Details of neighbourhood centres can be obtained from the Legal Action Group.

(3)   Trade Unions, Claimants' Unions and Pressure Groups
Most trade unions offer legal services to their members including assistance with social security claims and appeals (R. Lewis and G. Latta (1973) NLJ 386). Since this is an area in which the advice and assistance scheme is under-used and civil legal aid unavailable, and since many union officers are experienced in NI tribunal advocacy, this is often the best source of help for union members with social security problems. The more active claimants' unions may also be able to assist social security claimants; details of local unions can be obtained from local CABx.

Some pressure groups offer legal services to those with problems within their fields of concern, notably the Child Poverty Action Group whose Citizens' Rights Offices in London and Edinburgh advise on all aspects of social security and housing law, arrange tribunal representation and conduct test cases. Some local CPAG groups arrange advice sessions and tribunal representation. Both the national headquarters and some local groups of Shelter also take up housing cases.

(4) Duty Solicitor Schemes

In late 1973 there were twenty-three duty solicitor schemes in England and Wales. The typical scheme organizes a rota of volunteer solicitors, one of whom is available in the precincts of a magistrates' court to advise defendants in custody on such matters as plea and legal aid and to represent those otherwise without assistance. Few if any schemes achieve all this and in practice the services offered vary widely between areas ((1974) LAG BUL.207).

(5) Representation Schemes

As well as agencies which offer representation as part of their service, there are a few which offer exclusively representation before tribunals. Examples are the Surveyors' Aid Scheme for rent tribunal applicants in London and the Free Representation Unit, also in London, which takes cases before all the tribunals covered in this book ((1973) LAG BUL.240).

Any person, whether or not legally qualified, is able to assist an unrepresented party in court or tribunal proceedings as a 'McKenzie man'—'a friend of either party (who) may take notes, may quietly make suggestions, and give advice' (Collier v Hicks [1831] 109 ER 1290; McKenzie v McKenzie [1970] 3WLR 472, CA; cf. Mercy v Persons Unknown, 'The Times', 5 June 1974, CA). Before the tribunals mentioned in this book lawyers and non-lawyers have rights of audience but solicitors cannot be remunerated for tribunal representation under the statutory schemes. However, a solicitor can act as a 'McKenzie man' for a tribunal litigant under the advice and assistance scheme (Lord Chancellor's Office, 1973).

A county court has the power to allow a non-lawyer to represent a party (County Courts Act 1959, s89(d)). This permits, for example, social workers to represent inarticulate clients.

References

'Report of the Departmental Committee on Legal Aid in Criminal Proceedings', Chairman: Mr Justice Widgery, Cmnd 2934 (1966).
Legal Action Group (1972), 'Legal Advice Centres—An Explosion?'.
Lord Chancellor's Office (1973), 'Legal Aid in Tribunals', working paper.

Tables

TABLE 1 Contribution conditions for NI benefits

Benefit	Eligible classes	Contribution conditions	Earnings factor
Unemployment and sickness benefit*	1	(a) Contributions paid before day of claim	25 × LEL
	1 or 2	(b) Contributions paid or credited in previous year	50 × LEL
Maternity grant	1, 2 or 3	Husband or wife has:	
		(a) Paid contributions in any year	25 × LEL
		(b) Contributions paid or credited in year before confinement	25 × LEL
Maternity allowance*	1 or 2	(a) Contributions paid in any year	25 × LEL
		(b) Contributions paid or credited in year before maternity allowance period	50 × LEL
Widow's allowance	1, 2 or 3	Husband paid contributions in any year before death or pensionable age	25 × LEL
Widowed mother's allowance* Widow's pension*	1, 2 or 3	(a) Husband paid contributions in any year before death or pensionable age	50 × LEL
		(b) Husband paid or credited with contributions in one year for every two years of his working life	50 × LEL in each year
Category A and B retirement pensions*	1, 2 or 3	Claimant satisfies same conditions as for widowed mother's allowance. Women married before 55 must satisfy (b) in at least half the years of their working life between marriage and pensionable age (excluding the years in which they married and reached that age) to be entitled to Category A pension	
Child's special allowance	1, 2 or 3	Former husband paid contributions in any year before death or pensionable age	50 × LEL
Death grant	1, 2 or 3	Contributions paid in any year before death or pensionable age	25 × LEL

'Year' in any contribution condition means a complete year calculated from the first Sunday in January. The lower earnings limit (LEL) is that for the year specified in the contribution condition.
*These benefits may be paid at a reduced rate if the second condition is not fully satisfied.

TABLE 2   Rates of NI benefits and increases for dependants as at 17 November
1975

(a) Weekly benefits (£pw)

Benefit	Rate	1st child	2nd and other children	Adult dependant
Unemployment and	Higher 11.10			
sickness benefit	Lower 7.80	3.50[1]	2.00[1]	6.90[1]
Invalidity pension	13.30	6.50	5.00	7.90
Invalidity allowance	Higher 2.80			
	Middle 1.70			
	Lower 0.85			
Non-contributory invalidity pension and invalid care allowance	7.90	6.50	5.00	4.90
Attendance allowance	Higher 10.60			
	Lower 7.10			
Maternity allowance	11.10	3.50	2.00	6.90
Widow's allowance	18.60	6.50	5.00	
Widowed mother's allowance	13.30	6.50	5.00	
Widow's pension	13.30			
Guardian's allowance	6.50			
Retirement pensions:				
Category A	13.30 ⎫			⎧
Category B	Higher 13.30 ⎪			⎱ 7.90
	Lower 7.90 ⎬ 6.50[2]		5.00[2]	
Category C and D	Higher 7.90 ⎪			⎰ 4.90[2]
	Lower 4.90 ⎭			⎩
Age addition	0.25			
Child's special allowance	6.50		5.00	

(b) Grants

Maternity grant	£25.00

Death grant:
Age of deceased at death

(i) under 3	£9.00
(ii) 3-5	£15.00
(iii) 6-17	£22.50
(iv) over 18 and under 55 (50 if a woman) on 5 July 1948	£15.00
(v) others over 18	£30.00

1 If claimant is over pensionable age, increases are as for category A and B
retirement pensions.

2 Dependant's increases are not paid with category D retirement pension.

TABLE 3 Rates of II benefits and increases for dependants

INJURY BENEFIT[1] (£pw)

Higher rate 12.55
Lower rate 9.80

DISABLEMENT PENSIONS[1] (according to degree of disablement) (£pw)

	Higher rate	Lower rate
100%	19.00	11.60
90%	17.10	10.44
80%	15.20	9.28
70%	13.30	8.12
60%	11.40	6.96
50%	9.50	5.80
40%	7.60	4.64
30%	5.70	3.48
20%	3.80	2.32

DISABLEMENT GRATUITY maximum (i.e. assessment at 19% for life) £1,260

INCREASES of injury benefit and disablement pension for dependants (£pw)*

	1st child	Each other child	Adult
If entitled to unemployability supplement	6.50	5.00	7.90
Other cases	3.50	2.00	6.90

OTHER INCREASES of disablement benefit (£pw)*

Unemployability supplement	13.30
Increase if at initial entitlement aged under 35	2.80
under 45	1.70
under 60 (55 in the case of women)	0.85
Special hardship allowance	8.72
(or the difference between disablement pension received and	21.80 whichever less)
Constant attendance allowance (lower maximum)	8.70
Exceptionally severe disablement allowance	8.70

*With effect from 17 November 1975.

1 Higher rate paid to claimants over 18 or entitled to increase for dependants; lower rate to claimants under 18.

DEATH BENEFIT

Weekly Benefits (£pw)

Widow's pension: for first six months		16.20
after six months	12.15 or 30% of NI widow's pension[1]	
Widower's pension		12.15
Allowance for first child:	higher rate	5.65
	lower rate	4.15
each other child	higher rate	3.10
	lower rate	1.60
Parent's pension—if living with other parent who is entitled		0.75
—other cases		1.00
Relative's pension[2]		1.80
Allowance to woman with care of deceased's children		1.00

Gratuities

Widow's remarriage gratuity	52 times death benefit at date of remarriage
Parent's gratuity	£52
Relative's gratuity	£52

1 Higher rate paid if widow entitled to child allowance or over 50 at deceased's death or permanently incapable of self-support.
2 These rates paid if parent or relative was wholly maintained by deceased; in cases of lesser maintenance, pension is amount of maintenance or these rates, whichever less.

TABLE 4   SB Requirements as at 17 November 1975

(a) Scale rates (£pw)

	A	B	C
Husband and wife	17.75(19.00 or 19.80)	21.55(22.80 or 23.60)	21.80(23.05 or 23.85)
Person living alone (if a householder)	10.90	13.70	13.95
Any other person aged:			
not less than 18	8.70(12.15)	11.00(14.95)	11.25(15.20)
16-17	6.70(7.60)		
13-15	5.60		
11-12	4.60		
5-10	3.75		
less than five	3.10		

(Figures in brackets are blind person's requirements; for a husband and wife, the higher figure in brackets is paid if both are blind, the lower if one is blind.)

(b) Attendance requirements

Higher rate	£10.60 pw
Lower rate	£7.10 pw

(c) Non-householder rent requirements   £1.00 pw

TABLE 5   Requirements of SB claimants in Part III Accommodation (£pw)

Accommodation charges	
Person over 16	9.30
Child accompanying person over 16 aged:	
under 5	2.75
5-10	3.30
11-12	4.05
13-15	4.95
Personal requirements	2.30

TABLE 6   Contributions, legal advice and assistance scheme

Disposable income (pw)	Maximum contribution
£15 or less	Nil
over £15-16	£1.50
over £16-17	£3.00
over £17-19	£6.00
over £19-21	£9.00
over £21-23	£12.00
over £23-25	£15.00
over £25-27	£18.00
over £27-29	£21.00

Appendix **Agencies**

The Appendix provides addresses and a brief indication of the work of the agencies, official and voluntary, mentioned in this book, and a few others. It is not intended as a directory of agencies which an adviser in the poverty law field might wish to contact; more comprehensive lists already exist for that purpose in, for example:
Coote, A. and Grant, L.(1972), 'Civil Liberty: The NCCL Guide', Penguin, Harmondsworth; and
Matthews, G.(1974), 'Knowhere to Go' (sic), The Cyrenians, Canterbury.

1. Advisory Committee on Rent Rebates and Allowances
    Department of the Environment
    2 Marsham Street
    London SW1P 3EB
    Has a watching brief over rent rebates and allowances: see ch 11(A), (B).

2. Catholic Housing Aid Society
    189A Old Brompton Road
    London SW5 0AR
    (01-373 4961)
    Housing aid services in many parts of the country, various publications.

3. Child Poverty Action Group
    1 Macklin Street
    London WC2
    (01-242 3225/9149)
    Campaigns for more effective measures to counter poverty, publishes 'Poverty' quarterly which includes a welfare law section, runs Citizens' Rights Office at same address (01-405 4517/5942): see ch 13(B)(3).

4. Commissions for Local Administration
    21 Queen Anne's Gate
    London SW1H 9BU
    (01-930 3333)
    The local government 'ombudsmen': see ch 1(D).

5. Community Action
    7A Frederic Mews
    Kinnerton Street
    London SW1
    (01-235 3465)
    Assists tenants' and residents' groups in housing matters, publishes
    'Community Action' bi-monthly and other publications: see ch
    12(A)(2).

6. Council on Tribunals
    6 Spring Gardens
    Cockspur Street
    London SW1
    A statutory supervisory body for tribunals; receives complaints
    about tribunals: see ch 1(D).

7. Cyrenians
    The National Cyrenians
    13 Wincheap
    Canterbury
    Kent CT1 3TB
    (0227-51641/2/3)
    Provide overnight shelters and residential houses mainly for the single
    homeless, various publications.

8. Free Representation Unit
    College of Law
    27 Chancery Lane
    London WC2
    Provides free representation before tribunals in the London area: see
    ch 13(B)(5).

9. Health Service Commissioners
    Church House
    Great Smith Street
    London SW1
    The NHS 'ombudsmen': see ch 1(D).

10. The Law Society
    113 Chancery Lane
    London WC2A 1PL
    Responsible for operation of legal advice and assistance and civil legal
    aid schemes: see ch 13(A)(1),(2).

11. Legal Action Group
    28A Highgate Road
    London NW5 1NS
    (01-485 1189)
    Campaigns for improved legal services, especially for deprived areas,
    members receive monthly bulletin covering developments in poverty
    law.

12. National Federation of Claimants' Unions
    (contact nearest local union via CABx)
    See ch 13(B)(3).

13. Public Health Advisory Service
    159 Cleveland Street
    London W1
    (01-387 5155)
    Advises on public health aspects of housing and inspection of
    defective buildings, publishes directory of public health inspectors
    available for general consultation.

14. Shelter—National Campaign for the Homeless
    86 The Strand
    London WC2R 0EQ
    (01-836 2051)
    Campaigns and raises funds for better housing conditions; takes up
    individual cases: see ch 13(B)(3).

15. Surveyors' Aid Scheme
    (contact through CABx)
    Provides surveyors' services, including rent tribunal representation,
    to those who cannot afford them subject to a means-test; confined to
    London: see ch 13(B)(5).

Index